The
Best-ever
Games
for Kids

hamlyn

The Best-ever Games for Kids

501 ways to have fun!

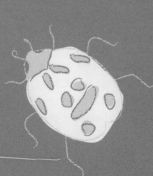

An Hachette UK Company
www.hachette.co.uk

First published in Great Britain in 2009 by
Hamlyn, a division of Octopus Publishing Group Ltd,
2—4 Heron Quays, London E14 4JP
www.octopusbooks.co.uk
www.octopusbooksusa.com

Distributed in the U.S. and Canada by Octopus
Books USA:
c/o Hachette Book Group
237 Park Avenue
New York NY 10017

ISBN: 978-0-600-61928-4

A CIP catalogue record for this book is available
from the British Library

Printed in China

10 9 8 7 6 5 4 3 2 1

This material was previously published as *Card
Games for Kids*, *Pencil and Paper Games*, *Outdoor Fun
and Games* and *Family Party Games*.

The publisher cannot accept any legal responsibility
or liability for any injury or accident resulting from
playing these games. For some of these games it may
be advisable to ensure an adult helper is present
to supervise.

Contents

Introduction

Keeping kids entertained is no mean feat. The combination of boundless energy, limited attention spans and the seemingly never-ending round of questioning leads many frazzled parents and babysitters to reach for the television remote control in order to just get a minute's respite. It's an ongoing battle to try and find diverting activities to keep restless kids amused without breaking the bank on outings, or toys that get used for a week or two and then either broken or forgotten.

Playing on their terms

Kids love games and attention so the prospect of both of these in one sitting will generally be greeted with much enthusiasm. However, timing is the key to success and it's important not to introduce a brand new game to children who are tired or over-stimulated; they simply won't appreciate it. It is also important to choose the right game for the situation and the age group. It should be something that challenges them but isn't too difficult to understand. Make sure you are fully up to speed with the rules yourself and, if possible, have a couple of trial runs before you start teaching the game to your children.

Keep it simple

A pack of cards, a pencil and paper or a few other props, plus a little imagination and bags of enthusiasm – that's all you really need to have endless fun with kids. In today's technological world, children have their attention drawn to computer consoles and electronic games and this can be quite a sedentary and isolated form of recreation. So, it's actually quite liberating to take a step back and browse through a book where you will discover games and activities that will keep kids entertained for hours. The nature of many of the games in this book makes them perfect for pulling out in potentially fraught situations. The card games and pencil and paper games, in particular, could provide a bit of diversion in an airport, or in a restaurant when you're trying to keep the kids amused while you wait for the food to arrive.

Fair play

Game playing is an important part of a child's development and many valuable lessons can be learnt in this relaxed and natural environment. Card games can help with memory and maths skills, pencil and paper games will aid creative leanings, whilst outdoor games provide essential physical activity. On top of this, all games will help children to build their concentration levels, as well as develop key social skills such as sharing, taking turns and interacting with other children. It can also be a great way to build some quality family time into busy schedules.

Even the youngest child loves scribbling, chasing a ball or playing a simple game of snap and this book has games for every age and level. For young children, you need to choose fairly quick games, in order to keep their concentration, and you shouldn't worry too much about sticking to the rules – feel free to adapt them to suit your own child. As children grow older so the games can become more involved and the children can build on their experience and move on to more difficult games. However, it can often be successful having older and younger children playing together as the older ones feel a sense of responsibility while the younger ones get the help they need.

Using this book

The book is divided into four sections: Card Games; Pencil & Paper Games; Outdoor Fun; and Party Time. Each chapter contains more than enough ideas to put a dent in the energy levels of even the most restless child. There is a comprehensive index at the back of the book listing every game by title, as well as by age, so that you can quickly and easily locate suitable games for your children.

Whether there's just one child at home, or you're hosting a party for twenty kids, you'll find plenty of inspiration for games and activities that will keep them amused and entertained. There are simple card games for one or two people, drawing games for the whole family and endless ideas for party activities for a whole gaggle of excited children. If you have this book close at hand, you will be able to keep your kids entertained whatever their age, whatever the occasion and whatever the weather.

Card games

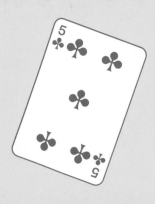

Klondike

or Canfield, Patience, Solitaire

Age range 10+
Skill level 5
Good for Rainy days and train journeys

This is probably the best-known and most popular patience game. It's very hard to win, and will be a real test.

Aim of the game

To get all the cards from your hand and the layout into four piles, one for each suit, with the Ace on the bottom and King on top.

Preparation

Shuffle the pack and deal out 28 cards, as below.

How to play

If you see any Aces face up, put them above your layout (to start your four foundation piles). Then turn over any cards underneath the Aces. If there are any twos now, put those on the relevant Aces.

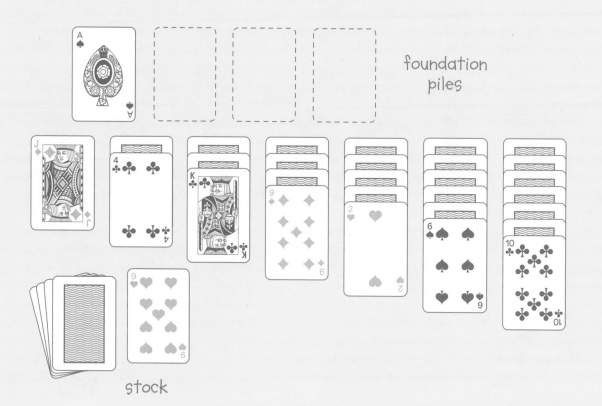

foundation piles

stock

When you have dealt, place the rest of the pack in front of you – this is called your stock.

Next, put any cards that are one less in number directly underneath the higher cards (eights under nines, fives under sixes etc). BUT NOTE! They have to be opposite colours (so red must have black under it, and black has to have a red under it).

When you've done all you can, deal three cards from your stock face down and turn the pile up. If the top card of your new pile can go onto your layout, play it. The second card then comes into play. If you can't play the top card, deal three new cards. The good thing is you can move whole columns of cards within the layout, or parts of columns, so you can get to a card you want to play.

Kings can be put on the blank spaces left if you've moved a whole column onto a foundation pile.

You have won when all the cards have been put onto the four foundation piles, topped with the King of their suit. Then gather up the cards, shuffle them really well (because remember they're all in number order!) and deal a fresh layout.

We did say it was tough!

Tip for beginners

* Is cheating naughty? Yes. But remember you'll only be cheating yourself! When you've found you can't move the cards around any more, go through the stock one card at a time rather than three; or if you really have reached your wit's end, look through the face-down piles, find a two and play it.

Dundee

or Second guess

Ages 5+
Skill level 2
Good for Whiling away time on trains, planes and automobiles

Dundee is a compelling game of chance that will keep kids occupied for hours, and what's more, it's simple and can be played almost anywhere.

Aim of the game

To turn over all 52 cards in a pack without predicting one correctly … sounds a bit bizarre, but trust me, it will make sense!

Preparation

Shuffle the cards and settle down … you will be playing for some time.

How to play

Hold the shuffled deck face down.

Before turning over the first card, you must announce a rank of card, for example, 'Five'. Say the word out loud and be clear – you will only cheat yourself if you mumble or kid yourself that you've forgotten what you said.

You must try to avoid predicting the card you are about to turn over. If your announcement coincides with the rank of card revealed, your turn reaches an immediate end. So, back to our example, if you'd announced 'Four' and then turned over the four of hearts, the game's up. Then the cards must be shuffled again and the game recommences.

The game continues in this way until either you predict a card or you get through the entire deck. This latter situation is extremely rare. The game is also made harder by the rule that you cannot make the same prediction in consecutive turns.

You have won when you've turned over the entire deck and have no cards held in hand. If you don't make it to the end of the pack, you can count up the remaining cards and make a mental note of how close you got. Keep trying to beat your personal best and, if you've got a sibling to play against, see if you can outperform him.

Ages 7+
Skill level 3
Good for Patience players with small tables

Aces up

or Idiot's delight

A simple patience game that is nice and quick to set up and can be played almost anywhere.

Aim of the game

To discard cards from the layout until you have only the Aces left.

Preparation

Deal four cards face up onto a table from a shuffled deck. The four face-up cards are your layout in Aces Up. Hold the remaining cards in your hand, keeping them face down.

layout

How to play

If any of the four cards in the layout are from the same suit, you can discard all but the highest ranked of them (Aces are high). So, for example, if the four cards were the King of hearts, the Jack of clubs, the four of hearts and the two of clubs, you would discard the latter two cards.

Gaps in the layout are then filled with cards from the stack.

The game continues in this way, with cards being discarded and replaced until either the cards are exhausted or the game becomes blocked.

A successful game ends when the layout is made up of the four Aces.

Tip for beginners

∗ If the game becomes blocked, younger players should be given one free move; in other words they are allowed to discard the lowest-ranked card in the layout irrespective of suit. If this doesn't get the game moving again, it's time to gather up the cards, shuffle and re-deal.

Stop the clock

or The clock, Clock patience

Age range 7+
Skill level 3
Good for A little bit of suspense on a rainy day

Straightforward rules and a swift outcome make this an addictive solo game for younger players.

Aim of the game
To turn over all the cards on the clock face before you uncover the fourth King.

Preparation
Shuffle the pack and deal out the cards into 13 piles of four cards each. Twelve of the piles should be set out face down in a circle that approximates a clock face. The remaining set of four cards is then placed in the middle of the layout.

Tip for beginners
* Once you've made a mistake the game cannot be continued, so take your time and do not rush. Younger players may benefit from having a watch or clock face to refer to when playing; alternatively, you might like to draw out the layout on a piece of paper so that they have a model to follow. It is also imperative that the cards are spaced evenly, without overlapping, and that the game is played on a flat surface.

How to play
Start the game by turning over the top card in the central pile. Suppose the card turned over is a six, you must then place that card face up under the pile of cards at the bottom of the clock face layout (in the position that corresponds to six o'clock on a conventional dial).

Having laid down your six, you continue the game by turning over the top card of the same pile. The revealed card is placed under the relevant pile and the top card turned over and relocated to its home.

When you reveal the fourth card in a pile and there is no face-down card left to turn over, you turn over the top card of the next highest pile in the layout.

You win the game if you manage to get all 12 piles of cards on the circular layout face up. You lose the game if you turn over the fourth King before you have managed to get the circular layout complete. Simple really – it's you against the Kings.

Golf patience

Age range 8+
Skill level 3
Good for Competitive types who enjoy a sporting challenge

Easy to set up, addictive and with the option of a head-to-head two-player version, Golf played with cards is more fun than hitting a small ball around a park in the cold.

Aim of the game

To remove as many cards as possible from the layout before the cards in hand run out.

Preparation

Shuffle the pack and deal out seven rows of five cards overlapping and face up. This 35-card layout is called the links. The remainder of the cards are held in hand (face down) and dealt one by one onto a waste pile. The objective of the game is to move the cards in the links onto the waste pile.

How to play

Turn over the first card that you have held in hand. The card that is revealed is then used to start the waste pile and this can be built on with any of the exposed cards (i.e. the bottom card in each column) in the links.

Place the cards moved from the links face up on top of the waste pile. You can play cards out of the layout in either ascending or descending order and irrespective of suit. So, for example, if the card on top of the waste pile is a four of diamonds, you could add either a five or three of any suit to it from the links.

When a card has been removed from the bottom row of the links, the card beneath it becomes available for play.

Continue adding to the pile by moving cards from the links until there are no cards left that you can play. The sequence can go up and down at will, so

Two-player option

* The great thing about Golf patience is that it can also be played competitively as a two-player game. You'll need two packs of cards, a large table and a couple of hours, but the rewards are worthwhile.
* Each player deals out her cards as above and the two hands are played simultaneously.
* You can either record the scores for each hole, and the player with the lowest aggregate score at the end of '18 holes' is the winner, or you can adopt 'matchplay' scoring.
* Under matchplay rules, each hole is either won, lost or halved (drawn), so at any stage a player is 'two up', 'four down' or a similar score as in the real matchplay game. The round continues until one player has an unassailable lead.

just because the first card added to that four of diamonds was a five, you don't have to keep going up. A five can be followed by a four and then another five, and so on.

Aces are low (that is, they count as one), and they can only be added to by a two; Kings, similarly, can only be built on by a Queen. In other words, you can't take the sequence 'round the corner' (King-Ace-two).

When you've exhausted all the available moves, turn over the next card held in hand and add it to the waste pile.

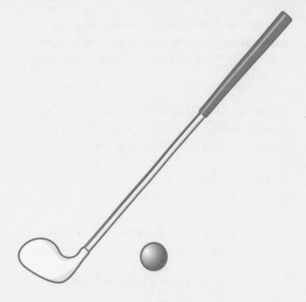

Continue playing until either the links are empty or your stock of cards in hand has run out.

Scoring

You calculate your score for the hole (hand) by counting up the cards left in the links at the end of play. If, however, you manage to empty the layout, you count up the cards left in hand and award yourself a minus score. Just as in real golf, low scores are best. Ideally, you should aim to play 18 holes for a complete round. Keep a note of your score and see if you can get a score of less than 72 strokes for the round.

Puss in the corner

Age range 8+
Skill level 3
Good for Players who want a patience game that is both winnable and demanding

A solo card game that is challenging without being impossible is a rare gem indeed … **Puss In The Corner** is just such a game.

Aim of the game

To build onto the four Aces in sequence and colour (though not suit) until all 52 cards are in the layout.

Preparation

Separate out the four Aces from a standard deck of cards and place them in a square in the centre of a large, clear table. The Aces are the foundation cards in this game and are built upon in ascending order.

The remaining 48 cards are shuffled and placed face down in the player's hand.

How to play

Turn over the cards held in hand one by one. Cards can be played onto the layout if they follow in sequence and are matched in colour, so, for example, a two of hearts can be played onto either the Ace of hearts or the Ace of diamonds.

If the card revealed cannot be added to the layout, it is placed face up into one of four waste piles positioned at the corners of the four Aces (see diagram right).

When the opportunity arises, the top card from any of the waste piles can be played onto the layout.

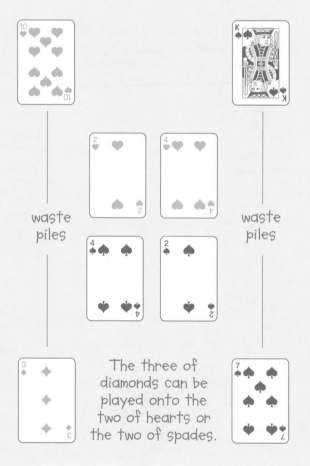

waste piles

waste piles

The three of diamonds can be played onto the two of hearts or the two of spades.

Players should try to play cards of similar rank onto particular waste piles. One pile should be reserved for cards ranked two to four; the next for cards five to seven; the next for cards ranked eight, nine and ten; and the last for court cards. By adopting this approach, players reduce the likelihood of finding themselves blocked later in the game.

Play continues in this fashion until the stock of cards runs out. The cards are then gathered up from the four waste piles (take care to place the lowest-rank pile at the top of the stack). Cards from the new stack are turned over one by one and are either played onto the layout or a single waste pile. The top card from the waste pile can be played onto the layout at any time.

If you have grouped your cards sensibly, it should be possible to get the remainder of the cards into the layout without too much effort. But you only get one deal, so when the stack of cards has been emptied onto the layout and the waste pile, that's your lot.

When all 52 cards in the deck have made it onto the layout, the game is complete. You should win more games than not. If you can't bear losing, however, you can always give yourself one more chance to go through the waste pile.

Tip for beginners

* The key to success in this game is to make sure you organize your waste piles properly. Group the cards as outlined left to start with, but as the game develops you will need to think more tactically. If you empty a waste pile, for example, you may want to fill the space with a card that you will soon be needing. Similarly, you may want to avoid covering a card that will soon become playable. Think ahead and try to keep your options open.

Bisley

Age range 10+
Skill level 4
Good for Bright kids who need a break
from computers and other techno gadgets

**Bisley is a patience classic that tests the
brainpower of adults and children alike.**

Aim of the game

To move all of the cards from the layout onto
foundation piles that begin with Aces and Kings.
Players build from the Aces in ascending order and
from the Kings in descending order. Cards must be
built in suit.

Preparation

Remove the Aces from the pack and lay them out
(in any order) as the first four cards in a row of 13.
Lay the cards face up and add three further rows of
13, with cards forming columns of four cards each.

How to play

The bottom card in each column is active and can be
moved either onto the foundation piles (the Aces at
the top of the layout) or can be used to build on
other columns. Players can build on columns either
up or down, but the card moved must be of the
same suit as the one it joins (unlike games like
Klondike, see page 10, which build in
alternating colours).

Your first objective should be to free
the Kings from the layout. When a
King is exposed, it is moved to the
top of the board and positioned
directly above the corresponding

active
cards

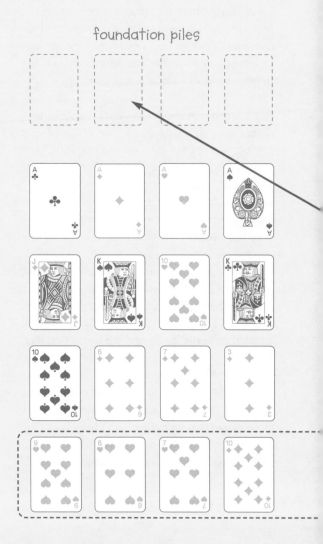

foundation piles

Ace. The King becomes a second foundation card and can then be built on in descending order.

Only single cards can be moved: shifting whole or part of a column is not allowed, and space left vacant by the removal of the last card in a column is not filled.

Success is yours when you have removed all of the cards from the layout onto the foundation piles. It doesn't matter whether you build more cards onto the Ace or the King of a particular suit and it is irrelevant where the two sequences end up meeting. When there are no cards left in the layout, you've won.

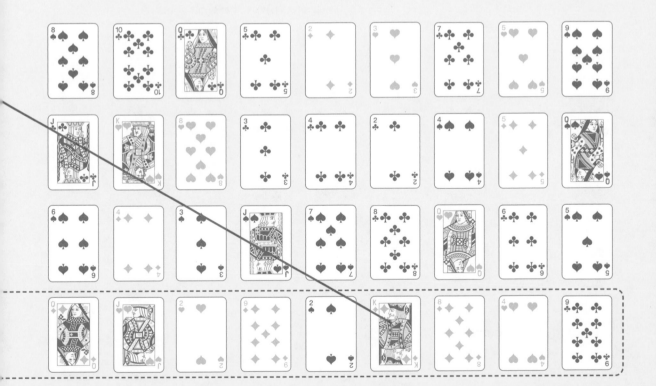

King Albert

Age range 11+
Skill level 5
Good for Clever kids who need to be stimulated

This demanding patience game is simple to play ... unfortunately, winning is not quite so straightforward.

Aim of the game

In common with many patience games, the aim is to take the cards from the starting layout and build them into four complete suit-based foundation piles; just like Klondike (see page 10) but with rather more scope to go wrong.

Preparation

Shuffle the pack and deal out 45 cards in rows of nine cards, then eight, seven and so on, down to a single card. The cards should be placed overlapping and face up on a table or board.

You should have seven cards left (if you haven't, you've either lost some cards or you're not very good at counting). The seven cards in hand are your 'reserve' and should be placed face up on the board. That's the easy bit done ...

layout

foundation piles

reserve

How to play

Your first objective is to release the Aces from the layout and establish your foundation piles; to do this, you must move other cards out of the way and onto other columns or foundation piles.

You can only move cards onto other columns in descending sequences of alternating colour, and you can only move single cards or complete columns – nothing in between.

If you move an entire column, you will be left with a gap in your layout that can be filled with any active card. This is a critical part of the game as your decision on which card to move may have a profound impact upon the shape of the game.

The seven reserve cards are used for building on the foundations or for 'packing' on the exposed cards in the layout. The reserve cards are a critical part of King Albert, providing the player with the chance to get things moving if the game stalls.

Victory is yours when you've managed to build complete suits of 13 cards on each of the foundation piles. Enjoy the smug, warm glow of triumph as you place the final King on the last foundation pile … it won't happen too often.

Tip for beginners

* The use of the reserve cards and the fact that all cards are exposed (face up) throughout reduces the element of chance in King Albert as compared to many other patience games. Study the cards and consider your decisions very carefully. Moving a King to a vacant column in the layout, for example, may seem like a logical action, but sometimes it is better to move a much lower card, which will help you open up further columns in less time.

Demon

or Fascination, Thirteen, Canfield

Age range 12+
Skill level 5
Good for Patience prodigies and those in need of a real challenge

Demon is a demanding game that calls for concentration in abundance and a large helping of brainpower.

Aim of the game

To build the cards in suit onto foundation cards … sounds simple.

Preparation

Deal 13 cards from a well-shuffled deck into a stack. The cards are placed face down on the table and become 'the heel'. The top card of the heel is turned over.

To the right of the heel, deal out one card to establish the rank of the foundation cards for the hand. Unlike many patience games, Demon does not use Aces or Kings as its foundations but instead uses this variable rank, which is defined by the deal. The remaining three cards of this rank then move to the foundation row as they emerge in play. Cards are built onto the foundations in ascending order and go 'round the corner'; so, for example, if the foundation card is a three, players must next play a four onto it, then a five and so on. They carry on building upwards until they get to the King, then complete the suit by playing the Ace and, lastly, the two.

Finally, deal out four face-up cards from the deck beneath the foundation row to start the layout.

How to play

Start by seeing if any of the cards in the layout can either be built onto the foundations or onto one another. Single cards can be moved from the bottom of one column to another, providing they are of alternating colour and descending sequence to the bottom card of the column they join. Entire columns can also be moved, but fragments of columns cannot.

Any spaces made in the layout must be immediately filled by the top card from the heel. Once a card has been played from the heel, the next card in line is turned over. When the heel is exhausted, players may fill gaps in the layout from the waste pile (see opposite) but they are no longer obliged to fill these gaps immediately and can, instead, wait for an opportune moment or card.

Tip for beginners

* Many youngsters will struggle initially to summon up the powers of concentration needed to succeed at Demon. However, you should encourage them to persevere and, most importantly, to take their time. Only by checking each card carefully against both the layout and the foundations do you stand any chance of success.

The remaining undealt 34 cards form a stock, which is held in hand. The stock is dealt to a waste pile three cards at a time, although at the end of the deal you may find there are fewer than three cards, in which case you should turn the cards one by one. Cards from the stock can be played either onto the foundation cards or onto the layout. The stock is dealt and re-dealt until either the game is won or becomes blocked.

The aim is to play all the cards from the stock and the heel onto the foundation piles: when all 52 cards are on the foundations, you've won. But be warned – this game is hard and it may take a while to win!

When a card of the same rank as the first foundation card appears, it should be moved to the foundation and replaced with the top card of the heel. The next card in the heel is then turned face up.

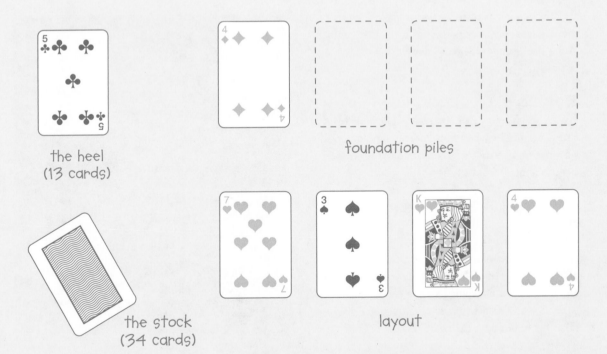

the heel
(13 cards)

foundation piles

the stock
(34 cards)

layout

Snap!

Age range 3+
Skill level I
Good for Exuberant youngsters and anybody who wants a simple, non-strategic but competitive game of cards

Simple, fast and noisy ... the perfect card game for young ones.

Aim of the game
To collect all your opponent's cards.

Preparation
Shuffle a standard 52-card deck and deal out all the cards between the two players. Alternatively, if you don't want to take the time to deal, you can simply cut the cards into two similarly sized stacks. Snap! is hardly a game of science, so it doesn't matter if one player has a few more cards than his opponent ... although it is probably wise to make sure that the youngest player gets the better of any inequity in the deal (otherwise you'll never hear the last of it).

How to play
Players hold their cards (face down) in their hands. The game begins when both players simultaneously turn over their top cards and place them on the table face up in front of them.

If the two cards revealed are of different values, the two players each turn over the next card in their stack (placing it on top of the previously played card) as before. The game continues in this way until cards of equal value appear together. Upon sight of a matching pair, the players must shout 'Snap!' The first player to utter the word takes his opponent's cards.

The person who snaps up all the cards and sits smugly with a hand full of 52 cards is the winner. The loser is the player complaining passionately that she has been cheated. An adjudicator may be required in cases of extreme controversy.

There are no tactics involved in Snap! Players could improve their reaction times by doing exercises, but this would, of course, be a little over the top, even for the most competitive among us! The best advice is to play for fun and accept that you will win as many games as you lose.

Variations
* Younger players often struggle to master the concept of playing cards simultaneously and their hesitancy can often lead to allegations of cheating, scuffling and (worst of all) snivelling. If you have this problem, an alternative way of playing can be employed. Players simply play their cards alternately onto a central waste pile and shout 'Snap!' when the card played matches the value of the one on top of the pile.
* If you want to play Snap! with three or more players, you will need to use two decks of cards. The rules remain the same; just make sure that you properly shuffle all 104 cards.

Age range 6–10
Skill level 1
Good for Introducing young people
to card games

Beggar my neighbour

This is often the first card game children learn. It requires no skill and children love winning a big pile of cards.

How to play

The dealer deals out all the cards face down one at a time to all the players, including himself. It does not matter if some players get a card more than others. Players do not look at their cards, but square them up in a neat pile face down in front of them.

The player to the dealer's left turns over her top card and lays it face up in the centre. Each player in turn lays the top card of his pile face up on top of it until an Ace, King, Queen or Jack appears.

If a player lays down an Ace, the following player must lay down, one at a time, four cards from his pile on top of it; if a King is laid down, the following player must lay three cards, if a Queen two cards and if a Jack one card. If, however, while doing this he himself lays down an Ace, King, Queen or Jack, he stops turning over his cards and the next player must add cards to the central pile in the same manner – four for an Ace, three for a King, and so on.

As soon as a player lays down the required number of cards without turning up an Ace, King, Queen or Jack, then the preceding player wins the whole pile. He turns the pile over and places it face down

below his existing face-down pile. He then turns over his top card and places it in the centre of the table to begin another round.

As players lose their cards, they drop out until only the winner is left, holding the complete pack.

GOPS

Age range 6+
Skill level 2
Good for Decisive kids who can think quickly

Simple rules and an easy set-up make GOPS a popular game with younger children, while its strategic qualities hold the interest of older players. Definitely one for all the siblings.

Aim of the game
To outscore your opponent over 13 hands.

Preparation
Separate a standard 52-card pack into its four suits.

Player One is given the 13 club cards and Player Two takes the diamonds. The 13 hearts are put to one side, and then the 13 spades are shuffled and placed in a pile face down in the middle of the playing table.

How to play
The deck of spades are called the points cards and to kick off the game the top card is turned over by Player One. The two players must now bid to win the card that has been revealed. If they win it, the points value of the card is added to their score (Ace = 1; Jack, Queen, King = 11, 12 and 13 respectively).

The players bid with the cards they hold in hand and can put down any card at any time. All they must do to win is put down a card of higher value than their opponent. Ideally, they must try to put

down a card with a value of only one more than that which their rival plays.

The two players place the card they wish to play face down in front of them before simultaneously revealing them. That way there can be no cheating or hesitating to gain an advantage.

The player who plays the highest card wins the hand and claims the value of the point card (spades) to her

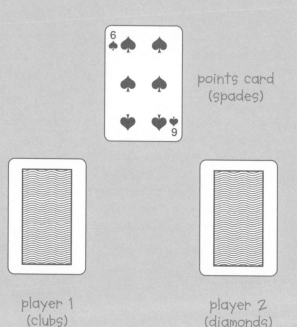

points card
(spades)

player 1
(clubs)

player 2
(diamonds)

score. If the two players put down cards
of equal value, they each take half the value of the
point card.

Once a hand has been played, the three cards used
are discarded. The second player now turns over a
points card and the game continues for a maximum
of 13 hands.

The first player to reach or exceed 46 points has an
unassailable lead and is the winner. Keep a written
running total of your scores and make sure that
each player agrees with what has been recorded.
Disagreement over scores can lead to abandoned
games, arguments and family feuds. Be warned!

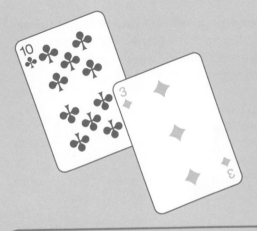

Variation

* A three-player version of GOPS can be
  played by simply including the discarded set
  of 13 hearts cards in the game. Player Three
  is given the hearts and joins the game as
  before. The only other modification required
  is that if all three players bid with cards of
  equal value, the points for the hand are now
  shared three ways.

Tip for beginners

* Impulsive youngsters can enjoy reasonable
  success by simply playing high cards to win
  high cards and vice versa. Of course, that
  approach will not always work and teenagers
  may want to think more strategically about
  their GOPS playing. The game itself takes its
  name from an acronym which stands for
  Game Of Pure Strategy, and there are many
  pages of theory about tactics for GOPS that
  can be found on the Internet. Unfortunately,
  these complicated algebraic ramblings,
  complete with Greek characters and
  probability symbols, make for impenetrable
  reading to anybody who has not taken the
  trouble to get a mathematics doctorate.

War

Age range 6+
Skill level 2
Good for Graduates of Snap!

The name alone will probably get boys queuing up for a game, while War's instant playability should appeal to even the most pacifist of females.

Aim of the game
To win all your opponent's cards.

Preparation
Shuffle a standard 52-card pack and deal out all the cards between the two players.

Players do not look at their cards, which are placed face down in a pack in front of them. They are now on the brink of War.

How to play
Both players simultaneously turn over the top card in their respective piles and place it face up in the middle of the table.

The highest-rank card is the one that wins the hand, and the relevant player can then collect all the cards played, and place them face down at the bottom of his pack. Aces are high and suits are ignored.

If the two cards played are of equal value, the two players must now go to War. They both now place the top cards of their packs face down in the middle of the table. These cards are not revealed;

player 1

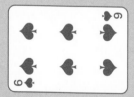

turned-up
cards

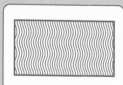

player 2

instead, the players return to their packs and take the new top card, turning it over and placing it face up on the table.

Whoever plays the highest card wins the hand and collects all six cards from the middle of the table, which are placed face down at the bottom of his pack.

If, however, the turned-up cards are of equal value, the War continues. Each player puts down another face-down card before turning over the next card in his stack.

Should a player run out of cards during a War, the game comes to an end.

Just like Snap!, the winner is the person who collects all 52 cards, leaving his opponent with nothing. It can take quite some time for the game to reach a conclusion … but that's not necessarily a bad thing.

Tip for beginners

* War is the perfect game to help your children understand and remember the traditional ranking system for playing cards. Each hand requires the players to make a decision about whether one card is higher than another, so after three or four games they should soon start picking things up. To help them get started, you might want to make them a simple reference chart, which will also help to prevent too many noisy arguments about whether a Jack is higher than an Ace. All you need to do is arrange a suit of cards in order and stick them to a piece of cardboard, or simply write down the following sequence on a piece of paper:

(highest) A K Q J 10 9 8 7 6 5 4 3 2 (lowest)

Sum

Age range 6+
Skill level 2
Good for Developing your child's mental arithmetic while playing cards

This is a game that encourages and rewards attacking play while at the same time challenging your child's maths skills – which has got to be a good thing ... especially if it keeps her quiet for an hour or two.

Aim of the game
To win cards from the layout by matching their sole or collective value to a card held in hand.

Preparation
Deal out 11 cards to each player and play six cards to the middle of the table, face up and in a row.

How to play
The non-dealer leads off and can take from the table any card she can match with one held in hand. So, for example, she can play a King to take another King from the table. Alternatively, she can take more than one card if their collective value is equal to the card she played. So, for example, she could play a King to take a four and a six or even a pair of threes and a four (court cards are all worth ten and Aces can be low or high).

The cards won by a player during her turn are placed face down in a stack, which is put to one side until the scores are settled at the end of the game.

If a player is unable to take any cards during her turn, she must instead discard one of the cards held in hand. The discarded card is added to the face-up row in the middle of the table. Similarly, if there are

no cards left to take, the player whose turn it is must play one of her own cards to the table.

When the players have no cards left, the remainder of the deck is dealt out and the game resumes. The game continues as before until the cards run dry.

At the end of the game the players turn over the stack of cards won and total up their scores. Pip cards count one, with court cards and Aces counting two. Ten bonus points are awarded to the player who has won the most cards and five bonus points are awarded for every seven points won by each player. ·

Tip for beginners

* The ten bonus points won by the player claiming the most cards is critical, so players should be encouraged to take multiple cards. A court card that claims a card of equal rank will net you two points, but if you can take three or four lower-rank cards, you will be better off as you will earn a point for each. This strategy will also provide the greatest opportunity for children to test their powers of mental arithmetic.

Possible combinations

* The seven of diamonds can be matched by both the seven of clubs and the sum of the four of diamonds and the three of clubs, etc.

Eights

or Switch, Fat ladies

Age range 8+
Skill level 4
Good for Tactical types and those who simply want an instantly playable head-to-head game

Eights is a quickfire game that is sometimes played impulsively, sometimes strategically, but always enthusiastically.

Aim of the game
To get rid of your seven cards before your opponent empties his hand.

Preparation
Shuffle a 52-card deck and deal out seven cards (one at a time) to both of the players.

The remaining cards are placed in a stock pile in the middle of the table, and the top card is turned over to become the game's starter card.

How to play
The basic gameplay in Eights is a little like many patience games – you play the cards from your hand onto a pile, building on the active card either in rank or suit.

The non-dealer plays first and must try to play a card from his hand onto the starter card. The card laid down must match either in suit or rank, so, for example, a seven of any suit or a club of any rank could be played onto a seven of clubs.

If a player does not have a playable card, he must take the top card of the stock pile and add that to his hand; if he still cannot play, he draws cards one at a time from the stock pile until he can.

player 1
(7 cards)

stock pile with
starter card

player 2
(7 cards)

Once a player has laid down a card, the turn passes to his opponent.

If the stock pile becomes exhausted, a player unable to take his turn simply has to pass.

Even if a player is able to play a card from his hand, he may still elect to first take a card from the stock pile. He must, however, eventually play a card, as players cannot pass while holding a playable card.

'So,' you're thinking, 'why is this game called Eights?' I was coming to that bit. In this game, eights are wild cards and can be played at any time onto any card. Players can elect to play an eight even if they have another playable card. When playing an eight, you must specify which suit it represents to clarify whether the previous suit continues or whether you wish to change to another suit (you have free choice). However, though the suit of an eight is wild, the rank is not. The next card played must either be another eight or a card that matches the stipulated suit.

The first player to get rid of all the cards in his hand is the winner. If, however, and as often happens, the game becomes blocked and neither player can make a move, there has to be a count-up to determine the winner. The player with the fewest cards is then the winner.

Variations

* For a more competitive form of Eights, which is suitable for teenagers, you can employ an aggregate scoring system over a series of games. The objective in this version of the game is to avoid reaching the critical score of 100 debit points; the player who reaches this total first is the loser. Points are awarded to players in respect of the cards they are left holding at the end of each hand. Different points are awarded for each card as follows:
EIGHTs = 50 points
KING, QUEEN OR JACK = 10 points
ACE = 1 point
CARDS TWO–TEN = 2–10 points respectively

* If the game ends in a block, each player is debited the value of the cards held in hand. Of course, a player who wins a game outright has no addition to his score.

Spit

or Speed

Age range 9+
Skill level 3
Good for Competitive siblings with quick brains and even quicker hands

Aim of the game

To move all the 15 cards out of your layout before your opponent empties his.

Preparation

Shuffle a standard 52-card deck and deal out the cards equally between the two players, who should be seated opposite one another at a table.

Players must now deal 15 of their own cards into a 'patience'-style layout. The cards are placed in five stock piles: the first contains one card, the second two … down to the fifth pile of five cards. The cards are set face down, with the exception of the bottom card in each pile, which is turned over.

The remaining 11 cards are the spit cards and they are held face down in a pile in the player's hand. Players are not allowed to look at the spit cards in advance of them being played.

How to play

When both players are ready to play, they each turn over their top spit card and place it in the middle of the table (between the two layouts).

The game begins as soon as the two cards are turned over and is played like a rapidfire version of patience. The basic objective is to play all your cards out of your layout and onto the spit piles. Players continue (they do not take consecutive turns) until they can make no more moves.

Cards are played from the bottom of the stock piles in the layout onto either of the two spit piles and turned face up. A card moved to a spit pile must be the next in sequence (either up or down), irrespective of suit.

Players are only allowed to use one hand to move their cards and can only play one card at a time.

As cards are played from the layout, the bottom card in each stock pile is turned over. If a stock pile is emptied, the gap in the layout can be filled by moving the bottom card of another stock pile into the space.

As soon as a card touches a spit pile or a space in the layout, it is deemed to have been played. There is no going back, and as soon as the card touches down, your opponent is free to play onto it.

When neither player can make any more moves, both shout 'Spit!' and turn over the top cards from the spit cards held in hand. The two cards are placed on top of the respective spit piles and play resumes.

The first player to empty the cards from his layout onto the spit piles is the undisputed Spit king. However, if the game reaches stalemate and neither player can make any further moves, the game can either be considered drawn or, if you are determined to get a positive result, you can count up the cards players have left in their layouts, awarding victory to whoever has fewest.

spit cards
in hand

turned–up
spit cards

spit cards
in hand

Colonel

Age range 9+
Skill level 3
Good for Rummy graduates looking for a fresh challenge

A compulsive and addictive Rummy variant (see page 50), which will have the noisiest of teenagers enraptured.

Aim of the game
To meld a hand of ten cards into sets of three or four, either by sequence or rank.

Preparation
Both players are dealt out ten cards, which are placed face down in front of them.

The remainder are placed face down in a stock pile in the centre of the table and the top card is turned over and placed to one side. This aspect of the game is identical to Rummy (see page 50).

Variation
∗ An optional twist on Colonel sees the introduction of a challenge. At any point during the game prior to the stock pile running out, one of the players can challenge his opponent to put down his cards and have a count-up. If the player challenged declines, the game continues as normal; however, if he accepts, play is brought to a halt and the cards are scored in the same way as when the stock pile runs out.

How to play
The non-dealer leads off and can take either the exposed face-up card (which is called the option card) or the unseen top card from the stock pile. Whichever he chooses, he must then discard one of his cards, which is placed face up and becomes the new option card.

At the end of his turn the player may now declare any sequences or sets of cards he has completed. He does not have to do this, but should he decide he would prefer to, the sets are placed face up on the table.

Either player can add to a declared three-of-a-kind or sequence during the game, provided he does so during his turn. So, for example, if Tom declares three Kings during his turn, his opponent, Joe, can lay off the odd King he holds when it is his turn.

Players take turns alternately, with each free to take either the stock or option card.

The first player to empty his hand and play out all his cards is the winner. Of course, this situation does not always arise, so if the stock pile is emptied before either player can play out his cards, the game can be decided on points. The players count up the value of the cards held in hand, with all the court cards and Aces counting ten and all others the value of their pips. The player with the lowest total is the winner.

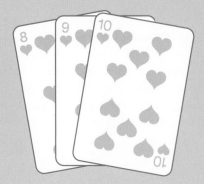

sequence

three-of-a-kind

Tip for beginners

∗ As in Rummy, the key is to keep your options open for as long as possible and to note the cards collected and ignored by your opponent. Avoid pursuing sets that can be completed by only one card: go after those that offer a greater chance of success.

Scoring

∗ Colonel can be played on a game-by-game basis, with the first to win a set number of hands declared the champion, or it can be played using a more complicated but traditional points system. In the latter scenario, the winning player receives points commensurate with the difference between the value of the cards held at the end of the game compared to his opponent's closing hand. So, for example, if Tom holds two Kings (value = 20) when the stock runs out but Joe has two Queens and a Jack (value = 30 points), Tom wins the game and adds the score of ten (30 − 20 = 10) to his total. The first player to reach an agreed figure is the champion.

Whist

or Trumps

Age range 9+
Skill level 5
Good for Teenagers who want to develop their card-playing skills and enjoy a competitive game

Whist is a great introduction to the world of grown-up card games and opens up a catalogue of games to the budding player. The instructions and example shown here are for two-player Whist, but the same principles can be applied to include more people in the game.

Aim of the game

To win more tricks than your opponent. A trick is the name given to one complete round of Whist; for example, if you have two players, the two cards on the table at the end of a round constitute a trick. The highest card played wins the trick and the victorious player gets to keep the cards, which will be counted up at the end to determine the game's winner.

Preparation

To determine who deals first, the players must cut the pack. The cards are placed in the centre of the table and each player in turn lifts off a small section from the deck. The card at the bottom of each section is shown to the other player and the player who has 'cut' the highest card (Aces are high) deals first. Should the two players draw cards of equal rank, a second cut is made. The job of dealer is swapped (or passes around the table in a clockwise fashion) with each hand. The dealer shuffles the cards and passes them to the other player, who cuts the deck and places the bottom half of the pack on the top half. The cards can now be dealt.

Cards are dealt one at a time and are placed face down in front of the players. If playing with more than two, the first card is dealt to the player on the left of the dealer, who works her way clockwise around the table.

How to play

For two-player Whist, each player is dealt seven cards. The player who has not dealt (or the player to the left of the dealer) starts the game and lays a card face up on the table. This card is now the lead card and the other player must follow its suit if she can. If the lead card had been a six of diamonds, the next player must play a diamond if she has one. To stand a chance of winning the hand, she must play a diamond card of higher rank than the six her opponent played. If she has no diamonds, she cannot 'follow' and must instead 'discard' a card of a different suit. You cannot win a trick with a discarded card, so its rank is irrelevant. The dealer retains his lead for the round of seven tricks.

For example, in the game shown in the diagram opposite, Player Two starts. The ticks show the winner of each trick. The first player to win four tricks is the winner. Player Two triumphs here, winning four tricks to his opponent's three.

player 1 player 2

trick 1

player 1 player 2

trick 2

trick 4

trick 3

trick 5

trick 6 ♣

trick 7

Variation
* Many Whist variants employ trump cards which can be used when a player is unable to follow suit. A trump will beat any other card except a trump of higher rank. The trump suit is defined by an extra cut of the deck prior to dealing.

Tip for beginners
* Whist is a more serious game and young players will have to learn to respect the rules of the game. It may seem quite stuffy to start dictating how the cards are to be shuffled, cut and dealt, but if you can manage to establish good habits now, you will avoid confusion in the future.

German whist

Age range 9+
Skill level 4
Good for Tactical types with time on their hands

German Whist is a game that calls for concentration, rigour and strategy. Impulsive younger siblings should resist the temptation to join in unless they are blessed with the tactical brain of a military commander.

Aim of the game
To win seven of the last 13 tricks.

Preparation
Thirteen cards are dealt to each player. The remaining cards are placed in a stock pile on the table and the dealer turns over the top card to reveal the trump suit for the game. This card is also the prize for the first trick winner.

How to play
The non-dealer leads off the first trick and the usual rules apply. The next player must follow suit or, if he can't, must play a trump. If he can do neither, he knocks on the table, surrenders one of his cards and loses the trick. The two cards played are put to one side and will not feature in the remainder of the game.

The winner of the trick collects the face-up card (the card turned over to set the trump suit), while the loser takes the top card from the face-down stack. The next card in the stack is turned over and is the prize for the next trick's winner.

Trick winners lead each subsequent hand and the game continues in this fashion until the stack of cards is exhausted. No scores are kept for this phase of the game, as the aim is to mould and strengthen your hand in readiness for the game's second phase, which now commences.

The trick playing continues, but with the stock pile gone, the players' hand of cards now diminishes with each trick. Scores are kept, with players receiving a point for each winning trick.

The first player to win seven tricks in the second phase of the game is the winner.

Tips for beginners

* German Whist is a game of two halves. In the first half the players attempt to engineer the best hand possible by winning (or sometimes losing) tricks; while the second half sees them go all out to secure the seven trick wins that bring ultimate victory. In the first half, it is important for players to think carefully about whether they want to win particular tricks or not, depending on the exposed card: the prize for victory. Decide how good a card it is worth playing to win the exposed card. In some cases, you are better off taking your chance with the face-down card!

* Strictly speaking, you must follow suit if you can and, if you can't, you must play a trump if you have one. However, if the exposed card is worthless, you may not want to sacrifice a more valuable card, in which case you must forget that you've got a playable card. Knock on the table, surrender another card and take the face-down card instead. Should you later need to use the card, you'll have to tell your opponent it was the one you picked up upon losing the earlier trick. Of course, you're only cheating yourself … but then, as they say, all's fair in love and Whist.

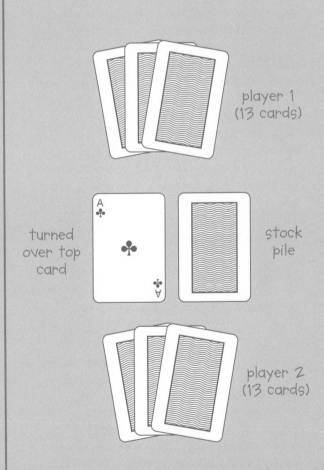

player 1
(13 cards)

turned
over top
card

stock
pile

player 2
(13 cards)

Cardgo

or Bingo, bango

Age range 5+
Skill level I
Good for Noisy parties and prize-chasing children

A card game that harnesses the inexplicable addictiveness of Bingo and the opportunity to win prizes is irresistible to any pre-teen partygoer.

Aim of the game
To get rid of your cards while there are prizes still to be won!

Preparation
This is definitely a game that requires supervision, so appoint a responsible adult to act as dealer and game caller. The dealer needs to make it clear in advance whether two cards of the same rank can be played at the same time or not if a player happens to hold more than one of them.

Once the dealer has all the players seated around a table, she deals five cards to each of them and places the remainder of the pack face down at her side.

Each player holds her five cards in her hand and well away from the glare of nosey opponents.

How to play
The game begins when the dealer turns over the top card of her stack and announces its value; so, for example, if the top card is a four of diamonds, she will simply say 'Four'. The dealer continues to turn the cards over, announcing them at a steady and unbroken pace until the game reaches its end.

The players check each newly revealed card against those they hold in hand. If they have a card of matching value, they must place it face down in front of them.

The flow of the game must be continuous; make it clear to the players that if they are distracted and miss a card, you will not pause the game for them to backtrack. Concentration is the key to this game.

The winner is the first player to turn all her cards face down. When this feat is achieved, the victorious player must shout 'Cardgo'. If two players put their cards down at the same time, it is the first to call 'Cardgo' who wins the game.

Variation
* If you want to get specific and make things a little harder, you can play the game with a divided pack. Simply split the pack by colour, separating the red cards from the black. Deal the reds to the players and keep the black cards as the stock. If you have more than five players, you will need two packs of cards.

Age range 7–10
Skill level 1
Good for A party with children, but adults can play too
What you will need Two packs of cards if more than eight players

Sevens

This is a game that goes under a variety of names, but children know the simplest version as Sevens.

How to play

A dealer is decided by any method. He deals all the cards out, one by one face down beginning with the player to his left. Some players may get one card more than others, so if a few games are played the deal should circulate to the left.

The player to the dealer's left begins play by laying any seven on the table. If she hasn't one, the next player to the left has the opportunity to lay one and so on. Once a seven is laid, then the eight or the six of the same suit can be played to it. A seven can always be played.

Once a suit is started, it gets built up in rows, from seven up to King in one direction, and from seven down to Ace in the other. Only one card is laid at a time. A player who cannot go must miss his turn.

A player must go if he can. He cannot hold back a card to stop the development of a suit. Of course, if he has a choice of cards to lay, he is entitled to choose the one that suits him best. The player who gets rid of all his cards first is the winner.

Cheat!

Age range 8–12
Skill level 1
Good for Amusing children with a noisy card game

This is a popular game in which sometimes, in fact often, you have to lie or cheat. Children love shouting out 'Cheat!' to each other, even though it might cost them a chance of winning if they're wrong.

How to play

Each player draws a card from the pack, and the player with the highest card (Ace is high) deals.

The whole pack (or double pack) is dealt out one at a time face down beginning with the player on the dealer's left. The object of the game is to get rid of all your cards.

The player on the dealer's left begins play by placing a card to the centre of the table face down, at the same time announcing its rank (for example, two, six or King). She may announce the true rank or she can lie and pretend it is any other card.

Suppose the player lays down a card and announces 'Queen'. The next player must lay a card face down on top of it and announce the next highest rank upwards, in this case 'King'. That player may have a King, and can lay it. But if she hasn't got a King, she must choose any other card she holds and lay it announcing 'King'. So here she is cheating. The next player must lay a card and announce 'Ace', but of course only she knows if it really is an Ace. In this game, Ace ranks both high and low, so the

sequence runs Queen, King, Ace, two, three and so on – in other words it is a never-ending sequence.

Each player on her turn must lay a card and must announce the requisite rank, whether the card is that rank or not.

The laying of cards continues until a player challenges another with the cry of 'Cheat!'. The player who is challenged must then turn over the card she has just laid. If she has been caught out cheating, and the card is not of the rank she said it was, she must take all the cards on the table into her hand, plus any two cards that the successful accuser wants to give her from her own hand. However, a player cannot hand over these two bonus cards if they are the only cards she holds – she must retain at least one card in her hand. Getting rid of these two cards is a bonus for the successful accuser, and it is to encourage players to cry 'Cheat! – it is tempting for some ultra-cautious players to leave all the challenging to others.

If the player who is challenged has not been cheating, and the card is as she said, then the challenger takes all the cards into his hand.

If two or more players call 'Cheat!' at the same time, then the player nearest to the left of the player challenged is the one deemed to have made the challenge.

What you will need Two packs of cards if more than eight players

The player forced to take the cards into her hand begins the new round of play by laying any card from her hand and announcing its rank (truly or falsely, as she wishes, of course).

The first player to get rid of her cards wins. Of course, as soon as a player lays her last card somebody should cry 'Cheat!'. It is probable she is cheating, so instead of winning she will have to pick up the pile from the table. The game can thus go on for a long time before somebody actually does win.

Children love this game and will probably demand countless repeats.

Old maid

Age range 7–10
Skill level 1
Good for Amusing young children
What you will need Two packs of
cards if more than six players

**Instead of a single winner, this game has
a single loser, so avoid it if there are
sensitive souls present.**

Preparation
Remove from the pack (or two packs) one of the
queens, so that an odd number of queens are left.

How to play
The cards are dealt until all are exhausted (it does
not matter if some children have one more card
than others).

The children look at their cards and lay down in
front of them on the table any pairs (for example,
two threes, two Kings) they hold. If a player holds
three of a kind, he lays down a pair and keeps the
third card.

The first player to go holds his remaining cards face
down and offers them to the player to his left. She
takes one and adds it to her cards. If the card she

receives makes a pair with a card in her hand, she
lays the pair down with the others.

Whether the accepted card makes a pair or not,
she shuffles her cards and offers them in a fan face
down to the player on her left who takes one, and
so on.

Players gradually drop out as the cards get discarded
as pairs, and finally only the odd Queen is left. The
player holding it is 'Old maid', and the loser.

Children are always anxious that a Queen in their
hand gets passed on, and often show their pleasure
when it is. As a result, the whereabouts of the odd
Queen is often known, but this just seems to add to
the excitement.

Age range 6–10
Skill level 1
Good for Entertaining children with
a simple card game.

Fish

**This is a very simple game, but it's also
easy to cheat, so keep a close watch.**

How to play

One child is chosen as dealer, and deals five cards to
each player including himself, the remainder being
put face down in the centre of the table as the stock.

The object is to form sets of four cards of the
same rank (for example, four sixes or four Aces). The
player on the dealer's left begins by naming another
player and asking her to hand over all her cards
of a certain rank ('Hannah, give me your nines'). If
Hannah has any nines, she must hand them over.
A player cannot ask for cards, however, without
holding at least one card of the rank himself.

Should a player asked not hold a card of that rank,
she says 'Fish', and the asking player takes a card from
the stock. If the asking player successfully obtains a
card he requests either from the player or the stock
(in which case he shows it), he is entitled to another
turn, and keeps the turn until he is unsuccessful,
when it passes to the player on his left.

As soon as a player obtains a set of four cards, he
lays them down on the table in front of him. The
winner is the player with most sets at the end,
by which time all the cards will be on the table.
If, on his turn, a player has no cards, he takes one
from stock, but must wait until his next turn
before asking for a card from another player.

Warning
* Young children who have collected three
cards of the same rank have been known to
throw tantrums when asked to hand them
to a player holding the fourth one. You have
been warned.

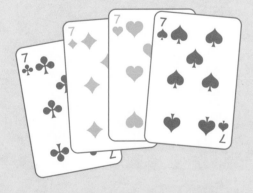

Rummy

Age range 6+
Skill level 3
Good for Teaching grandma who's the best at cards

Rummy is one of the most popular family card games in the world, and with good reason. The rules are simple, the gameplay is slick and victory is always sweet.

Aim of the game

To meld your hand into sets of cards that either run sequentially (for example, Jack, Queen, King of hearts) or that are equal in value (for example, three Aces). Alternatively, you can win the game with a run of seven cards (for example, Ace to seven of clubs).

Preparation

Rummy can be played with 2–7 players. The players cut to deal: the lowest card determines the dealer.

Each player is given seven cards, which are dealt individually and face down. When all players have their seven cards, the dealer gives an eighth card to the player seated to her left. The stack of remaining cards in the deck is placed face down in the centre of the table.

How to play

The player who has the eight cards starts the game by throwing away one of her cards. The discarded card starts a new, face-up pile next to the stack placed in the centre of the table.

The turn passes around the table in a clockwise direction. Players now have two options: they can either take the top face-up card or, if that card is

Variation

* To increase the pace of the game, some slight changes can be made. Firstly, you can introduce jokers to represent any card in a set. Twos are also traditionally used for this purpose. Secondly, you can rule that a run of six cards in sequence is considered a winning hand providing the seventh card has a pip value of seven or less.

Tip for beginners

* The key to success in Rummy lies in pursuing the right cards. Keep your options open for as long as you can: for example, the Ace and two of spades can only make a set of cards if one card (the three of spades) comes up. But if you hold the four of hearts, the four of clubs and the three of clubs, your chances of making a set are greatly increased as any one of four cards can complete a playable trio.

not appealing, they can turn over the top card of the face-down stack. Whichever option they choose, they must throw away one card onto the face-up stack at the end of their turn. They can, of course, discard the card they just picked up.

The game continues, with players taking alternate turns until either one player declares that she is ready to 'Go down', or the stack of face-down cards runs out. If the latter occurs, the adjacent pile of face-up cards is simply inverted and the game subsequently resumed.

The winner is the player who is first to successfully assemble all of her hand into sets of complete cards. A set of three plus a set of four (either runs or cards of equal value) is enough to secure victory. So, for example, a trio of Kings plus the seven, eight, nine and ten of hearts would make for a winning hand.

To find out who comes second and third, the remaining players must reveal their cards and count up the pip value of any cards that do not form part of complete sets. If, for example, you had a trio of Queens, a pair of twos and a pair of fours, your deficit score for the hand would be 12. The Queens count as a complete set so have a value of zero, but the sum of the other cards, which are not in complete sets, counts against you. The player with the lowest deficit score comes second.

Pairs

or Concentration, Memory,
Pelmanism

Age range 3+
Skill level 2
Good for Getting competitive
youngsters to concentrate and test their
powers of memory.

**A game of concentration and memory,
there could be wide variations in the skill
levels of children of different ages.**

Aim of the game

To locate matching pairs and collect more cards
than your opponents by the time the table is bare.

To start

For this game to run smoothly, it is imperative that
the cards are laid out properly at the start of the
game. The cards (which must be shuffled) are placed
face down on a flat surface (for example, a table)
and spaced evenly in a grid made up of 13 rows of
four cards.

How to play

The game begins when the youngest player turns over two cards in the layout. If the cards revealed are of equal value, the player picks them up and puts them to one side. He or she may now reveal another pair of cards, and their turn continues until they choose two cards that do not match.

When two unmatched cards are revealed, they remain in the layout and are turned face down once more before the next player takes their turn.

It is important that players take great care not to make a mess of the layout. If cards move out of line and start overlapping, the game can easily descend into chaos.

Players then take alternate turns and continue until there are no cards left to play because they have all been taken. At the end of the game players count up how many pairs of cards they have each collected. The player with the most cards is the winner.

Variation

* If matching cards by their face value becomes too easy, you can also make the game colour-specific. So, for example, if you reveal the two of hearts, you will only complete a match if you locate the two of diamonds next.

Tip for beginners

* Pairs is essentially a game that tests the players' ability to memorize card positions. To improve your chances of winning, you must endeavour to employ strategies that will help you recall the positions of the cards revealed throughout the game. Some people use repetition, chanting to themselves as if they were saying a mantra (for example, 'top left Ace, bottom right Queen'), while others try to visualize the cards they have seen. More sophisticated memory systems like 'chunking' can be researched through self-help books if you're feeling very competitive. Be warned, though – children often have very good memories compared to those found in the addled brains of adults. If you're not careful, your precocious six-year-old might well give you a sound thrashing at Pairs.

Dry Jack

Age range 7+
Skill level 3
Good for Rainy days on holiday and those rare occasions when there's no TV, no stereo and no phone reception

Dry Jack is another multi-player game that can be played for prizes or for pride ... whichever you choose, it's a great way to while away a few hours.

Aim of the game

To win as many scoring cards as you can and take dry tricks whenever possible.

Preparation

Cut the cards to select a dealer; the player who draws the lowest card gets the job and deals six cards to each player. If you have more than four players, you will need to use two packs of cards.

Four cards are then dealt face up into a neat pile in the centre of the table. The remainder of the deck is put to one side in readiness for the next deal.

How to play

The player to the left of the dealer leads off and plays a card from her hand onto the top of the face-up pile. If she plays a card of equal rank, she wins the cards beneath. The cards won are put to one side until the end of the game, when the scores are finally settled.

If she plays a card of another rank onto the face-up pile, the turn simply moves around the table in a clockwise direction.

player 1
(6 cards)

stock
(4 cards)

player 2
(6 cards)

The gameplay is relatively simple and moves quickly from one player to the next. The only complicating factors are that:

Jacks operate like trumps and take the face-up pile irrespective of the value of the top card.

If a player wins a new pile that consists of just one card, that player is said to have completed a 'dry trick' and wins a bonus ten points.

When the stock pile is taken, the next player must start a new pile by laying a card face up into the centre of the table. The game continues in this way until the players have each used their six cards. The dealer then deals out another hand of six cards to each and adds four cards to the stock pile.

The game reaches its end when there are not enough cards left to complete a fresh deal. At this point, the players turn over the cards they have won and points are awarded on the following basis:

The player who has won the most cards – 5
The player who has the most hearts – 5
For each Jack held – 1
For the Ace of spades – 2
For the ten of spades – 2

Don't forget to take into consideration the ten bonus points awarded to any player completing a dry trick.

Tip for beginners

* Players must choose very carefully when to make an attack. It would obviously be unwise to forgo the chance to make a dry trick, but in other circumstances you may like to wait before playing a matching card. Jacks, in particular, should be saved up until a scoring card has been played or until there are several hearts in the pile.

I promise

or 'Oh well', Nomination trumps

Age range 8+
Skill level 4
Good for Family parties and other mixed gatherings

Whether played for stakes or fun, I Promise is an engaging trick-based game that is a favourite with kids and adults alike!

Aim of the game

To successfully predict how many tricks you will win in any given deal.

Preparation

Cut the cards to select a dealer; the player who draws the lowest card gets the job. The dealer distributes the cards until there are not enough to make another complete round of the table. Each player must have the same number of cards as his rivals, with any spare cards put to one side.

Before the players look at their cards, the dealer turns over the last card dealt to himself as this card indicates the trump suit for the deal.

The players now assess their cards and begin making their 'promises'. The player to the left of the dealer starts the process and must declare how many tricks she 'promises' to win during the hand. The number announced is recorded by the dealer.

How to play

When all players have made their predictions, the trick playing begins, with the player sitting to the left of the dealer laying the first card.

In the fashion of Whist (see page 40), all players must either follow suit or, if they can't, play a trump. If they can do neither, they discard a card. The player laying the highest trump, or if no trumps are played, the highest card that follows in suit, wins that particular trick.

At the end of each trick, the dealer records who won. The trick winner then gets to lead off the next trick.

Play continues until the cards run out. The scores are then counted up and players are awarded one

Variation

* Variations on the game include reducing the number of cards by one each time, moving the deal around the table and predicting how many tricks you won't win. In this version, a player has all his points deducted for that round if he ends up winning the amount of tricks he said that he wouldn't win.

point for each winning trick, plus a bonus of ten points if they successfully predicted the number of winning tricks they would make. So, for example, if Tom said he'd win three and did so, he'd earn 13 points for the hand, but if Meryl had said she'd win five but only won four, her total would be four points. Players continue playing hands in this way and the first person to reach a total of 100 points is the winner.

This player could bid three tricks fairly safely.

Tip for beginners

* Avoid reaching your predicted total too early in the hand, as you may find that your opponents gang up on you to ensure you win an additional trick that will mean you lose your ten-point bonus. For example, if you predict you will win three tricks and take the first two of eight, you would be unwise to play a high-ranking trump at the next hand. Sure, you'll take the trick, but with five hands remaining you cannot afford to win any more, and you may find yourself vulnerable should your opponents decide to conspire against you. If they all play low-ranking cards, you may be forced to take an unwanted victory.

With only two high cards, this player would be safer bidding two tricks or three if spades or diamonds were trumps.

Knock-out whist

or Trumps

Age range 9+
Skill level 4
Good for Kids who think they've mastered Rummy and want to impress with their trick-playing prowess

Absorbing, tactical and time-consuming, Knock-out Whist is perfect for those competitive teenagers with a desire to win.

Aim of the game

To survive the early rounds of the game and win the final trick of the final hand.

Preparation

The gameplay of Knock-out Whist is not greatly different to that described for two-player Whist (see page 40). It is, in essence, a simple trick-based game and can be played by up to seven players with a standard deck.

After the pack has been cut and the player with the lowest card has been appointed dealer, the players are each dealt seven cards. The remainder of the deck is placed on the table and the dealer turns the top card over to set the trump suit for the hand.

How to play

The player to the left of the dealer leads off the first trick and can play any card to start the game.

The turn moves around the table clockwise and, in the usual fashion, players follow suit to continue the trick. Alternatively, they can play a trump card, or failing that they must knock on the table to indicate that they cannot play a card onto the trick. The knocking player must then surrender one of his or her cards.

The trick is won by the highest trump card (Aces are high) or the highest card that follows suit if no trumps are played. The dealer keeps score along the way, writing down the number of tricks won in each hand by each player.

Tip for beginners

* When choosing trumps, opt for the suit from which you have most cards. If you have equal numbers of cards from two suits, go for the one from which you have the lowest-ranking cards. A high-ranked non-trump will still offer a good prospect of victory.

The winner of a trick leads the next trick, and the winner of the most tricks in a hand gets to choose the trump suit for the next deal.

With each hand the number of cards dealt reduces by one, so the second deal sees each player receive six cards and at the seventh and final deal the players receive just one card each.

The knock-out element of the game comes into play at the end of each hand, when any players who have failed to win a trick during that deal are knocked out. These players play no further part in the game.

The winner is either the player who wins the final trick of the final hand or the last player left when all rivals are eliminated.

Variation

* The first player knocked out of the game can (if all parties have agreed prior to the game) be granted what is known as a 'dog's life'. They are given a single card at the next deal and can play the card on any trick they choose, so if the other players have six cards, they can pass on five tricks before making their move. If they win the trick, they rejoin the game and are dealt a normal hand on the next deal. If, however, they fail, they are knocked out of the game along with any other players who have failed to win a trick during the round. A further variation that, again, must be agreed by all parties is to provide the first player out with one more chance of staying in the game after failing with the 'dog's life' through a 'blind dog'. Here the player is given a card face down and can choose to play the unseen card on any of the tricks. Though the chances of winning a trick are slim, it's a great feeling to win and get back into the game simply on the turn of a blind card.

Samuel Spade the gardener

Age range 8+
Skill level 3
Good for Parties where children are the same age, and of roughly the same capabilities, such as a group of school friends

This game is similar to the well-known card games called Fish and Happy families, and is as simple. The fun comes from the outlandish names the children have to remember.

How to play

For up to six players: from the pack of cards take the Ace, King, Queen, Jack and ten of each suit.

For seven or eight players: take the Ace, King, ten and nine of each suit.

For nine or ten players: take the Ace down to the eight of each suit.

The dealer shuffles the cards and deals them out one at a time to the players, beginning with the player on his left, and including himself, until all the

Special names for the cards:

* **King of spades:** Samuel Spade the gardener.
* **Queen of spades:** Samuel Spade the gardener's wife.
* **Jack of spades:** Samuel Spade the gardener's son.
* **Ace of spades:** Samuel Spade the gardener's servant.
* **Ten of spades:** Samuel Spade the gardener's dog.
* If used, **nine of spades:** Samuel Spade the gardener's cat.
* If used, **eight of spades:** Samuel Spade the gardener's canary.
* **King of hearts:** Henry Heart the butcher.
* **Queen of hearts:** Henry Heart the butcher's wife, the **Jack** is his son, the **Ace** is his servant, the **ten** is his dog, the **nine** his cat and the **eight** his canary.
* **King of diamonds:** Dominic Diamond the jeweller, the **Queen** is Dominic Diamond the jeweller's wife, the **Jack** his son, the **Ace** his servant, the **ten** his dog, the **nine** his cat and the **eight** his canary.
* **King of clubs:** Clarence Club the policeman, and the **Queen** his wife, the **Jack** his son, the **Ace** his servant, the **ten** his dog, the **nine** his cat and the **eight** his canary.

cards are gone. It does not matter if some players have one more card than others.

The object is to collect together all the cards of one family. When a player has obtained the whole of a family – for example, Dominic Diamond the Jeweller and his wife, son, servant and dog, and, if being used, his cat and canary – he lays them down on the table.

When the players have picked up their cards and looked at them, the player to the dealer's left starts the game by asking one of the other players for a card. For example, he might say: 'Hannah, have you got Clarence Club the policeman's dog?' If Hannah has this card she must hand it over, whereupon the asking player adds it to his hand. He then asks Hannah, or any other player, for any other card. So long as the player asked has the card, it must be handed over. The asking player keeps asking until the card he asked for is not held by the player he asked, when his turn ends; the turn to ask passes to the player on his left, and so on.

The asking player must ask for the card by its proper name. For example, he must ask for 'Clarence Club the policeman's dog' and not the 'ten of clubs'. If he gets the name wrong, his turn ends.

An asking player can ask for any card he likes, whether or not he has a card of the relevant suit in his hand. For example, he can ask a player for

Tip for beginners

* In this game, fortunes may swing quickly, as a player with many cards in his hand can lose the lot at one turn. For example, the player whose turn it is when there are only two players left knows that all the cards not laid on the table and not in his hand are held by his opponent, who only has to ask for them one by one to acquire the lot, and at least one set. But of course he might still make a mistake in asking for a card by its wrong name!

Samuel Spade the gardener's wife whether he has a spade in his hand or not. It follows that when the second asking player's turn arrives, he can ask for any cards the first asking player might have picked up on his turn. Of course, he's got to be able to remember them.

A player who runs out of cards, either because he has laid down a set or because he has had to give them to other players when asked, drops out of the game (but might still win if he has laid a set or two down).

The game ends when all cards have been laid down and the player with most sets is the winner.

My ship sails

Age range 8–12
Skill level 2
Good for Amusing up to seven children

This game is similar to Pig (see page 70), and will please children as they try to collect seven cards of the same suit.

How to play

Anyone can deal (there is no advantage), and the dealer deals seven cards face down to each player.

Each player's object is to collect seven cards of the same suit. So when players pick up their cards and examine them, they will decide (without telling the other players, of course) which suit (hearts, clubs, diamonds or spades) they will collect. It will be the suit they have most cards of to start with.

Once players have looked at their hands, they all place a card face down to their left. When everyone has done this, the dealer calls 'Go' and each player picks up the card to her right which her neighbour has placed there, adding it to her hand.

This continues for round after round, with players retaining cards of the suit they are collecting, and passing on to their left-hand neighbour cards of the other suits.

Eventually one player will have a hand that holds a set of seven cards all of the same suit. Instantly she calls out 'My ship sails', and lays the seven cards out in a line.

It is possible that two or more players complete a winning hand on the same round, in which case the player who calls 'My ship sails' first is the declared winner.

Sometimes, of course, two players will, without knowing it, be collecting the same suit, which will make it harder for them to win. If there are more than four players, this is a certainty as there are only four suits.

Rolling stone

Age range 8–12
Skill level 3
Good for Amusing a small group
of children

This is an intriguing game that contains an element of trick-taking.

Preparation

You will need to reduce the pack according to the number of players. For six players, remove the twos, making a 48-card pack. For five players, remove the twos, threes and fours, making a 40-card pack. For four players, remove the twos, threes, fours, fives and sixes, making a 32-card pack.

How to play

Each player takes a card from the pack, the player with the highest (Ace high) becoming dealer. She deals out the pack one at a time face down to all the players, who should each receive eight cards.

The object is to be the first player to get rid of all your cards.

Players look at their hands, and the person to the dealer's left lays a card face up on the table. Each player in turn to the left must lay a card of the same suit on top of it.

If all players are able to do this, the player who laid the highest card (Ace high) wins all the cards, which are called a 'trick'.

She lays the cards to one side, and they take no further part. She then lays down a card face up from her hand to begin the next trick.

If a player doesn't have a card of the suit laid on the table, she must on her turn pick up all the cards on the table and place them in her hand. She then lays down a card of another suit to begin the next trick (she is not allowed to lay down a card of the suit she has just picked up).

The tricks won are of no value – the winner is the first player to get rid of all her cards. It is an amusing game because time and again a player will get her hand down to one card and then be forced to pick up others.

Rockaway

Age range 8–13
Skill level 3
Good for Parties with children over 8 years old

This is a simple game to understand, which nevertheless occasionally gives the opportunity for skilful play. Players should hold on to Aces as long as they can and try to keep a good selection of suits and numbers in their hands to give them the maximum chance of being able to go when their turn comes round next.

How to play

The first dealer is chosen by any method – there is no advantage to going first. After shuffling, the dealer deals seven cards face down to each player, then turns the next card face up in the centre of the table. This card is called the 'widow'. The rest of the cards are placed in a pile face down beside it, and are called the stock.

Players take their cards into their hands, and the player to the dealer's left plays first. He must play a card to the widow, which can be one of three: a card of the same suit, a card of the same rank or an Ace.

If he has none of these, he must draw a card from the stock, and continue to do so until he draws a card that will go, which he plays. The following player must play a card to the new top card of the widow, and so on.

If the stock becomes exhausted and a player cannot go, he merely 'knocks' and misses his turn. The hand ends when a player gets rid of all his cards, called 'going boom'. All other players then expose their hands and are debited on the score sheet with the total value of the cards they hold: Aces count 15, court cards (King, Queen, Jack) count ten each, and the other cards have their pip value.

The deal passes round the table clockwise, and when everyone has dealt once, the winner is the player with the lowest debit score.

Variation
* In Rockaway, the Ace is of special value in that it can always go. Thus players should keep hold of Aces at least until an opponent is down to one card and therefore likely to go out next round, when it might be wise to ditch the Ace as it costs 15 points if caught in your hand. Some players give even more value to the Ace, in that a player who lays an Ace can change the suit to whatever he wants, e.g. if he lays the Ace of spades the suit doesn't automatically change to spades but to whatever suit the player specifies.

What you will need Two packs of cards if there more than five players; pencil and paper to score

Example hand

Players A, B, C, D hold the hands in the illustration. Player A dealt, and the widow is the ♥K. Player B is first to play and has to play ♥2. Player C plays ♥6 and Player D ♥J.

On the second round, Player A plays ♥3 (at this stage he holds back ♥A, even though it would cost 15 points if he were caught with it,

because an Ace can always go). Player B is now out of hearts but can play ♣3. Player C now has the choice of playing ♣K or ♦3. Although he would be pleased to get rid of his high-scoring ♣K, he would be advised to play ♦3, thus retaining at least one card of each suit in his hand. This guarantees that he will be able to go on the next round. And so on.

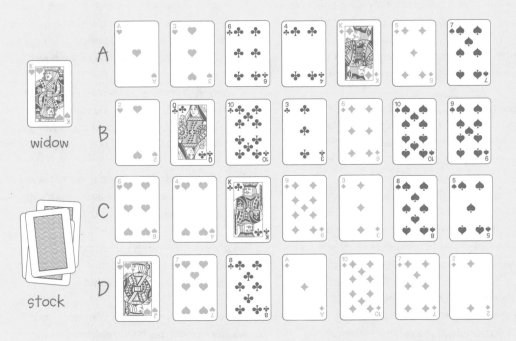

widow

stock

Ranter go round

Age range 8–12
Skill level 2
Good for Large parties of children, as up to 30 can play if necessary
What you will need Three counters or coins for each player; a receptacle for the counters

This is a simple, fun game that could entertain as few as four or five children, a dozen sitting round a table, or even more sitting in a circle on the floor. Also called Cuckoo or Chase-the-Ace, it has been popular for at least three centuries and you can even buy specially made packs without suits to play the game.

How to play

All players are given three counters, one of which they will have to forfeit each time they lose a life, so if you are playing round a table, a bowl, saucer, or other receptacle should be placed in the centre of the table to receive the counters. In this game the cards rank from King (high) down to Ace (low).

Any player may deal. The dealer shuffles the cards and gives one card face down to each player, including herself. The object is to avoid being left holding the lowest card.

Each player looks at his card, and play begins with the player to dealer's left. He decides whether to keep his card or swap it with the player on his left. If he has a card that he considers is unlikely to be lowest, he will keep it. So if there are eight players and he holds a ten, he would think it extremely unlikely that all other players would hold a card of value ten or above, so he wouldn't want to change it for what would probably be a lower card. However, if he had a three, he would change,

knowing that he would only lose if he was given a two in exchange.

To change, a player pushes his card towards his left-hand neighbour and says 'Change'. His neighbour must hand over his card, pick the one offered him and then has the option of changing with his left-hand neighbour, and so on.

The only occasion when a player may refuse to exchange cards is if he holds a King, which is the highest card. He merely says 'King' and exposes it, forcing whoever wished to change to keep his card. The player to the left of the player with the exposed King then can change or not with the player to his left.

If a player, in obeying a command to change, passes to his right an Ace, two or three, he must announce this. This could tell succeeding players that their card is safe, so they would not demand a change.

The dealer is last to play, and if she wishes to change she must cut the remaining pack and change with the card at the top of the bottom half of the pack.

All players then expose their cards, the player or players holding the lowest card losing a life and putting a counter into the middle.

The deal passes to the left after each round. A player who loses his three counters drops out, and the last player remaining is the winner.

Twenty-nine

Ages 8–12
Skill level 2
Good for A small party where four or six children would like to play

This is a neat adding-up game for either four or six players, which requires little more skill than the ability to count to 29.

How to play

With four players, the full pack is used; with six players you remove any ten, nine, eight and two, thus reducing the pack to 48 cards.

In this game each card has a value. Picture cards count as one point only, as do the Aces, while all the other cards count as their pip value.

Any player may deal first (everyone gets the chance to deal once during a game). The dealer shuffles the cards and deals them one at a time to each player, including herself, beginning with the player on her left.

The player to the dealer's left chooses a card and plays it face up to the centre of the table, announcing its value. The next player to the left places a card face up on top and announces the value of the two cards added up. For example, if the first player lays a ten, and calls ten, the second might

Variation

* The game can be played with five players by removing a 10 and 9 from the pack, reducing it to 50 cards, or 10 per player. The game is played in the standard way, but the last pile will add up only to 10, and not 29. The last player to put a card on it wins it.

decide to lay an eight, in which case he would call 18. Players continue to add cards to the pile in turn clockwise round the table. The object is to try to make the total 29. If a player can make the total 29, he wins all the cards in the pile and puts them face down in front of him. The player to his left begins a new pile.

The suits are immaterial. The total of the pile can never exceed 29, and a player must always go if he can. So if the total reaches 26, the next player can win the pile by laying a three. If he hasn't a three, but has a one or two he must lay it. If he has only cards of value more than three, he cannot go. Once a player has played all his cards, he takes no further part in that deal.

Once all the cards have been played, each player scores a point for each card he has won. When each player has dealt once, the scores are added up and the player with the highest total wins.

Authors

Age range 6+
Skill level 2
Good for Mixed gatherings and children's parties

Lively, interactive and demanding, Authors is the perfect game for three to nine players at a party or family gathering.

Aim of the game

To collect complete sets of the same denomination.

Preparation

Authors can be played with as many as nine players and as few as three. Get everybody seated around a table and ask each player to draw a card from a shuffled deck. The player who draws the highest-ranking card is appointed the dealer for the first hand; thereafter the job of dealer moves around the table in a clockwise fashion.

The dealer deals cards one at a time to each player, starting with the person seated to his left. The whole deck is used and distributed as evenly as possible. Some players will end up with more cards than others (unless, of course, you have four players), but this inequity will even itself out providing the deal rotates.

Players should keep their cards concealed from their opponents and should take some time to familiarize themselves with their hands, grouping the cards together by rank.

How to play

The player to the left of the dealer (let's call him Charlie) starts the game by asking any other player (in this case Linus) to give him a particular card, say, for example, the Ace of diamonds. If Linus has the Ace of diamonds, he must give it to Charlie.

Players can only ask for a card if they already hold another card of the same rank. So, back to our example, for Charlie to ask for the Ace of diamonds he must already hold an Ace from one of the other three suits.

If Charlie's bid is successful, his turn continues until he asks for a card from a player who doesn't hold the card he seeks. When this happens, the turn passes to the player asked.

Tip for beginners

* Authors is more a game of fun than strategy and should not be taken too seriously. However, for those competitive souls who must be first at everything, it is advantageous to make a mental note of the cards asked for by opponents.

When a player has collected all four cards of a particular rank, he must place the cards face down in front of him.

If a player runs out of cards, he can take no further part in the current deal. If his hand is emptied by the completion of a set of cards (rather than by another player successfully bidding for his final card), the turn passes to the player from whom he collected his last card.

When all the cards have been played, the players count up the number of completed sets of cards they have collected. The player with the most is the winner of that hand and is given a bonus of ten points. Each player is also awarded a point for every set of cards gathered during the deal. Scores are recorded and the player with the highest aggregate total over a set number of deals is the winner. Alternatively, the game can be played in a 'first past the post' style, with the first to exceed 25 points crowned champion.

Pig

Age range 6+
Skill level 2
Good for Those looking for an alternative to Pass the Parcel and other party game 'classics'
What you will need Pencil and sticky labels (optional)

Whether played for prizes or fun, this is a game sure to delight children, who will relish the opportunity to play cards, act silly, point to their noses and call one another pigs!

Aim of the game
To collect a hand made up of four-of-a-kind.

Preparation
Seat the children around a table or in a circle on the floor. Clear the general area and stand back.

Take a standard 52-card deck and sort the cards by rank so that you end up with 13 complete sets. You will need one complete set per player, so, for example, if you have five players, you could just use the tens, court cards and Aces. It doesn't matter which rank of cards you choose as the object of the game is to be the first player to assemble four-of-a-kind with no preference given to the value of the cards. Put the remainder of the cards to one side and, presuming our example of five players, shuffle the 20 cards you have selected.

Each player is dealt four cards face down in front of her. When all the cards are dealt, the players pick up their hands and prepare to play.

How to play
The gameplay in Pig is continuous rather than alternate, so instead of one player leading off, the supervising adult calls 'Start'. The game commences with the players discarding a card to their left-hand neighbours and picking up the card that, by the same process, arrives at their right.

The game continues, with players discarding and receiving cards one by one, until one of the players completes a four-of-a-kind hand. When this feat is achieved, the triumphant player points to her nose without saying anything.

As soon as a player points to her nose, the others should do likewise. The last player to point to her nose loses the hand.

Tip for beginners
* To maintain the interest of players who are 'out' – and thereby avoid that awkward situation where only two are engaged in the game and the rest are bored – you can introduce a fun new rule. The redundant pigs are allowed to try to distract the active players by talking to them, but should any of them speak back to the ostracized swine, they are out too.

player 1

player 2

player 3
(four-of-a-kind)
PIG!

player 5

player 4

When a player loses a hand, she is given a letter from the word 'pig' as a penalty. The object of the game is to avoid collecting three letters and spelling out the word, at which point you are out. If you are playing Pig at a children's party, you may want to avoid any confusion and argument by writing the letters on some sticky labels and handing them to the losing player at the end of each hand. The game continues until only one player is left, who is then declared the winner.

Newmarket

or Boodle, Stops

Age range 7+
Skill level 2
Good for Rummy graduates
What you will need Twenty counters for each player; two packs of cards

A versatile game that can keep things moving at family parties but that can also occupy rowdy youngsters eager for success or those in search of a boredom cure on a rainy day.

Aim of the game
To be the first player to get rid of all your cards … and along the way to collect more counters than your opponents!

Preparation
Players each take a card from the deck, and expose it: whoever has chosen the lowest card becomes the dealer.

Tip for beginners
* Consider carefully your options when leading off, as this is your opportunity to control the game. Watch the cards played and try to work out which cards your opponents hold. As the game develops, you may be able to frustrate your rivals by playing high-ranking cards that rid you of a particular suit without allowing them the opportunity to do likewise.

After shuffling and cutting the deck, the dealer distributes the cards as evenly as possible to the players. He also deals out a dummy hand, which he then places to one side along with any spare cards.

Before the players look at their cards, the dealer takes four cards from a separate pack and lays them face up on the table. These are called the boodle cards and they must be an Ace, King, Queen and Jack each from different suits; so, for example, the Jack of spades, Queen of diamonds, King of hearts and Ace of clubs.

The players are each given ten counters, which they must place on the boodle cards (they are also given another ten counters, which they keep in reserve). They can place all ten counters on one card, but more often will spread them around.

How to play
With the stakes placed, the player to the left of the dealer leads off. He can play a card of any suit, but it must be the lowest card that he holds in that suit.

Play is continuous rather than alternate, and the next player to go is the one who holds the next-highest card in the suit. So, for example, if Player One had laid the seven of hearts, the player who holds the eight of hearts would go next.

The play continues in this way until either the play is blocked because the card needed is tucked away

   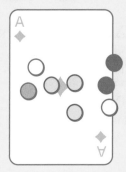

in the dummy hand, or because the run is complete (Aces are high, so the appearance of an Ace automatically brings the run to an end).

Play is restarted by the person who played the last card, and resumes with him leading the lowest card of another suit. If, however, he does not hold any cards from another suit, the job of leading off passes to the player on his left.

When a player plays a card identical to one of the boodle cards, he receives all the counters that have been staked on that particular card.

The player who gets rid of all his cards first wins the hand. The victor receives one counter from the other players in respect of every card they still hold at the time they emptied their hand. If no player manages to get rid of all his cards, the winner is the player with fewest cards when the game becomes blocked. In these circumstances, the winner is entitled to one counter from all of his rivals in respect of the difference between the cards he has left and those they still hold in hand. So, for example, if David had three cards left at the end of the game and his rivals Stewart and Sharon each had five, they would both have to pay the victorious David two counters.

Fee-fi-fo-fum

Age range 7+
Number of players 4–6
Skill level I
Good for The usual ranks of over-excited partygoers

With a fairy-tale chant and prizes on offer, Fee-Fi-Fo-Fum is sure to make your party go with a swing.

Aim of the game

To lay as many stop cards as possible and be the first player to empty your hand.

Preparation

Deal out a well-shuffled pack between all the players. It doesn't matter if some players have an extra card; this inequity will even itself out if the starting point for the deal rotates with each hand.

Tip for beginners

* You can play this game strategically if you wish, plotting which card will give you the best opportunity to lay a stop card and thereby give you the chance to lay a Fee card. However, the feverish excitement of a children's party is no environment for ponderous tactical thinking. Keep the game moving quickly and play for fun.

How to play

The player to the left of the dealer starts. He can play any card he wishes, setting it down face up in the centre of the table. As he lays the card, he says 'Fee'.

The player who has the next card in ascending sequence and matching suit follows, playing the card and announcing it by saying 'Fi'. So, for example, if the game had opened with the six of clubs (Fee), the next card would be the seven of clubs (Fi). The play continues with whoever holds the eight, nine and ten, each player announcing his cards with calls of 'Fo', 'Fum' and 'Giant's tum' respectively.

The sequence ends when a player lays a card and calls 'Giant's tum'. The player who brought the run to a

fee   fi   fo   fum   GIANT'S TUM!

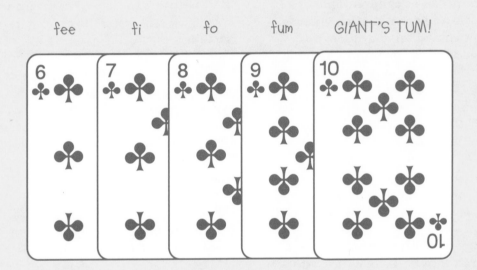

halt in this way starts the game off again by laying a new Fi card from his hand. Sequences do not go 'round the corner', so when a King is laid (irrespective of whether it is a Fee, Fi, Fo or Fum card), the sequence must stops and must then be restarted by the player who played the King. Aces are low.

As the game develops, more and more cards will become stop cards because the next card in sequence has already been played. For example, following the opening sequence of the four to eight of hearts, the three of hearts would now become a stop card. When it is played, the run ends and the player who laid it starts a new sequence with a fresh Fee card.

The first player to play all his cards is the winner. Continue playing until only one player is left holding cards. If you wanted to add a little spice to the proceedings, you could lay out individually wrapped sweets as prizes. Put out enough sweets for all but one of the players … he who comes last gets nothing.

Red dog

or High card pool

Age range 7+
Number of players 2–10
Skill level 2
Good for Getting any children's party buzzing
What you will need Sweets or counters as stakes

Red Dog is a game of chance that is best played for prizes at children's parties ... quick, tense and dramatic, it's great for between two and ten players and is guaranteed to get your soiree swinging.

Aim of the game
To trump the top card of the stock with a higher-ranked card of the same suit.

Preparation
Give every child a bag of individually wrapped confectionery to use as stakes and seat all the players around a table.

With younger children it is probably best to appoint an adult to act as dealer (and as de facto arbitrator in the event of any disputes). Older children can draw cards from a shuffled deck to determine the dealer; lowest card gets the job.

Before the cards are dealt, the players each put an agreed number of sweet treats (units) into the centre of the table to establish a pool. It is probably best to start with two per player.

Five cards are now dealt to each player (although if the number of players exceeds eight, each will receive only four). The players pick up their cards and assess them. A good hand is one that includes high-ranking cards of all four suits, with the four Kings offering the perfect hand and guaranteed victory. The remaining cards are placed face down in front of the dealer in a stock pile.

Players must now place their stakes prior to the game commencing. The player to the left of the

Tip for beginners
* If you have a great hand with lots of high-ranking cards, you will be tempted to stake big, but you may be wise to play more discreetly. A big stake may discourage your opponents from making a big bid themselves. A couple of overconfident, gung-ho players can soon boost the pool, so let them believe they are going to win and watch them throw their sweets away!

dealer starts the bidding and must stake at least one unit. The maximum bid by any one player must not exceed the total number of units held in the pool (so, in our example, if there were five players, no individual could stake more than ten pieces of confectionery).

How to play

The player to the left of the dealer goes first. The dealer turns over the top card of the stock and turns it face up on the table.

If the player can beat it (with a higher-ranked card of the same suit), she shows the other players her superior card and collects the sweets from the pool. The winning player keeps her remaining cards and the pool is restocked with another two units

from each player. If the active player cannot beat the card turned over by the dealer, she must turn over her hand of cards and her stake is then added to the pool.

The game continues until all players have had their turn. If, after this, you wish to continue playing, then the cards must be gathered up and a fresh deal made.

The player with the most sweets is the winner … though her dentist may also consider themselves somewhat fortuitous. Of course, if you prefer not to give your children sweets, you can play for counters that can be totalled up at the end of the game, with a non-confectionery prize awarded to the final victor.

31s

Ages 6+
Skill level 3
Good for Those who are tired of Pontoon
What you will need Sweets as stakes

As long as they can all add up to 31, up to 15 players can take part in this game, and what's more they'll all love it ... but especially the winner.

Aim of the game
To hold a hand of 31 ... the clue's in the name.

Preparation
A full deck of cards is used and all players should be given an equal amount of individually wrapped sweets to use as stakes.

Before the deal is made, players agree a stake for the hand, which is placed into a central kitty.

The cards are cut to determine who will be the dealer, and the deal passes around the table clockwise with each hand.

All players are dealt three cards, which are placed face down in front of them. Three additional cards are laid face up in a row in the centre of the table (this is called the widow hand).

How to play
In traditional fashion, the player to the left of the dealer goes first. She must swap one card from her hand for one of the cards in the widow hand. She cannot pass and cannot exchange more than one card at a time.

The turn passes around the table clockwise, with players swapping cards one by one.

The game comes to a halt either when one player has a hand of 31 (Aces count 11) or when any player 'knocks' because she is confident that her hand – though imperfect – is better than her opponents'.

The situation when a player has 31 should be obvious enough – she automatically wins and collect the kitty.

Tip for beginners
* Hang onto any pairs of cards in the early part of the game; if you get the chance to complete a trio while your opponents are still pondering their options, you are likely to catch them off guard. Going for a perfect hand of 31 is unwise unless you hold an Ace; you cannot achieve such a hand without capturing one of these four elusive cards. By contrast, snaring two of the 12 court cards to complete the hand should be easier, as you only need two cards from 12. As always, play the percentages and give yourself the best chance of winning those sweets.

The scenario where a player knocks is less obvious. A player can knock at any time during the game and at that point all cards are turned face up. The hands are checked and the winner is the player with the best hand.

A hand of 31 is the grail; thereafter, a hand that contains three cards of equal rank is next in value;

failing that, the winner is the player who has the highest total in any one suit.

However, when a player chooses to 'knock', her opponents get one more turn at exchanging their cards with the widow hand before turning over their cards.

Blind hookey

Ages 7+
Skill level 2
Good for Children's parties and large family gatherings
What you will need Counters as stakes

It may be a game of chance, but children will take Blind Hookey very seriously. Losing is not easily accepted, but winning is often greeted with greater glee than you might expect. Between three and ten people can play.

Aim of the game
To reveal a card of higher value than the banker.

Preparation
Players sit around a table and a full pack of 52 cards is needed. You will also need a stock of counters (of the kind used for board games) to use as stakes.

Tip for beginners
* Without recommending you cheat by looking at your cards – which would obviously be wrong – there is little you can do to improve your chances of winning a hand of Blind Hookey. It sensible to stake wisely throughout the game and don't throw your counters away early in the game. Leave your opponents to be the ones to play boldly and badly.

The cards are cut to determine the banker for the hand; it is the player with the lowest card deals.

The shuffled deck is passed to the player on the left of the banker, who removes a small stack of cards (probably around five or six) and places them face down on the table in front of him. The remainder of the deck is passed to the player on his left, who does the same.

The deck of cards moves around the table in a clockwise direction until it reaches the banker, who also removes a small stack of cards in the same way as the other players. The remainder of the deck is set aside and won't be needed until the next deal.

How to play
The players now place their stakes. An upper limit should be set, with perhaps five counters maximum per deal. Counters are placed above the relevant stack of face-down cards according to the player's confidence of revealing a card that is higher in value than the banker's. Aces are low.

When all stakes are laid, the banker turns over his stack of cards to expose the bottom card. The others now turn over their cards one by one, starting with the player to the left of the banker.

The banker wins from all players whose exposed cards are lower than or equal to his, but pays to anybody who shows a card of higher value.

player 1   player 2   player 3   player 4   player 5   player 6   player 7

banker

Continue to play successive hands until everybody has had a turn as banker. Any players who run out of counters drop out of the game. The winner is the player with the most counters at the end of play. If you are playing at a children's party, you may want to exchange the victor's pile of counters for a small prize ... perhaps a book on children's card games?

Twenty-one

or Vingt-et-un, Pontoon,
Black Jack

Ages 7+ (younger players will enjoy
playing a simplified game without stakes)
Skill level 3
Good for Break-time card players and
other competitive souls
What you will need Counters as stakes

With up to ten people able to join in,
no complicated set-ups and no
impenetrable rules, Twenty-one is the
king of prize-winning card games.

Aim of the game
To hold a value of 21 or as near as possible.

Background
Twenty-one is, in principle, a simple game. Each
player starts with two cards and can take additional
cards from the deck one by one, as they try to
complete a hand of 21 without exceeding this
figure. The traditional banking version of Pontoon
takes this simple game and adds a legion of
complicated rules, which can often take the fun out
of the game for kids. By way of compromise, I have
outlined a variant of the game that combines
elements of the senior game with the simplistic
game frequently played by children without stakes.

Preparation
An adult or reliable child is given the job of banker
(or dealer). In our game, the banker does not play
but merely deals the cards and distributes the
winnings. She starts by giving each player a set
number of counters (25 is a good number to start
with). The remainder goes to the bank.

The banker gives each player one card, dealt face
down on the table. Players look at their cards and
place their stakes. A maximum and minimum starting
stake should be set (I would recommend a minimum
of one counter and a maximum of three counters).

How to play
Once all players have placed their stakes, the dealer
hands round a second card to each player.

The players look at their cards and assess their
options; they each now have a chance to improve
their hand if they are bold enough! The player to
the left of the banker goes first, with the turn
moving around the table clockwise thereafter.
Players can either:

'Buy': This is where they take an additional card and
add to their stake. The additional stake must not

Variation
* In some games, the rules allow 'wild cards'
that can represent cards of any value. This is
particularly useful in games where runs or
sequences are built up. The cards most
commonly used as wild cards are the Jokers,
the twos (also known as deuces, giving the
call 'Deuces wild') and the Jacks, although
other cards can be used if wanted. If only two
wild cards are wanted, it's usual to use the
black Jacks rather than the red ones.

Card values

* In Twenty-one, the Aces are high or low (that is, they count as one or 11) and the court cards (King, Queen and Jack) count as ten.

exceed the maximum, but can be no less than the original amount they staked at the start of the game. Players can immediately buy a fourth and fifth card if they want, but on each occasion they must add to their stake again. Alternatively, they can stop buying cards and twist (see below). For example, a player who has a ten and two may decide to buy a card at first, but if the card dealt is another two, she may decide to be cautious and twist for her fourth card.

'Twist': If a player decides to twist, she does not add to her stake but simply takes another card from the dealer. Once a player has started twisting, she cannot subsequently 'buy', so her stake remains the same.

'Stick': If a player is happy with her two cards, either because they add up to 21 or close to that total, she may decide to stick with them. She puts them on the table face down and takes no further cards. In our game we will make it a rule that players cannot stick with a total of 15 or under.

Players continue to twist and buy cards until either their total exceeds 21, at which point they are said to have 'bust', or they decide to stick.

When all players have finished their bidding, the banker asks them to turn over their cards.

The winning hand is that which totals closest to 21. A hand comprised of an Ace and a ten is called 'pontoon', but an Ace and a court card supersedes this and is called 'royal pontoon'. If no player holds such a hand, then any combination that adds up to 21 is victorious. Failing that, the total closest to 21 wins. In the event of two players holding a hand of equal value, the bank pays both. All losing players are obliged to pay their stakes to the banker, while the victors receive payment equal to their stakes from the banker. Sweets can always be used as prizes instead of real money.

Sweet Sixteen

Ages 7+
Skill level 3
Good for Youngsters who are bored of Pontoon but eager for a competitive game of cards
What you will need Counters as stakes

Two cards, a banker, up to ten people and a simple target – this game is as sweet as its name.

Aim of the game
To hold two cards with a combined value of 16.

Preparation
Before the game can start, the players must agree upon stakes and upon the number of deals over which the game will be played. It's probably best to play for five deals and to award points according to the scoring guide outlined opposite. Counters can be used to aid scoring. Each player should start with ten counters, but don't forget that the bank will need to be well stocked too!

Next, a banker must be appointed, with the players each cutting the deck; whoever gets the lowest card gets the job. The banker removes the eights and sixes (with the exception of the eight of diamonds) from the deck. The remaining 45 cards are shuffled and passed to the player seated to the left of the banker, in this case that man is Sam.

How to play
Sam takes the top two cards from the deck, which is positioned face down in front of him. His aim is to hold two cards with a value of 16 (Aces are low and court cards each count ten).

He can swap his cards one at a time, discarding one of the cards held onto a waste pile and taking the top card from the deck. Sam can continue changing cards to get closer to the grail of 16. However, if he exceeds 16, his hand will 'bust' and his turn comes to an end. He may choose to avoid this situation by electing to stick on any total under 16.

A player does not tell his opponents what he has scored – even if he has bust – but instead simply puts his cards face down in front of him. He now

shuffles the deck, mixing in the cards from the
waste pile, and passes it to the player seated to
his left.

The game continues until all players have had their
turn. The cards are then revealed, with each player
turning his hand over simultaneously on the word
of the banker. Counters can then be awarded on
the following basis:

Players with 16 exactly receive as many counters
from the bank as there are players in the game.
**Players with 16 exactly in a hand that
includes the eight of diamonds** receive two
counters from the bank for each player in the game.
Players with less than 16 pay the banker one
counter.
Players with more than 16 pay the banker one
counter for every pip above 16.
Ten bonus counters are awarded to the player
with the best hand. In the event of a tie, the
counters are shared.

At the end of ten deals, the counters are totted up.
The player with the most wins the prize ... which
could be a week without having to do the dishes or
some sweets if you're feeling generous.

Racing

Ages 7+
Skill level I
Good for Noisy children's parties and rowdy get-togethers
What you will need Counters as stakes

What it lacks in strategy and equine presence, this game makes up for in pure excitement. Never has such drama been unleashed with just cards, some counters and a few confectionery-based prizes.

Aim of the game

To predict which suit's Ace will be first to reach the finish line.

Preparation

Before the game starts, you'll need to gather up some counters. Give each player ten counters and make it clear that the game will be played over five races (deals).

Appoint a reliable child or an adult as dealer/banker and pass her a standard 52-card deck.

The dealer removes the Aces from the deck and places them in a row at the top of the table. She

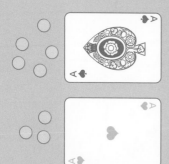

then places the top seven cards from the deck in a vertical column below the Aces. The layout should look like a T when complete.

How to play

The players now place their stakes, putting their counters next to the Ace they think will win the race. They can bid as many counters as they want; if they choose the winning Ace correctly, the banker will give them back their stake plus an identical number of counters. Of course, if they lose, their counters go to the bank.

When all stakes have been laid, the remaining 41 cards are shuffled and turned face down in a stack on the table. The dealer now turns the cards over one by one. The rank of the card revealed is unimportant but the suit is not; each time a particular suit appears, the corresponding Ace moves forward one place in the layout. So, for example, if the dealer turns over the five of clubs, the Ace of clubs will move forward one place.

The winning post is the seventh card in the layout, so the first Ace to pass that point is victorious. At the end of each hand, the banker distributes the winnings (in counters) to the players who successfully guessed which Ace would win.

The person with the most counters at the end of five hands is the winner. A set prize, perhaps a chocolate bar, is awarded to the triumphant player.

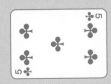

Tip for beginners

* The seven cards laid out vertically in the layout (the stem of the T) offer the only hint of what might happen when the race begins. If there are three or four cards of a particular suit in the layout, the chances of the corresponding Ace winning the race are greatly reduced. Aside from that, Racing is purely a game of chance.

Lift smoke

Ages 7+
Skill level 3
Good for Introducing children to card games that use 'tricks'

This is an engaging but straightforward trick-based game for four to six players that is sure to stir the interest of budding card players and veterans alike.

Aim of the game

To win more tricks than your opponents and thereby be the last player left with cards held in hand.

Preparation

A shuffled deck is placed face down in the centre of the table and each player turns over the top card in turn. The player revealing the lowest-ranked card (Aces are high) is appointed dealer.

The player to the left of the dealer cuts the deck to establish the trump suit. The cards are then shuffled once more and dealt.

player 3

player 4

stock

player 2

player 1

Each player is given the same number of cards (one by one) as there are players taking part in the game. The remainder of the cards are placed in the centre of the table to form a stock.

The players now take up their cards and hold them in hand, away from the view of their opponents, and the trick playing begins.

How to play

The player to the left of the dealer starts the game, playing one of his cards onto the table to lead the trick.

The turn now moves around the table in a clockwise direction. The second player must try to build on the trick but must follow in suit, or if he cannot play a card of the same suit, he can trump. If he can do neither, he discards a card onto the trick, thereby reducing his hand.

The dealer plays last and when he has had his turn the trick is complete.

The trick is won by the highest-rank trump played or if no trumps have been played, the highest card in the suit led.

The dealer gathers up the completed trick, places it to one side and gives the winner of that trick the top card from the stock. The winner, who now has

more cards than his opponents, then leads the next trick.

When a player runs out of cards, he drops out of the game. Play continues until either only one player is left holding cards or the stock of cards runs dry. In the event of the latter situation occurring, the winner of the next trick is deemed the game winner.

Reward each trick winner with a small confectionery prize. Additional prizes can be awarded to the overall game winner.

Tip for beginners

* As with any trick-based game, the key to success is to make a mental note of the cards played and of the suits your opponents are unable to follow.

Monte bank

Ages 8+
Skill level 3
Good for Those who enjoy the role of being banker
What you will need Counters as stakes

Monte Bank is a simple game of chance for four to six players that can be played at parties or for fun, but it must always be played for stakes.

Aim of the game

To predict which section of the layout includes a card of the same suit to that revealed by the banker.

Preparation

Players each cut a shuffled deck to determine who will be banker; the player revealing the highest-ranked card becomes the banker.

Each player is given ten counters to use as stakes. Each player's counters should be of different colours or in some way discernible from those of their opponents … we don't want the banker getting mixed up and paying out to the wrong player!

The banker removes the eights, nines and tens from the pack of cards, shuffles them once more and deals out four cards face up in a grid. The top two cards are called the 'top layout' and the bottom pair are the 'bottom layout'.

How to play

The players now place their stakes. You can have as many players as you wish, but you should set minimum and maximum stake limits (one and five counters respectively is a good starting point). Counters are then staked on either the top or bottom layout.

When all stakes are laid, the dealer takes the top card from the remainder of the deck. This card is called 'the gate', and if it is of a matching suit to any of the four face-up cards, the banker must pay out to those players who placed their stakes next to that half of the layout. See the example illustrated opposite.

If the gate is of a different suit to all four cards in the layout, the banker collects all the counters.

After five deals, the job of banker rotates around the table, with the player to the left of the current incumbent taking over.

Sweets or other prizes can be exchanged at the end to the value of the stakes won.

Tip for beginners

Tip for beginners
* Monte Bank is entirely a game of chance. If it's your day, you'll clean up; if not, you'll win nothing. Whichever way, don't take it personally.

top layout

the gate

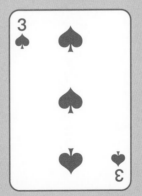

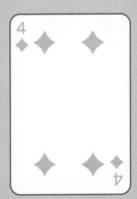

bottom layout

Brag

Ages 11+
Skill level 3
Good for Aspiring Poker players who want to play a more 'serious' game of cards
What you will need Counters or sweets as stakes

Simpler than Poker, but with all the drama of placing stakes and bluffing plus the opportunity to say 'I'll see you', Brag is a teenage card sharp's dream game for up to ten people.

Aim of the game

To hold – or convince your opponents that you hold – a superior hand to your opponents.

Preparation

Each player is given a pile of counters or individually wrapped sweets to use as stakes. The players then agree minimum and maximum stakes (one to five counters or sweets per bid is suggested).

After the cards have been cut and the lowest player has been appointed dealer, he places a minimum stake into the pot (the centre of the table). He then deals out three cards to each player, placing them face down one at a time onto the table.

The players collect their cards and assess their hands. The stake laying now begins.

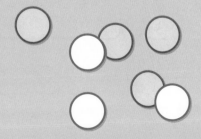

How to play

The player to the left of the dealer starts the bidding. He stakes as much or as little as he wants (provided he stays within the prescribed minimum and maximum levels). A high bet suggests he is confident that he holds a winning hand … although, of course, it might be a bluff.

The turn moves around the table in a clockwise direction, and each player can either match the bet, raise or fold. If a player folds, he does not have to stake any more and simply return his cards to the dealer. He will take no further part in the hand.

The betting continues, moving round and round the table for as long as it takes until all players still in the game bet the same amount and no player wishes to raise the stakes further. Of course, if one player out-stakes all the others and none of his opponents are prepared to match him, he wins the hand automatically. In this situation he does not have to show his cards to the rest of the players – they will never know if the player was bluffing or had genuine cause for confidence.

With the bidding over, the cards are turned over and the hands assessed. Three cards are wild and can be used to represent any other card to make a winning combination; these three cards – the Ace of diamonds, the Jack of clubs and the nine of diamonds – are called the braggers.

Combinations of cards rank in the following order (with the best first):

Trios
Three of a kind will always beat a pair, irrespective of rank.
Three natural Aces (no braggers)
Three Aces (including any two Aces and one of the other braggers)
Three natural Kings
Three Kings (two Kings plus any of the braggers)
The pattern continues down to the three twos.

Pairs
The ranking of pairs is in keeping with the above, so a natural pair will always beat a pair of the same rank that consists of one natural card and a bragger.

Singletons
If there are no pairs, the hand is won by the player who has the highest-ranked single card. Suits have no bearing on the outcome, so if two players have cards of the same rank, the pot is shared.

The player with the best hand – as you might expect – takes the kitty.

three natural Aces.

natural pair.

three Aces (with bragger)

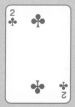

singletons

Three-stake brag

Ages 11+
Skill level 3
Good for Teenage parties and other adolescent gatherings
What you will need Counters or sweets as stakes

With three times the opportunity for stake laying, this is a Brag variant that is sure to delight those with a penchant for bluff and bravado.

Aim of the game

To convince your opponents that you hold superior cards to them.

Preparation

The preliminaries of Three-stake Brag are the same as for the single-stake variant of the game (see page 92). However, in this game, stakes are placed after each card is dealt.

How to play

After the dealer has dealt one card to each player, the play is temporarily halted while stakes are placed. The players look at their card and bid as much or as little as they want, whilst remaining within the minimum and maximum levels which should have already been decided. Just like in the single-stake variant (see page 92), a high bid suggests that the player is confident, but it may well be a bluff. The players continue staking until they wish to go no further.

The cards are revealed and the player with the highest-ranked card takes the pot. If two players have cards of equal status, the winnings are shared. There are no braggers (wild cards) in this first round.

The players then leave their first card face up on the table and the dealer now hands them each a second card. Another round of stake laying takes place, and once it has reached its conclusion the cards are revealed again. Braggers (the Ace of diamonds, the Jack of clubs and the nine of diamonds, see page 92) are now effective, so, for example, the Jack of clubs and the Queen of hearts count as a pair of Queens. The player with the highest-ranked pair wins the hand (natural pairs always beat an equally ranked pair that includes a bragger). If there are no pairs, the same rules apply as for the first round.

In Three-stake Brag, this hand is impossible to beat.

10 pts

10 pts

11 pts

These cards are also left on the table and the dealer passes out a third card to each player. The now-familiar stake laying follows before the cards are revealed. This time, however, the rules about the best hand change, and the player whose cards total closest to 31 (either above or below) takes the kitty. Aces count as 11 and court cards are worth ten; all other cards have a value commensurate with their pips. Braggers are of no additional significance.

Tip for beginners
* As in all versions of Brag, the ability to bluff rather than tactical genius is the greatest gift a player can have. You could spend hours trying to assess probabilities, but you are better off working on your powers of deceit and subterfuge!

Pencil & paper games

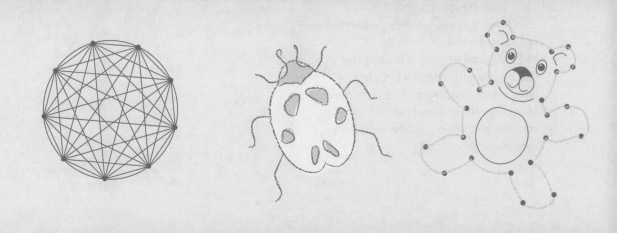

Chain drawings

Age range 5+
Number of players Up to four

All children enjoy the element of surprise in this game. By adding his own contribution to each of the drawings as they pass around the table – and in seeing how much fun the resulting pictures are – your child will quickly learn to be more imaginative in the figures he creates.

How to play

Each player has a sheet of paper and begins by drawing the head of a person, as far as the neck. The player folds the top of the sheet over to hide the head, leaving just the neck showing. He then passes his sheet on to the next person, who draws the body, including the arms, but not the hands. The paper is folded again, with just the waist and wrists left showing, and the papers are passed on. This time, each player draws the legs down to the knee and the hands. Finally, each player draws the lower legs and feet. The papers are passed on for the last time, and the players unfold their pictures for everyone to enjoy.

Tips for beginners
* Take fewer turns: for example, draw the head first, then the rest of the body.
* Make suggestions such as drawing the hair big and curly, adding a large belt or jewellery, or shoes with funny, curly toes.
* Using different coloured pens for each body part makes it obvious where the different sections begin and end.

Variations
* Draw more complicated figures, such as wild beasts, or mythical animals.
* Have more players or take more turns: for example, the paper could be folded after the head, upper body, lower body, knees, ankles and feet.

What you will need A sheet
of paper and a pencil, or coloured
pen, for each player

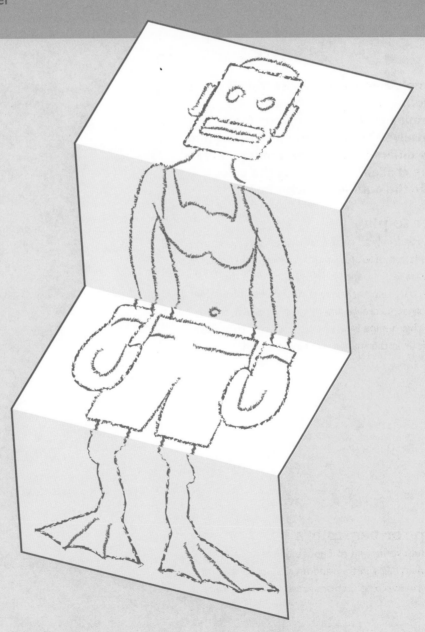

Pencil walk

Age range 4+
Number of players One
What you will need A sheet of paper and a pencil; coloured crayons or felt-tipped pens

A simple colouring exercise, this is great for younger children, who are just beginning to discover drawing for themselves. They will enjoy choosing and using different colours and many will rise to the challenge of keeping the colour within the outline of each shape.

How to play

Draw randomly all over a sheet of paper. Use any combination of loops, squiggles or straight lines, but do not take the pencil off the paper until the pattern is complete. Make sure the lines cross over each other to create a number of irregular shapes. Once this outline is finished, show your child how to colour in the shapes you have created.

Variations

∗ Older children can draw the random outline themselves.

∗ Draw a simple picture, such as a tree or teddy. 'Scribble' lightly over the image to disguise it, and mark a dot on each part of the scribble that contains your picture. Ask your child to find out what it is by colouring in all the dotted sections.

Tip for beginners

∗ Help your child to choose different colours when filling in the random shapes so that no two adjoining sections are the same colour.

Age range 6+
Number of players One
What you will need A sheet of paper and a pencil; scissors, glue, an eraser (all optional)

Mirror, mirror

This game will really test your child's hand-to-eye coordination as well as her observation skills. She has to 'read' a drawing you give her in terms of outline, scale and detail in order to match what you have drawn. She will also need to check your drawing constantly to make sure she is on the right track.

Preparation

First, make a simple drawing of one half of a symmetrical image, such as a face or a house with windows on either side of the door. You may find it easier to draw the whole picture, then cut it down the centre and stick one half onto a fresh sheet of paper, ready for the game. Or you could draw the whole picture and erase half of it.

How to play

Give your child the half-completed drawing. She has to complete the image by copying your picture as accurately as possible, in 'mirror image', on the opposite side of the paper.

Variations

* Try drawing funny opposites – for example, a man with a bushy moustache on one side and a woman with long flowing hair on the other.
* Older children can add extra details to the finished picture, such as curtains in the windows of a house, or flowers by the door – as long as they appear on each half of the image.
* Your child can colour in the finished picture.

Tips for beginners

* Hold the half-completed image up to a real mirror, perpendicular to the surface, so that your child can get a clear idea of how the completed picture should look.
* Try the game with symmetrical letters (for example, H, M, O); or shapes such as squares, circles and diamonds.
* Use squared paper to help your child with more complex images.

What a match!

Age range 5+
Number of players Two or more
What you will need A sheet of paper and a pencil for each player

Each child in a group has to follow the same set of verbal instructions in drawing a picture. It is fascinating to see just how different the finished drawings are from one another. This may be quite a challenge for your child, who has first to rely on his ability to visualize what is being described, and then to transfer that to paper.

How to play

Each player sits with his sheet of paper hidden from the other players. One player starts to draw a picture, describing it out loud as he draws, but without naming exactly what it is straight away. The other players then start to draw the same picture, following the description as carefully as possible. For example, the drawer might say: 'I am starting with a small circle, and drawing lots of little circles around the edge of it. It is a flower with petals. Now I am drawing its long stalk and a leaf on either side. There is a butterfly flying right next to it, and a big sun shining up in the sky. But there are two clouds – maybe it is going to rain.' As everyone finishes, all the players show their pictures, and see how closely they match each other – or how differently each person has interpreted the same description!

Tip for beginners
* Suggest very simple picture ideas at first, such as a square inside another, larger square; or a smiley face with long ears to make a rabbit.

Variation
* Older children can describe a more complicated scene to draw.

Age range 3+
Number of players One or more
What you will need A sheet of paper and a pencil

Odd one out

A good game from an early age, this teaches your child to recognize basic shapes and to make associations between groups of similar objects. The drawings can be as simple or as complicated as you like, depending on the age and ability of your child.

Preparation

Draw a row of images, where one is a misfit. For example, draw a row of dolls with one teddy; a row of smiley faces with one frowning; or a row of trees with one flower.

How to play

Quite simply, your child has to look at the drawn items and point to the odd one out.

Variations

* Spread the items around the page rather than in a straight line.
* 'Hide' the odd one out in a bigger picture. For example in an underwater scene, draw lots of identical little fish with a bigger one lurking behind some seaweed.
* Write out a sequence of numbers or letters from the alphabet, with a number or letter out of place. Ask your child to draw a line to lead the stray number or letter back to where it should be.
* Older children can create their own odd-one-out pictures.

Gone fishing

Age range 5+
Number of players Two or more
What you will need A sheet of paper and a pencil; a felt-tipped pen for each player (optional)

In this game, your child has to identify which object is on the end of each tangled fishing line. This is a good exercise for hand-to-eye coordination skills and will also test your child's powers of concentration as he follows each line to its end.

Preparation
Draw four objects along the bottom of the paper – four different fish or other items such as a boot, a tin can, a key and a glove, for example. Along the top of the sheet, draw four fishermen with fishing rods. Now draw a fishing line coming from the first item, drawing randomly up the paper to meet with one of the fishermen at the top. Repeat with the remaining three items, crossing the fishing lines over each other to create a jumble.

How to play
Ask your child to trace along each of the tangled fishing lines, using either a finger or a felt-tipped pen, to discover which of the fishermen has caught each of the items.

Variations
* Draw up to ten items and fishermen, with a dense tangle of lines.
* Place the items randomly across the whole sheet of paper, rather than just along the bottom, before adding the fishing lines.
* Use the lines to match up other pairs, such as mother and baby (sheep and lamb, dog and puppy, hen and chick); or items that go together (knife and fork, cup and saucer, hammer and nail).

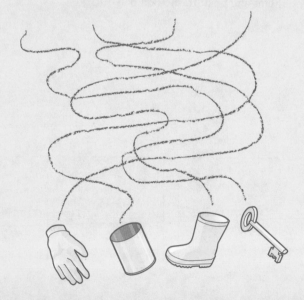

Pretty patterns

Age range 4+
Number of players One
What you will need A sheet of paper and a pencil; coloured crayons (optional)

This game is a good test of your child's mental skills – challenging his ability to recognize a pattern emerging in a row of figures or symbols, and to work out what should come next. You can adapt the game to test a wide range of skills: visual, numerical, knowledge of the alphabet, and so on.

Preparation
Draw a row of shapes that follow a basic repeating pattern, leaving enough space at the end of the row for your child to add to it. For example, the pattern could be a row of alternating squares and circles; or two circles followed by a triangle; or two vertical lines followed by two horizontal lines.

How to play
Ask your child to study the pattern carefully. He then has to draw in the shapes he thinks are missing to complete the row.

Tip for beginners
* Use different colours for each shape as an extra visual clue to help your child recognize the emerging pattern.

Variations
* Create more complex patterns. For example, choose three different shapes. Draw one of each to start with, followed by two of each, then three of each. See if your child works out that he now has to draw four of each.
* Use numbers or letters, for example, 1, 12, 123, 1234, or alternate letters of the alphabet – a, c, e, g, and so on.
* Leave gaps to fill within the pattern, not just at the end.

Build it up

Age range 8+
Number of players Any even number, split into two teams
What you will need A sheet of paper and a pencil for each team

Played with two teams, each player in a team takes her turn to write a word on a piece of paper that is passed from player to player. The idea is to complete a sentence as the words build up on the page. The challenge is for one team to complete a sentence before the other.

Tips for beginners
* Allow team members to discuss which words would be appropriate.
* Write words in grammatical order rather than randomly.

Variations
* Give each team the same starter word.
* With a small team, each player can take two turns to write a word.
* Do not allow any conferring between the team members.
* The final player's word must be the one to complete the sentence.

How to play
The first player from each team takes the pencil and writes down any word on the piece of paper. Then she hands the paper and pencil to the next player, who adds a second word. Each team member has a turn adding a word to the paper, where each word must be able to form part of a sentence on the page (although not necessarily in order). The winning team is the first to have completed a sentence.

Example of play
Five players might write their chosen words in the following order:

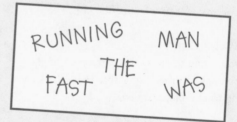

Together, the words can read:

THE
MAN WAS
RUNNING FAST

Letter sandwich

Age range 10+
Number of players Any number
What you will need A sheet of paper and a pencil for each player; an egg timer or a stopwatch

A group of children have a set time to think of as many words as they can beginning and ending with the same letter. This is a great test of your child's vocabulary and poses an extra challenge in having to find unusual or long words.

How to play

Each player has just five minutes to write down as many words as she can that begin and end with the same letter. Each player scores a point for every word, with a bonus point for any word that no one else has thought of. Allocate extra points for longer words, too.

Sample words

Taught
Taut
Rear
Roar
Sees
Sausages
Mum
Dad
Trumpet
Fluff
Pop

Variations

* One player chooses one letter that all words have to begin and end with.
* Choose one letter for the beginning and a different letter for the end of the word. The winner is the first to think of a word that fits. For example, a word that begins with 'g' and ends with 'e' could be 'game'.
* Try to find words that are written the same backwards and forwards – for example, level and toot.

Tip for beginners

* Give clues to help new players. For example, 'a lion makes this noise'.

Join up words

Age range 9+
Number of players Any number
What you will need A sheet of paper and a pencil for each player; an egg timer or a stopwatch

In this game, your child has to think of as many two-word combinations as he can that all start with the same word. It is a good test of his vocabulary. The game is played with a number of children, so each one is encouraged to think hard to write combinations that no one else will come up with.

Preparation

Choose a number of starter words that take on a new meaning when a second word is added. For example, you could have 'door', which can become 'door step', 'door stop', 'door knob', 'door handle' and 'door bell'.

How to play

Call out a starter word and give the children five minutes to add other words, so making as many new combinations as they can. Give an example to start them off. At the end of the time each child reads out his answers and scores one point for every word combination that no one else has thought of. The person with the most points wins.

Good starter words

Moon	Train
Flag	Sea
Ice	Egg
Bread	Bed
Over	Ring
Fire	Shoe

Tip for beginners
* Give some clues for the combinations, such as 'I am thinking of something that goes with rain and falls from the sky' (answer = raindrops).

Variations
* Try having the starter word at the end rather than the beginning of the combination. For example, 'boat' could become 'motor boat', 'sailing boat', 'rowing boat' and 'fishing boat'.
* Allow the starter word to be used at either the beginning or end of the combination. For example, 'paper' could become 'paper clip', 'paper bag', 'paper cut' or 'newspaper'.

Age range 7+
Number of players Any number
What you will need A sheet of paper and a pencil for each player; an egg timer or a stopwatch

Telegrams

Each child in this game has to make a sentence, where each new word begins with a specially chosen letter. It is amazing to see how varied the resulting sentences are, and just how versatile your child is when it comes to playing with words.

Tips for beginners

* Use fewer letters for younger players – for example, C, E, G could be cows eat grass.
* Have an adult choose all the letters, to avoid tricky ones, or suggest ways to start the sentence. For example instead of 'Hugh was ...' a sentence could start 'Hippos wear ...'

Variations

* Include the name of at least one person present in each telegram. (To do this, be sure to include initials in the list of letters.)
* Select a word that must be in everyone's sentence – for example, the T in the example on the right has to be teapot.
* The sentences must be on a particular theme. For example, sports or holidays.

How to play

Each person in the game takes a turn to call out a letter, which every player writes down on the left side of his sheet of paper. This continues until the players have up to 15 letters written down in the same order in which they were given. With just one minute to play the game, each player must write down a 'telegram' or 'sentence', using the written-down letters – in the correct order – to start each new word. For example, if the letters were H, W, P, P, O, B, T, I, A, C, B, one telegram could be: 'Hugh was painting pictures of blue teapots in a cardboard box.'

At the end of the minute, each player reads out his version to the others and the best one wins.

Hugh
Was
Painting
Pictures
Of
Blue
Teapots
In
A
Cardboard
Box

Sentence scramble

Age range 7+
Number of players One
What you will need A sheet of paper and a pencil

Here is a word game that tests your child's ability to make a sentence from a jumble of words. Older children will have fun making up their own confused sentences for their friends to attempt to unravel.

How to play

Think up a sentence and write it down on the sheet of paper, but mix up all of the words randomly. Hand the paper to your child and ask her to work out the right order for the words so that they make sense as a sentence.

Sample sentence

kite air flew the red up in The

might become

The red kite flew up in the air

Variations
* Make longer sentences.
* Spread the words randomly over the page, instead of in a straight line.
* Write each word in a different size, with some in upper case, some in lower.

Tip for beginners
* Keep sentences very short, for example: The dog is wet; Fish like swimming; Tea is hot.

Words within words

Age range 7+
Number of players Any number
What you will need A sheet of paper and a pencil for each player; an egg timer or a stopwatch

This game has been a favourite among children for many years. Quite simply, it is a test of your child's vocabulary. One player in a group chooses a word and the other players in the group have to use its letters to make as many new words as they can. The challenge here, is to write down words that no one else will think of, because that is the only way to earn points.

Variations
∗ Use words with fewer vowels and more difficult consonants, such as 'xylophone'.
∗ Allow letters to be used more than once.
∗ Impose a shorter time limit.

Tips for beginners
∗ Use shorter starter words.
∗ Use words that feature plenty of vowels, such as 'elasticated'.
∗ Play the game in teams.

How to play
An adult chooses a long starter word, such as 'nonsensical', and asks each of the other players to write the word at the top of her sheet of paper. Each player then has to write as many words as she can, using letters from within the starter word. She can use each letter only once.

At the end of five minutes, each player reads out her words in turn, with the other players crossing off any that appear on their own lists. At the end, each player counts up her score for the words she has left: four-letter words (and under) score one point; five-letter words score two points; six-letter words score three points, and so on. The player with the highest score is the winner of that round and chooses the next starter word.

Nonsensical
No   Lone
Can   Ice
Clone   One
Con   Loan
Less   Nice
Slice

Triplet challenge

Age range 10+
Number of players Any number
What you will need A sheet of paper and a pencil for each player; an egg timer or stopwatch

Each player in this game has to think of words that include the same three letters, which makes it a good test of both your child's vocabulary and his ability to visualize words in his mind. The same three letters can appear in any order and any number of times in the words your child writes down, which adds to the challenge before him.

How to play

One player chooses any three letters, which each player writes down at the top of his sheet of paper. Within a five-minute time limit, the players have to think of as many words as possible that include all three of those letters. They can use each letter as many times as they like, and a point is scored for each word. For example, the letters T, O and H can be used to make the words:

though
thorough
hot
touch
hoot

And the letters S, E and M can be used to make the words:

message
smile
seam
messy
emeralds

Variations
* Use less common letters, such as I, K and J.
* Set a limit on how short the words can be – for example, no fewer than five letters.

Letter leader

Age range 10+
Number of players Any number
What you will need A sheet of paper and a pencil for each player; an egg timer or stopwatch

When it comes to playing this game, your child will wish he was a walking dictionary! The idea is to take the same three letters and use them to start as many different words as possible. It sounds easy, but with one of the players deciding what the three starter letters should be, some rounds of this game may be challenging.

How to play

One of the players suggests three letters, which each player writes down at the top of his sheet of paper. Players then have five minutes to think of as many words as possible beginning with those three letters. For example, with the letters COM, a player may come up with the following:

comedy

come

compare

compass

communicate

With the three letters MON, a player might come up with:

mongrel

money

monk

monkey

monochrome

With the three letters SAL, a player might write down the following:

salt

saliva

saline

sallow

saloon

Players score a point for each word no other player has thought of and the winner is the player with the highest score.

Variations

* Take each letter of the alphabet in turn when choosing the three starter letters (see below).
* See how many words each player can make within a one-minute time limit.
* Suggested starter letters are:
  AND, BAT, CAR, DOT, ENT, FIL, GRO, HOL, INC, JUG, KNI, LAM, MOD, NON, OFF, PUM, QUI, RUN, SIT, TRI, ULT, VIR, WEL, YEA.

Criss-cross words

Age range 7+
Number of players Up to four
What you will need A sheet of paper (squared if possible) and a pencil

In this game, each child takes it in turn to write a new word in a grid. Younger children will be thrilled when they find a space, while older children will try to gain maximum points.

Preparation

Draw a 100-square grid on the sheet of paper, ten across by ten down.

How to play

The first player writes a word in the grid, either vertically or horizontally, and up to six letters long. One point is scored for each vowel in the word (a, e, i, o, u) and two points for each of the other letters. The next player writes a new word in the grid, which must overlap the first word either horizontally or vertically. The remaining players take it in turns to add new words to the grid, until it is no longer possible to fit any more in. The last person to add a word wins a bonus five points. The winner is the player with the highest score.

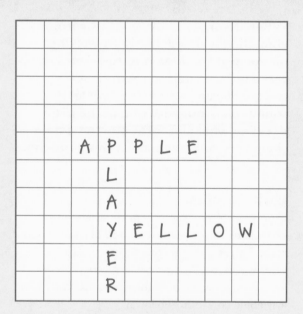

Variations

* Draw a larger grid for a longer game.
* Choose a theme such as animals or school.
* Have a minimum length of word that can be used – say four, five or six letters.

Tips for beginners

* Use a smaller grid.
* Suggest a space where a word will fit.
* Suggest a word, and explain there is a space where it will fit.
* Allow a fresh start elsewhere on the grid if the players get stuck.

Age range 3+
Number of players One
What you will need A sheet of paper and a pencil

Misfits

This game encourages your child to use her observational skills. Can she spot the odd one out?

Preparation
Write down the names of five objects, where four are related and one is not. Depending on the age of your child you can vary the game to make it more challenging.

How to play
Show the list of words to your child and ask her to identify which is the odd one out. Ask her to explain why. You could try the following lists:

Variations
* Have more objects in the list.
* Have two or three odd items.
* Make it odd for different reasons, for example, all the others begin with the same letter.

Tips for beginners
* Read out the list of words slowly.
* Draw a picture of each word.
* Put the odd word in the same place in the row each time.

Pig, cow, duck, sheep, crocodile

Plane, boat, car, train, drill

Sue, Mary, Kate, Vanessa, Robert

Trumpet, piano, saxophone, flute, kettle

Look inside

Age range 7+
Number of players One
What you will need A sheet of paper and a pencil

This clever game will test not only your child's spelling ability, but also her observational skills as she has to search for words that are hidden among the other words in a sentence.

Preparation

Choose a theme – say animals, transport or toys – then select a few words from the theme to hide in a sentence. For example, from animals you could choose 'cat', 'donkey', 'fish' and 'badger'. Make up sentences, where each contains one of your chosen words.

Sample sentences

The magic **at**las had a talking map.

In Lon**don key**s are kept on hooks.

A tin roo**f is** hot in summer.

Oh no, that **bad ger**bil has nibbled the wire again!

How to play

Write down the words you have hidden, for example, the names of the four animals, then show your child the sentences you have made up and ask her if she can spot the words hidden within them. Explain how she will need to look between the words to find them, and show her a sample sentence to get her on the right track.

Tip for beginners

* Keep both words and sentences short.

Variations

* Hide two words within one sentence.
* For an older child, try hiding a secret message within several sentences, such as a task that she has to carry out. For instance, if your secret message is 'Touch your nose', your sentences could be:
  He said it fel**t ouch**y!
  Luck**y our** food lasted out.
  There are **no se**ttlers here.

Match the words

Age range 10+
Number of players Any number
What you will need A sheet of paper and a pencil for each player

This is quite a challenging spelling game that can even catch out adults. The aim is to write down correctly two words that sound the same, but have different spellings. This will really appeal to children who enjoy playing with words.

Preparation
Write a list of five words that sound identical, but that have alternative meanings and are spelt differently. (See right for examples.)

How to play
Read two sentences to the children, telling them that each one contains a word that sounds the same but is spelt differently each time. Explain that the words also have different meanings. As the children listen, they have to write down the word, spelling it correctly in each case.

For example, if your word is 'which/witch' you might say 'The naughty girl took my pencil, which was better than hers'; followed by 'the witch flew through the air on her broomstick'. Treat each word pair the same way, then check the answers. The child with the most correct spellings wins.

Word pairs

Great	Grate
Blue	Blew
Too	Two
Toe	Tow
Sore	Saw
See	Sea
Weight	Wait
Shoe	Shoo
Knight	Night
For	Four
Would	Wood
Flour	Flower
Sole	Soul
Fir	Fur
Poor	Pour
Die	Dye
Buy	By

Variations
* Spell one of the words in each pair and ask a child to invent a sentence using that word.
* See if the children can make more pairs.

Slithering snakes

Age range 4+
Number of players One
What you will need A sheet of paper and a pencil; coloured pencils (optional)

This is a simple counting game with a twist. Your child has to count the number of snakes you draw on a sheet of paper – but all the snakes are jumbled up. A good test of visual as well as numerical skills.

Preparation

Draw a pile of wiggly snakes on the sheet of paper (see illustration, below). The first one you draw will be the top one. Now draw one beneath – making sure you do not overlap any lines where the snakes cross. Continue to draw more snakes, always being careful to connect the lines correctly. Do not give any of the snakes eyes.

How to play

Ask your child to look closely at the pile of snakes and see if he can count how many there are all together. Challenge him further by seeing if he can also work out which snake is at the bottom of the pile and gradually work up to the one on top.

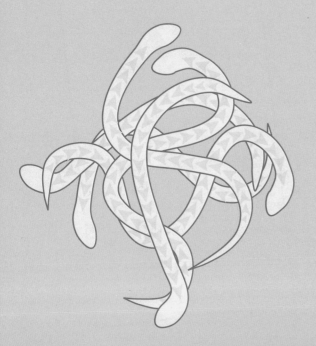

Tips for beginners

* Give the snakes eyes to make it easier to count them.
* Tell your child to colour in each snake as he counts it.

Variation

* Draw two eight-legged spiders and one seven-legged spider, with as many legs as possible crossing over each other. Ask your child if he can disentangle the spiders to find out which one has only seven legs.

Picture letter

Age range 6+
Number of players One
What you will need A sheet of paper and a pencil

Can your child read a letter that has been written half in words and half in pictures? Children love this game and will enjoy working out what your letter says. An older child can make up his own picture letter in reply to yours.

Preparation
Write a simple letter, replacing some of the words with pictures (see illustration, right).

How to play
See if your child can work out what the pictures mean, and thereby read the letter out loud.

Variation
* Split a word so that half is a picture, while the rest is made of letters.

Tips for beginners
* Read the main portion of the letter out to your child, leaving him to decipher the picture clues.
* Only replace nouns with pictures.

Dear Billy,

Please come to my [house]

You can play with my

[train] and see my [cat].

We will have a [cake]

for tea and watch

[television] . I hope you

can come.

[heart] from Susan.

Lion and tiger

Age range 6+
Number of players Two
What you will need A sheet of paper; a pencil for each player; two coloured pencils (optional)

Also known as Boxes, this game is a well-known favourite, in which players take it in turns to try and form squares by joining dots on a grid. Older children can draw the grids themselves.

Preparation
Draw a 25-dot grid, five dots across by five dots down (see illustration, right).

How to play
Decide who is going to be the lion and who is going to be the tiger. Each player takes it in turns to join any two adjacent dots with a straight vertical or horizontal line, until one of them draws a line that completes a square. The person who forms the square puts her initial (L for Lion, T for Tiger) inside the 'box' and joins two dots somewhere else on the grid. If this line completes another box, she gets another turn. More squares are made as the game progresses and play continues until it is impossible to complete any more squares. The lion and the tiger count up how many squares they each have, and the winner is the one with the most.

Variations
* More advanced players can use a larger-sized grid.
* Try speed play, which leaves no time to linger over your choice of line.

Tip for beginners
* Use a different coloured pencil for each player so that counting up the initials in the squares is easier.

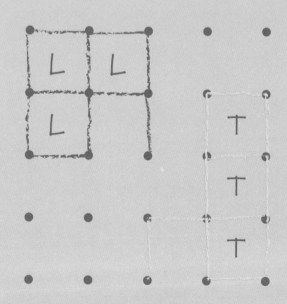

Age range 6+
Number of players Two
What you will need A sheet of paper and a pencil; an eraser; two same-coloured counters for each player (for example, two blue and two green)

Round the bend

This is a simple game involving moving counters on a grid. Younger children will enjoy finding somewhere to move to, while older children will love to see if they can work out the perfect strategy for winning.

Preparation
In pencil, lightly draw a rectangle (landscape format) with two diagonal lines joining the four corners. Erase the top line, and mark a circle at each of the four corners and at the point where the diagonals intersect.

How to play
Place two blue counters on the top two corners, and two green counters on the bottom two corners. The first player moves one counter along a line to the centre circle. The second player moves her counter along a line and into the first player's old space. The game continues like this until one of the players can no longer move either of her counters and is the loser.

Tip for beginners
∗ Suggest where your child should move if she finds the game difficult to start with.

Variation
∗ Two older children can play the game, either drawing the grid themselves, or asking an adult for help.

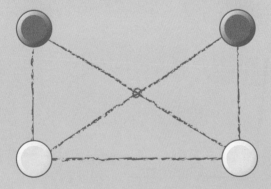

Streets ahead

Age range 7+
Number of players One
What you will need A sheet of paper and a pencil

The aim of this game is to see if your child can match a visual clue to a written one. You can make the game more fun by telling a story to help your child identify the different streets.

Preparation

Draw a very simple grid of a number of parallel roads, each with a feature or characteristic of its own – say a tall tree, a cat, a flowerbed, a cottage and a lamp post. Write a list of road names beneath the grid, in no particular order, but where each street name can be easily linked to one of your visual clues.

Examples of street names

Tall Tree Avenue
Pussy Cat Walk
Posy Place
Cottage Close
Lamp Post Lane

How to play

Ask your child to write the correct name along each of the roads you have drawn, matching them up to the visual clues you have drawn.

Variation

* Make your map more complicated, adding crescents (Moon Crescent), wiggly roads (Snake Pass), roundabouts (Flowerbed Roundabout), and parks (Boat Lake Park).

Tip for beginners

* Write the road names in the order in which they appear on your map.

Age range 7+
Number of players One
What you will need A sheet of paper and a pencil; a damp teabag (optional); crayons (optional); coins (optional)

Treasure map

Children love games of hide and seek and this is no exception. You have to find your child's hidden treasure and having the upper hand in this game will encourage your child to be artful in avoiding a quick discovery.

How to play

Ask your child to draw the outline of a large, empty treasure island and offer suggestions of features that he might like to draw on his island. For example, he could draw a sandy cove; a slimy swamp; a waterfall; a dark forest; a bottomless lake; caves; cliffs; and mountains – appeal to his sense of adventure.

Once the island is complete, your child must choose one location to 'hide' his treasure – he should not tell you where it is. Taking the picture from your child, pretend to be a pirate seeking the treasure. Draw a dotted line as you move around the island, with your child saying 'hot', 'cold' or 'warm' each time you approach a new area. When you reach the right spot, he shouts 'Gold!' and you can mark the spot with an X.

Tips for beginners
* Draw the map for your child.
* Draw the treasure chest in one corner, helping your child to make crayon rubbings of real coins for the treasure.

Variation
* You can give the map an aged look by tearing the edges of the paper and rubbing it over with a damp teabag before you start. Make sure the paper is completely dry before your child starts to draw, otherwise it might tear.

Dice code

Age range 8+
Number of players Any number

This game is similar to Words Within Words (see page 111), except that, here, the letters start out as numbers! This means your child has to be good at code breaking as well as at making up words under pressure.

Preparation
Write down all the letters of the alphabet on the extra sheet of paper and cut out each letter so that you have 26 individual squares. Add a small 'u' next to the 'q'. Place the vowels (A, E, I, O, U) in one bag and the consonants (B, C, D, F, and so on) in another bag.

How to play
Choose one person to be the 'caller'. The caller picks a letter from the vowels bag, say E, and calls out 'I is E'. The players write this down. Then the caller selects another vowel and calls out '2 is A'. The caller selects four consonants in the same way, until each player has a list of six numbers and their corresponding letters on her sheet of paper. For example:

1 = E
2 = A
3 = P
4 = R
5 = S
6 = T

Variations
* Play a second round using the same number code – the die will throw new combinations – or by selecting a new set of letters from the bags.
* Throw the die more times to get more letters and so make longer words.
* Allow each letter to be used more than once. From the example on the right you might also be able to make: steep, peep or state, for example.

What you will need A sheet of paper and a pencil for each player, plus an extra sheet; scissors; two bags; a die; an egg timer or stopwatch (optional)

The caller then throws the die and calls out the number it lands on. Everyone writes this down. The die is thrown five more times, until each player has six numbers on her sheet of paper. The players now have one minute to swap the numbers for letters and make as many words as they can, using each letter once only. For example: if the numbers were 3, 1, 2, 3, 5, 6 the letters would be P, E, A, P, S, T, which could be used to make the following words: pea, peas, peat, pat, sat, sea, tea, sap, tap, set, pet and so on.

At the end of the minute, each person reads out her list of words in turn, crossing off any word that someone else also has and scoring one point for every word left. The player with the most points wins the game.

3	1	2	3	5	6
P	E	A	P	S	T

Pea
Peas
Peat
Pat
Sat
Sea
Tea
Sap
Tap
Set
Pet

Tips for beginners
* Remove any difficult consonants from the bag (X, Z or Qu).
* Score a point for every word made, even if someone else has it.

Order, order!

Age range 7+
Number of players One
What you will need A sheet of paper and a pencil; scissors (optional)

Does your child know the seasons of the year and the days of the week? Test his knowledge by presenting words to him in the wrong order and seeing if he can put them right.

Preparation

Choose a set of words that always go in a familiar order, for example: the days of the week; the months of the year; the colours of the rainbow. Write the words on a piece of paper, but with the order all jumbled up.

How to play

Ask your child to write a number next to each word, so indicating the right order for them to go in. For example:

Tuesday 2

Sunday 7

Wednesday 3

Monday 1

Friday 5

Saturday 6

Thursday 4

Alternatively, cut out each word in the list and see how quickly your child can lay them down in the correct order.

Tips for beginners
* Choose a very short list to mix up, such as the seasons, or who is tallest or oldest in your family.
* Mix up the names of familiar nursery rhyme or story characters. For example: Gingerbread Dumpty; Humpty Man; Little Red Simon; Simple Riding Hood.

Variation
* Write out a familiar nursery rhyme or favourite poem, jumbling the words and asking your child to unscramble them.

Catch the thief

Age range 9+
Number of players One
What you will need A sheet of paper and a pencil

If your child does not know his left from his right already, this is a great way to teach him. In this game he has to follow a simple set of directions to help catch a thief.

Preparation

Copy the illustration to create a simple network of roads lined with blocks of flats. Mark a 'start' point somewhere in the drawing and give each block of flats a letter.

How to play

Explain to your child that a policeman is trying to catch a criminal who is hiding in one of the blocks of flats. Your child has to help the policeman by following your directions to the hideout. Write the location of the hideout on a piece of paper and turn it face down. Then ask your child to draw a route according to your instructions. For instance, 'Turn left and go along the road until you come to the first junction. Turn right and go past two turnings'

and so on. When your child has arrived at the correct location, ask him to stop and turn over the piece of paper to check whether he is right.

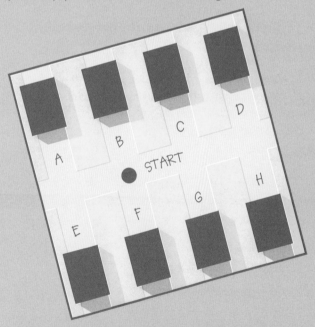

Tip for beginners

* Write a little 'r' on your child's right hand and an 'l' on his left hand to help him know which way to turn.

Variations

* Draw a more complicated map with road names and use these in your instructions.
* Instead of a policeman chasing a criminal, make it a squirrel looking for her stash of nuts, or two friends playing hide and seek.

Activity codes

Age range 9+
Number of players Any number
What you will need A sheet of paper and a pencil

This game involves giving your child a simple instruction, say, to scratch her nose. The problem is, that you give it to her in code. Once she's revealed the message she'll relish carrying out the task.

Preparation
Substitute a number for each letter of the alphabet, for example A=1, B=2 and so on, up to Z=26.

How to play
Write out a secret message in the number code and ask your child to crack the code by replacing numbers with letters again. Each child in a group could receive a different instruction, along the following lines:

Stand on one leg
Clap six times
Run up the stairs
Touch your toes
Curl into a ball
Jump three times

A = 1	J = 10	S = 19
B = 2	K = 11	T = 20
C = 3	L = 12	U = 21
D = 4	M = 13	V = 22
E = 5	N = 14	W = 23
F = 6	O = 15	X = 24
G = 7	P = 16	Y = 25
H = 8	Q = 17	Z = 26
I = 9	R = 18	

Variations
* Make your code more difficult by counting three letters along, so A=D, B=E, C=F and so on.
* If you have a word processor or a computer, you can transform a whole list of code sentences by changing the typeface into one that uses symbols (for example, Zapf Dingbats).
* Make a code by removing all the vowels from the words in each sentence and run the words together. For example: TOUCH YOUR KNEES becomes TCHYRKNS.

Spot the cities

Age range 10+
Number of players One
What you will need A sheet of tracing paper and a pencil; an atlas

In this simple memory game, your child has to see how many city names she can remember having looked at a map. This is a great way to learn the basic whereabouts of major cities in your country and others.

How to play
Give your child a simple map of your country and ask her to trace the outline carefully. Help her to mark in the major cities with dots, repeating the name of each one as you do so. Show her the simple map again and let her look at it for a while. Close the atlas and see how many of the city names she is able to fill in on the outline from memory.

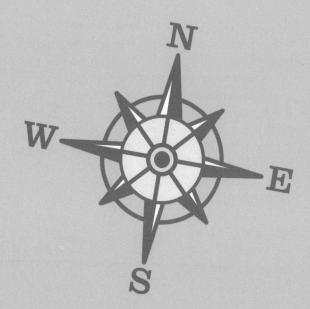

Tip for beginners
* Write the first two letters of each city's name beside each dot.

Variations
* Add in a few other details, such as rivers or mountain ranges.
* Try tracing the outlines of other countries and filling in the capital cities.
* Make up a country of your own for your child to trace, inventing fun place names for her to memorize.

Nine men's morris

Age range 10+
Number of players Two
What you will need A sheet of paper and a pencil; 18 counters (nine each of two colours)

Also known as 'Mill' in the United States, this board game has always been popular. By placing and moving his counters around the board, each player aims to remove his opponent's counters from the game. If he manages to reduce his opponent to two men, or to corner him so that he cannot make a move, a player has won.

Preparation
Copy the illustration below to create your own playing board.

How to play
Each player has nine counters, or men, and takes turns to place them on the board one at a time. He can place the counter either on a corner or where two lines intersect. As soon as a player has three men in a line (known as a 'mill'), he can remove one

of his opponent's men from the board. That man is then out of the game, or 'dead'.

Once both players have all of their counters on the board they continue play by moving them around the board. With each move, however, a player must move his counter to an adjacent point in a line. If a player makes a mill he removes an opponent's piece from the board. The game ends when one player has just two counters remaining, or is unable to move a piece on the board. He is the loser.

Variation
* When one player is down to three men (one man away from losing), let him jump over his own pieces to get to a new position.

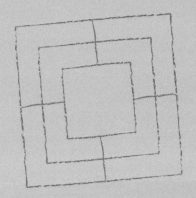

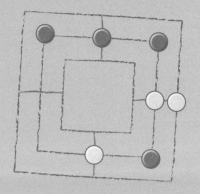

Safe cracker

Age range 11
Number of players Two
What you will need A sheet of paper and a pencil; felt-tipped pens (optional)

There is an element of chance to this game, in which one player has to guess his opponent's secret four-digit code. There is a call for some clever deduction too, however, which makes the game a real challenge.

Preparation
Draw a 40-square grid, ten down by four across.

How to play
The first player secretly writes a four-digit number on a piece of paper, using any figures from 1 to 8. The second player has to guess what those figures are, and writes his guess in the first row of the grid. The first player now marks the guess with a star for a correct number in the right place; a tick for a correct number in the wrong place; and an x for a wrong number.

The second player continues to guess the code, using the information from his previous attempts to revise his selection of numbers. If he gets the code right before reaching the top of the grid, he has cracked the code and is the winner.

Variations
* Play simultaneously on separate sheets of paper, taking turns to have a go.
* Play this game with different coloured dots instead of numbers.

Tip for beginners
* Play with fewer numbers.

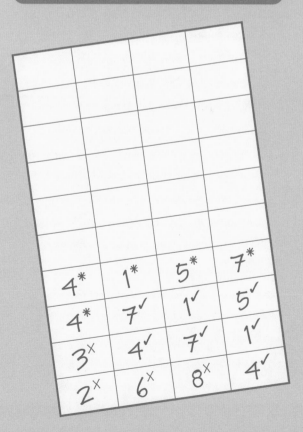

Spy letters

Age range 11
Number of players Two
What you will need A sheet of paper for each player; two sheets of squared paper and a pencil for each player; sharp scissors

This game will appeal to the spy master in your child. The aim of the game is to break a coded message. It sounds simple, and it would be if your child did not have to find the message first!

Preparation

Each player needs to think of a short message and write it down on a piece of paper. For example, one player may come up with MEET ME IN THE PARK. Agree on a code, say, moving each letter of the alphabet one to the right, so that A becomes B, B becomes C and so on. Each player now needs to convert her message using the code. The message above would now read: NFFU NF JO UIF QBSL.

Each player writes her coded message on her first sheet of squared paper. She has to write one letter in each square and can leave a random number of blank squares between the words. Laying the second sheet of squared paper over the first, the player marks the squares where the letters show through. If the player cuts these squares out carefully, and lays the second piece over the first again, she should now be able to read her coded message through the holes. Returning to the first sheet of squared paper, the player now fills in the blank squares between the words of her coded message with random letters, thereby 'hiding' her original message.

Tip for beginners
* Help your child when it comes to positioning the words and cutting out.

Variation
* Group the letters together in sets of four, with spaces between. This will make the decoded message harder to read.

How to play

The children swap both their sheets of paper. The race is now on for each player to work out her opponent's message. She lays the 'decoder' sheet – the one with the squares cut out of it – over the cryptic message. This reveals the coded message and the player then uses the agreed code to unscramble the secret message.

Age range 10+
Number of players Any number
What you will need A sheet of paper
and a pencil for each player; a ruler for
each player; coloured pencils (optional); an
egg timer or stopwatch (optional)

Busy hexagon

This game is an incredible test of your
child's visual skills. She has to count the
number of triangles hiding in a simple
hexagon. Every time she thinks she has
counted them all, she will spot another
one, and another, and ...

Preparation

Draw a large hexagon for each of the players.
Instruct them to use a ruler to draw a line from
each point of the hexagon to the three opposite
points on the shape (see illustration, right).

How to play

Each player has to count up how many complete
triangles there are within the hexagon. The winner
is the player who finds the most.

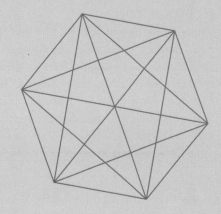

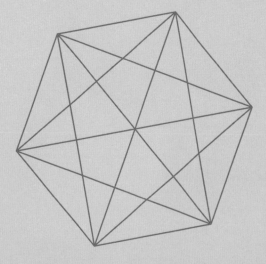

Tip for beginners

∗ Use different coloured pencils to outline the
   various-sized triangles to make it easier to
   count them.

Variation

∗ Set a time limit for how long players have to
   come up with their answer.

See page 384 for the solution

Lose your letters

Age range 5+
Number of players Any number
What you will need A sheet of paper and a pencil for each player; an extra sheet of paper; scissors; opaque bag

This game requires a keen eye as players cross off letters in a five-letter word as you pull them out of the bag. Each player has a different word, and the pressure is on to finish first.

Preparation

Write down the letters of the alphabet on the extra sheet of paper and cut each out so that you have 26 individual squares. Clearly write out a few five-letter words at the top of separate sheets of paper, one for each player. Useful words could include: house, stage, train, magic, watch, brush, woman and party. Make sure no words feature the same letter more than once.

How to play

Put the cut-up letters into an opaque bag and give each player a piece of paper with a five-letter word at the top. Pick a letter from the bag and call it out. If anyone has that letter in their word, they can cross it off. For example, if you call out the letter 'N' and one player has the word 'plane', the player could cross out the fourth letter of her word. Shake the bag of letters and choose a new one. The first player to cross off all of her letters is the winner.

Tip for beginners

* Keep all the letters lower case and clearly separated so they are easy to recognize.

Variations

* Choose words in which a letter is repeated – 'river'; 'treat'; 'small', for example – and return each letter to the bag after it is called out.
* For older players, use longer words or give them two or three words to do at once.
* Play the game with numbers from 1 to 20 instead of letters, and have a row of five numbers for each player to cross off.

What's in the picture?

Age range 5+
Number of players Any number
What you will need A sheet of paper and a pencil for each player; some magazines, books or postcards; an egg timer or a stopwatch

By asking your child a number of questions about a picture that she has looked at, but which is now hidden, you can use this game to test your child's observation and memory skills.

Preparation

Choose a large, detailed coloured picture from a magazine or book, or find some picture postcards. Think of a number of questions to ask the children in order to test their skills of observation and memory.

How to play

Allow a group of children to have a good look at the picture for one minute. Then remove it and ask a number of questions about the picture. For instance, if you showed them a picture of a seaside scene, you could ask if there were any boats in the picture and if so how many, or any sandcastles on the beach, or a café nearby, or anyone playing with a ball. Each player has to write her own answers on a sheet of paper.

If children of mixed ages are playing, ask individual questions – but keep a note of what you have asked each person so you can give them the right answers at the end of the game. When you have asked as many questions as you can, show the children the picture again and go through all the answers, scoring a mark for each correct one. The child with the highest score wins.

Variations

* Play in pairs, with one player asking the questions and the other player writing the answers.
* Try an abstract version of the game by drawing a page of different coloured shapes and asking related questions. For example, 'Was the circle blue or orange?', 'How many squares were there?'.

Sprouts

Age range 6+
Number of players Two
What you will need A sheet of paper; a pencil for each player; coloured pencils (optional)

In this game, all your child has to do is draw a line between two dots each time his turn comes round. The rules of play make this simple game quite a challenge, however, and victory quite often takes both players by surprise.

Variation
∗ Draw more starting dots for a longer game.

Tip for beginners
∗ Use different coloured pencils for each individual player.

How to play
To start the game, draw two dots at random on the sheet of paper. The first player either draws a line to connect the dots or a line that starts and ends on the same dot (see illustration, below). The player then draws a new dot on that line. Play passes to the next player, with each player taking his turn to draw a line and add a new dot. The players must follow the rules below when adding lines and new dots and, eventually, it will become impossible for play to continue. The last person to add a dot is the winner.

Rules of play
1. No dot can have more than three lines coming out of it.
2. A line cannot cross itself or another line.
3. A new line cannot go through a dot.

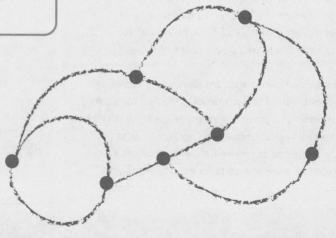

He said, she said

Age range 7+
Number of players Any number
What you will need A sheet of paper and a pencil for each player

This game is Consequences in its purest form. Each child takes it in turn to write the key facts in what happens when a boy meets a girl. Children love the element of secrecy here, and can barely wait to read out the silly stories at the end.

How to play

Each player takes a blank sheet of paper and writes a boy's name at the top. The player then folds the top of the paper over so that no one else can see the name. When everyone is ready the sheets of paper are passed to the left. Each player now writes down a girl's name and folds the paper over once more. The papers are again passed to the left and this time a location is added. Play continues by writing a short sentence a boy might say, followed by a short sentence a girl might say, and finally a consequence. Players continue to pass the sheets of paper each time something new is written.

When all the papers have been passed to the left for the last time each player takes a turn to read out his 'story'. For instance, one might read: Jim met Nancy on a ferris wheel. He said: 'I like chips.' She said: 'You're great!' And the consequence was: They rode off on a donkey into the sunset.

Tip for beginners
∗ Have a list of boys' and girls' names, locations, and so on, to choose from.

Variations
∗ Choose celebrity or pop star names for your boys and girls.
∗ Add more detail, such as 'he was wearing' and 'she was wearing' or a time of day, name of town or a country.

I like chips

You're great!

Treasure muddle

Age range 8+
Number of players Any number working in pairs
What you will need A sheet of paper and a pencil for each pair of children; an extra sheet of paper; scissors; some treasure

This game will appeal to all children who like playing with words – and finding treasure! Each hiding place has a scrambled clue, which the children have to work out before moving on to the next. It is a good idea to have treasure that can be shared among all players.

Preparation

Choose ten hiding places around the house – for example, dining table, umbrella stand, kitchen sink, and so on. Write down the name of each hiding place, but muddle up the letters in each case so that you have clues that read something like ginnid balet (dining table), ballerum dants (umbrella stand) and hitenck kins (kitchen sink). Space the clues out over your sheet of paper so that you can cut them out easily. Choose one hiding place for the treasure, and leave a clue in each of the remaining nine places.

How to play

Give each pair of children the first clue. They must unscramble the words to find the first hiding place, where the next clue is waiting. Each pair works through the clues – writing the next muddled word on their sheet of paper and leaving the original clue exactly as they found it – until the treasure is discovered in the final hiding place.

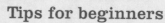

Variation

∗ Extend the game by having a short riddle to answer at each hiding place. For example, 'My first is in cup, my second is in jam, my third is in grit – can you guess me?'. The answer 'cat' could indicate that the next clue is in the cat basket.

Tips for beginners

∗ Pair an adult and child together.
∗ Use hiding places that have shorter names to muddle up – for example, bath or bed.

Football fun

Age range 9+
Number of players Two
What you will need A sheet of paper and a pencil; a coloured pencil for each player

This is a great game for rainy days that will appeal to your child's competitive nature. The skill is in moving forward without giving the opponent the chance to 'bounce' the ball for an extra turn.

Preparation

Draw an 80-square grid – ten across by eight down. This is your football pitch. Add two squares at each short end for the goals (see illustration, below). Mark a point in the centre of the pitch. This is your ball.

How to play

Using a different coloured pencil each, the players take it in turns to move the ball from the centre of the pitch to their goal. A player can cross one square at a time – horizontally, vertically or diagonally – drawing a line to indicate her move. Her opponent does the same, but moves in the opposite direction. Play continues with players zigzagging across the pitch until one of them reaches her goal. During play, if the ball touches either the sides of the pitch or a line that has been drawn already, it 'bounces' off and that player has another go.

Tip for beginners

* Explain the benefits of 'bouncing' moves.

Variation

* Draw a bigger grid for a longer game.

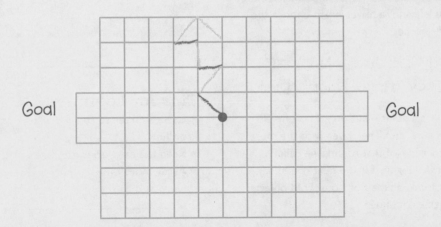

Goal   Goal

Categories

Age range 8+
Number of players Any number
What you will need A sheet of paper and a pencil for each player; an egg timer or stopwatch

This is a word game that tests your child's ability to think of words of the same type – animal names, for example – starting with a range of different letters. Not only that, but she has to play against both time and other players. There are no points for two players writing down the same word, so this game calls for great concentration.

How to play

One player – the 'caller' – chooses a five-letter starter word, such as 'plane', 'spade' or 'diver'. Each of the remaining players then writes that word across the top of her sheet of paper, with the letters well spaced out, heading each of five columns. The caller then announces a category, such as girls' names. The other players have two minutes in which to write down a girl's name beginning with each letter of the starter word. For example, if the starter word is 'plane', a player might choose the following girls' names:

P L A N E
Polly Lucy Anne Naomi Emma

Each name wins a point – but only if no one else has used the same one. The player with the most points is the winner of that round. The caller chooses a new category for the next round, say, boys' names, foods, animals or household objects, and so the game continues.

Variations

* Choose a starter word with unusual letters, such as 'quick' or 'amaze'.
* Choose longer starter words such as 'tickle' or 'ghostly'.
* Choose more difficult categories, such as countries, flowers, colours or gemstones.

Tips for beginners

* Use a shorter starter word, such as 'mat' or 'hen'.
* Keep the categories easy.
* Allow more time.

Age range 9+
Number of players Any number
What you will need A sheet of paper and a pencil for each player

Story circle

With each child in a group writing the next line of a story as paper is passed from one player to the next, this game is a test of your child's imagination and encourages her to think creatively as she builds on each story that comes her way during the game.

How to play

Each player writes the opening lines of a story at the top of her sheet of paper. She passes the paper on to the next player, who reads what the first player has written and adds the next sentence. The game continues like this until each player has had a turn. On the last round, each player must write a sentence to end the story. The players then take it in turns to read out their stories.

Variations
* Agree on main characters before starting the game, but keep each section of the story hidden from the other players until everyone has had a turn.
* Choose a theme, such as horror, comedy or romance.
* With just two or three players, go round several times before agreeing when to write the final sentence.

Tips for beginners
* All start with the same first line, and discuss what you are going to write.
* Say out loud what you are writing.
* Take dictation from other players.

Inside story

Age range 5+
Number of players One
What you will need A sheet of paper and a pencil; coloured pencils (optional)

Your child will be pleased if he spots all of the triangles within the triangle below, although there is a chance he will get caught out. You can increase the number of triangles and, therefore, the complexity of the game for older children.

Preparation

Copy the illustration to draw a large triangle divided into four smaller triangles.

How to play

Show the triangle to your child and ask him to count the triangles in the drawing. If he says 'four', point out that he has forgotten to count the original triangle holding all the others, so there are five in total.

Variation

* Draw a larger triangle split into more parts, or draw a square that is four squares across by four squares down (see below). This has 21 squares in total.

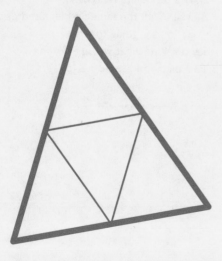

Tip for beginners

* Draw over each triangle in a different colour to emphasize how each one is made.

House builder

Age range 8+
Number of players One
What you will need A sheet of paper and a pencil

Can your child draw a house using one continuous line? This is a great visual trick – even if you demonstrate (with reasonable speed) your child will not be able to see how you did it. He will enjoy catching his friends out, too.

How to play

Copy the house onto your sheet of paper (see illustration, below) and ask your child to draw the shape without taking his pencil off the paper. He must use only eight lines and he may not go over the same line twice.

Variation

* There is more than one way to draw the house. Can your child find any others?

Tip for beginners

* Omit the crossed lines in the centre of the house, which makes it simpler to draw.

 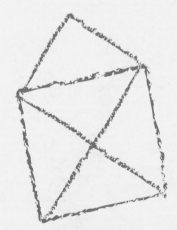 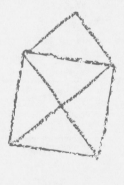

See page 384 for the solution

Sunshine

Age range 7+
Number of players Two or more
What you will need A sheet of paper
and a pencil; a ruler

**The radiating lines in this illustration
create an optical illusion, persuading the
viewer that the horizontal lines are not
straight, but curved. This picture is
simple enough for your child to draw
herself and try out on her friends.**

Preparation
Copy the illustration. Start by drawing a small circle
in the centre of the paper, with another smaller
circle within it. Draw a series of long, straight lines
radiating out from the larger circle in a sunburst,
but avoid drawing any that are completely vertical.
Now draw in the two straight lines of identical
length, above and below the circles.

How to play
Each player has to say in turn whether she thinks the
horizontal lines are straight or curved. The winner is
the one to guess correctly that both are straight.

Tip for beginners
* Give a player the ruler to check the 'curves'
  for himself, if he is not convinced.

Variation
* Make one of the straight lines thicker than
  the other. This has the effect of making the
  thinner line look even more curved.

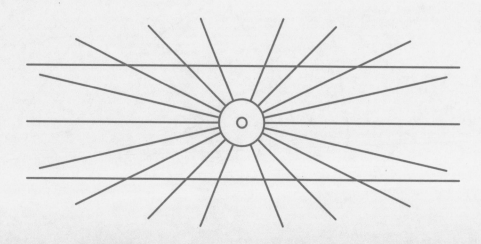

Age range 8+
Number of players Any number
What you will need A sheet of paper and a pencil for each player

Future fun

Does your child dream about her future? Does she wonder what life has in store for her? This game has all the answers – who she will marry, where she will live and how many children she will have!

Preparation

Draw a large square. Along the top, write the letters MASH; down one side write four boys' names (if the player is a girl); down the other side write four countries; along the bottom ask the player to choose four numbers between 1 and 10, and write them in.

How to play

Ask the player to choose a number between 1 and 6. Starting at the M, count around the square in a clockwise direction, crossing off whichever word you land on that corresponds with the number the player chose. If she chose 5, for example, the first word you should cross off is 'Ireland'. Continue to count around the square in multiples of 5 until there is only one item left on each side of the square.

You then reveal that:
M stands for **M**ansion
A stands for **A**partment
S stands for **S**hed
H stands for **H**ouse

In this example, therefore, the player will marry a boy called David, live in a shed in India, and have three children – not bad going!

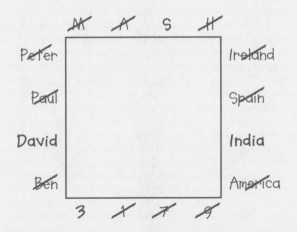

Mystic rose

Age range 8+
Number of players Any number

This drawing exercise is a great example of what you can achieve with just a pencil and paper. Your child will marvel at the beautiful shapes that emerge from nothing but straight lines, and will delight in colouring them in.

Preparation

Each child draws a large circle on a sheet of paper, using the rim of a mug or glass to make it perfect. Mark 12 dots evenly around the circumference.

How to play

Starting at any one of the dots, the child uses her ruler to draw lines joining that dot to each of the other dots in turn. Working clockwise, she repeats the process for each of the dots around the circle. A complex pattern will emerge gradually, becoming increasingly dense as more lines are drawn.

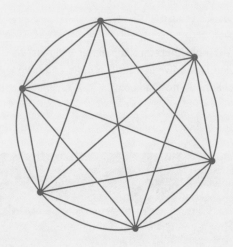

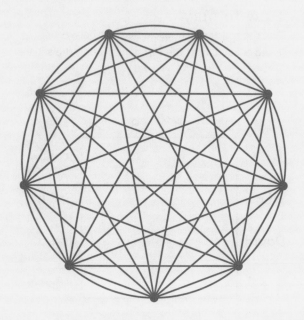

What you will need A sheet of paper and a pencil for each player; a glass or mug; a ruler for each player; coloured pencils (optional)

Tips for beginners

* Mark each of the dots with the numbers 1 to 12, like the face of a clock. This makes it easier to follow which dot is linked to which.
* Mark out only six dots if 12 makes the game too complicated.

Variations

* Mark 20 dots around the edge of the circle to make the pattern more complex.
* Colour in the intricate patterns within the whole rose.
* Try different links between the dots, for example link 1 to 3; 2 to 4; 3 to 5 and so on.

Which is bigger?

Age range 6+
Number of players Two or more
What you will need A sheet of paper and a pencil; a bottle top or cork

This is a straightforward optical illusion. See how long it takes your child to spot the fact that two circles are the same size, although one looks larger than the other.

Preparation

Draw two identical circles on the sheet of paper, spaced well apart and using a bottle top or cork to make sure they are the same. Copy the illustration to draw 12 smaller circles around the left-hand circle, in a petal formation. Draw fewer, larger circles around the right-hand circle.

How to play

Place the two flower pictures in front of the players, and ask each in turn which has the larger circle in its centre. It looks as if the left-hand circle is larger, so the winner is the first to realize that both circles are, in fact, identical.

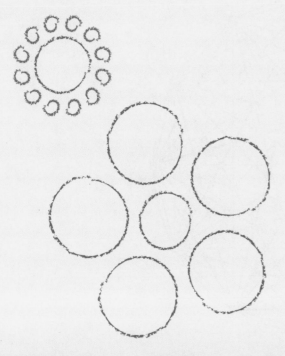

Variation

* Draw several of these circle illusions on different sheets of paper, but make one of them the odd one out, in that it actually does have different-sized circles. See which of the players can spot the difference when you show all of the pictures in turn.

Tip for beginners

* Help a younger player to draw his own two circles around the rim of an upturned cup. Add the extra circles around the edge so that he can see for himself how the illusion works.

Age range 8+
Number of players Any number
What you will need A sheet of paper
and a pencil; a ruler; scissors; a different
coloured sheet of paper for each player
(optional); an egg timer or stopwatch
(optional)

Where will it fit?

This game is based on tessellation and is a really good test of your child's visual-spatial skills. Can he 'read' the pieces of a puzzle to see how they might fit together to make a square?

Preparation

Draw a large 16-square grid on a sheet of paper, four squares across by four squares down. Divide the square into a number of tessellating shapes – that is, shapes that interlock – using the grid squares as a guide (see illustration, right). Cut out the main square, then all the individual pieces. Repeat the process for each player. (You can speed this up by cutting through several sheets of paper at the same time.) If you use a different coloured sheet of paper for each player you will avoid the pieces getting mixed up.

How to play

Mix up each player's pieces of paper and see how quickly he can put them back together to recreate the original square. You can either time each player's record, or ask all the players to start at the same time and see who finishes first.

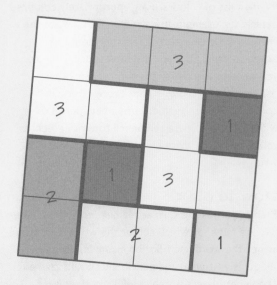

Tips for beginners

* Make a smaller square with less divisions.
* Use paper that is only coloured on one side so there is no confusion about which way up the pieces should be.

Variation

* Draw a larger square with more complicated tessellating shapes.

Colour coded

Age range 9+
Number of players Any number
What you will need A sheet of paper; coloured pencils; scissors (optional)

This game is a visual tongue twister! Your child has to read one thing but say another and it is amazing to see just how difficult this can be. The exercise is a test of your child's powers of concentration.

Preparation

Write a list of colours, using appropriately coloured pencils: for example, use a red pencil to write the word red; a green pencil to write green; a blue pencil to write blue; and a yellow pencil to write yellow. Repeat the process twice more. Now use a different coloured pencil to write each colour name. For example, use a blue pencil to write the word red; a red pencil to write green; a yellow pencil to write blue; and a green pencil to write yellow.

How to play

Each player takes a turn at reading out the colours, but she must say which colour the word is written in, not the word itself. So, for example, where yellow is written in red pencil, she should say 'red'. The other players watch carefully as the player goes through the list – and stop her as soon as she makes a mistake.

The winner is the player who gets furthest down the list without getting a colour wrong.

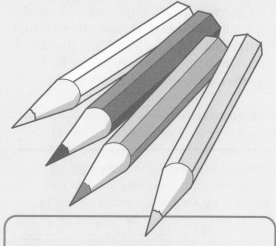

Tips for beginners
∗ Use only two colours to begin with.
∗ Allow plenty of time for each word.

Variations
∗ Make the game a speed contest so that the players have to read through the list more and more quickly.
∗ To vary the game, cut out each of the colour names and rearrange them any number of times to make a fresh game.
∗ Introduce extra colours.

Back to the beginning

Age range 10+
Number of players One
What you will need A sheet of paper and a pencil

This is a brilliant brain teaser based on mathematics. Your child chooses a number, does some simple arithmetic and ends up with the number she started with! This is one that she can try out on her friends.

How to play

Give your child the following instructions: Write down a number between 1 and 9. Multiply that number by 3. Add 1 and multiply by 3 again. Now add on the number you first thought of. Tell your child that you know she now has a two-figure number that ends in a 3. Ask her to cross off that 3 and she will be left with the number she first wrote down.

Tip for beginners

* Check on your child's maths as the trick goes along to make sure that she makes no mistakes.

Variation

* Try this one: Ask your child to choose a number between 1 and 10. Add 1 and multiply by 2. Add 3 and multiply by 2 again. Subtract 10. Now ask your child to tell you her final number – and amaze her by telling her the original number (which you arrive at by dividing her final number by 4).

5
5 × 3 = 15
15 + 1 = 16
16 × 3 = 48
48 + 5 = 53
5̶3̶

Switch it round

Age range 10+
Number of players One

This test of your child's visual skills involves using matchsticks to change the shape of a simple diagram. Many children find the game quite challenging until they have had some practice.

Preparation
Copy the illustration below (1) to create the four-square grid out of 12 matchsticks on a sheet of paper.

How to play
Instruct your child to make a new pattern of just three squares. He can move four of the matchsticks to make the new shape, but he has to use them all. See how few moves it takes your child to complete the task. (See solution, below right.)

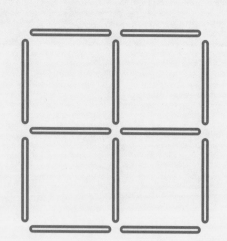

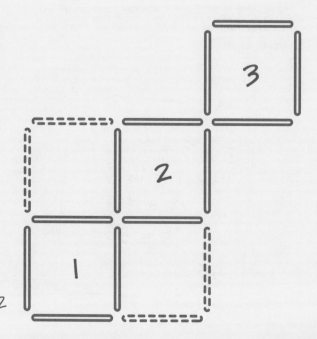

What you will need A sheet of paper; matchsticks; a pencil (optional); an eraser (optional)

Variations

* Try a more complicated shape, using 24 matchsticks to make up a nine-square figure. Your child must remove eight matchsticks to leave only two squares. (See solution, bottom right).
* The game can also be played using a pencil and eraser.

Tip for beginners

* Mark out the solution on a piece of paper so that your child can see how to move the pieces. Use a different coloured pencil for the lines that show the solution.

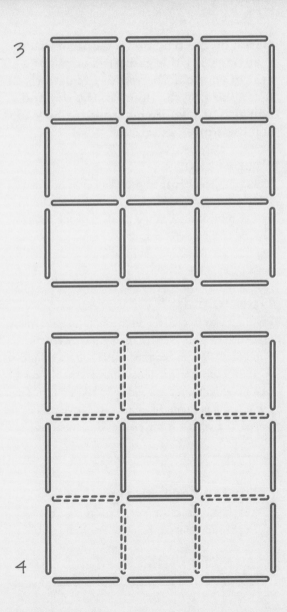

3

4

Time pairs

Age range 5+
Number of players Two
What you will need Two sheets of paper and a pencil; scissors

Based on the traditional game of Pairs (see page 52), this game is a very good test of your child's memory. It uses clock faces showing the hours of the day and will also help your child to learn how to tell the time.

Preparation
Cut each sheet of paper into 12 identical rectangles and draw a simple clock face on each one. On the first two cards draw in the hands showing midday. On the second two cards draw the hands showing one o'clock. Continue until you have two cards for each hour of the day.

How to play
Lay the cards face down on the table and ask the first child to turn over two cards. If they tell the same time, she can keep the cards and have another go. If they tell different times, she returns the cards, face down, while the second child takes a turn. The game continues until all of the cards have been paired. The winner is the player with the most pairs.

Tip for beginners
∗ Say the hour as your child turns over the card and point to the number on the clock face.

Variation
∗ To make the game harder, add in some extra cards, first showing some half-hours, then some quarter-past hours, and finally some quarter-to hours. Remember to make two cards of each, so there is a pair of each.

Highest and lowest

Age range 6+
Number of players Any number
What you will need A sheet of paper and a pencil

This is an interesting game in which your child needs to put a range of numbers in the correct numerical order. The challenge lies in the fact that some of the numbers are written as figures, while others are written as words.

Preparation
Write out three lists of five numbers that are not in numerical order, using both figures and words, and tailoring the lists to the age range of the children playing. For example:

six, 4, 1, five, 2
21, thirteen, 9, three, eleven
one hundred and one, 100, zero, 10, ninety-nine

How to play
Ask your child if she can rearrange each list so that all the numbers read in the correct numerical order. For example:

1, 2, 4, five, six
three, 9, eleven, thirteen, 21
zero, 10, ninety-nine, 100, one hundred and one

63 14
six eleven
     2

Variations
* If there are several children playing this game, have a race, with winners for each round and an overall 'best of three'.
* Instead of writing out the whole list, just ask them to write down the lowest number and the highest number.

Tips for beginners
* Suggest your child converts the written numbers into figures before putting the numbers in order, so that she is doing one thing at a time.
* Remind her to watch out for the number of zeros each number has.

Spotty ladybirds

Age range 4+
Number of players One

This fun numerical game will help your child understand the difference between even and odd numbers. Played in a similar way to Time Pairs (see page 154), all your child has to do is to count the spots on the ladybirds and collect either the odd or even ones in a pile.

Preparation

Cut each sheet of paper into ten equal-sized rectangles and draw the outline of a ladybird on each one (an oval with six legs and two feelers). Colour each ladybird red and add on black spots, giving ten ladybirds an even number of spots (2, 4, 6, 8 or 10), and ten odd (1, 3, 5, 7 or 9).

How to play

Lay the cards out face down in front of your child and decide who is going to collect the even numbers and who the odd ones. Take turns to turn over a card, one at a time, and count the spots on it. If the number of spots matches what your child is collecting, he can keep it. For example, if he is collecting even numbers and turns over a ladybird with four spots on it, he keeps the card. Otherwise, the card must be turned back over. The first person to collect all ten of his cards wins.

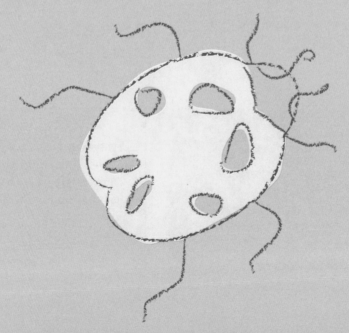

What you will need Two sheets of paper and a pencil; scissors; red and black crayons

Tips for beginners

* Write out the even and odd numbers in two rows for your child to refer to.
* For young children, lie all the cards out face up and sort them into two piles of even and odd spots together.
* Keep the number of spots small, say, no more than four on each one.

Variations

* Increase the number of spots according to your child's counting ability.
* Make caterpillars instead, with varying numbers of legs.

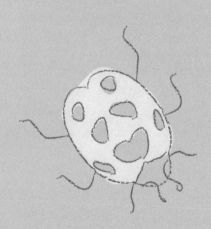

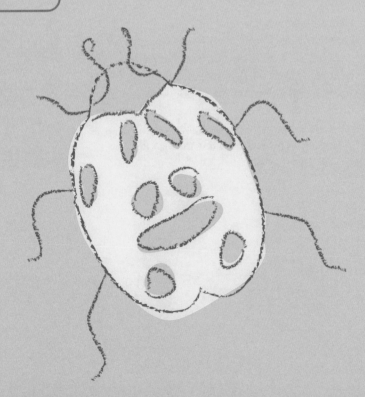

Noughts and crosses

Age range 4+
Number of players Two
What you will need A sheet of paper; a pencil for each player; coloured pens (optional)

Although this game does not use numbers, it does require an understanding of symbols and basic strategy when it comes to beating an opponent. The aim of the game is to be the first to make a complete line of either noughts or crosses.

Preparation
Copy the illustration below to draw a grid of nine spaces.

How to play
Let your child choose whether she wants to be 'noughts' or 'crosses' and instruct her to draw her symbol in any of the nine spaces. Then you draw your symbol in another space. Continue to take turns like this until one person has a complete line of three of her symbol (vertically, horizontally or diagonally) and can draw a line through it.

Tips for beginners
* Diagonal lines are hardest for young kids to spot, so give your child a hint if possible.
* Use different coloured pens to make the lines even easier for little ones to spot.

Variations
* Make a larger grid of 16, 25 or 36 spaces, scoring for each run of your symbol. Score one point for a line of three, two for a line of four, and three for a line of five.
* Older children may like to play the game between themselves.

Age range 7+
Number of players One
What you will need A sheet of paper
and a pencil

Number crossword

This game is a great test of your child's basic arithmetic. She must fill the gaps in the crossword by completing the sums. The challenge is that, in order to arrive at the answers, she must calculate each sum in reverse.

Preparation
Copy the 25-square grid – five down by five across – blacking out four squares and filling in the white squares with numbers as shown. The gaps are the squares that your child will fill in.

How to play
Show the grid to your child and ask her if she can work out what the missing numbers are.

A more difficult grid might include multiplication and division symbols (see illustration, below).

3	×		=	9
×		÷		−
	+	1	=	5
=		=		=
12	÷	3	=	

Tip for beginners
* Remind players to look at symbols carefully.

3	+		=	4
+		+		−
3	−	2	=	
=		=		=
6	−	3	=	3

Variation
* Older children can make up number crosswords of their own to try on friends.

It's a line up!

Age range 7+
Number of players Two

This game of strategy is a variation on the theme of Noughts and Crosses (see page 158). Each player needs to create a line of four squares with the same symbol, while preventing his opponent from doing the same.

Preparation

Draw a 42-square grid – seven across by six down (see illustration, below).

How to play

Using a different coloured pencil each, the players take turns to mark either noughts or crosses respectively in the squares. A player can only draw one mark at a time and he must build up from the bottom of the grid (imagine each column as a chute and the noughts and crosses as items dropped down the chutes). The idea is for a player to make a line of four squares of his symbol, while trying to stop his opponent from doing the same. The winner is the first to make a horizontal, vertical or diagonal line of four.

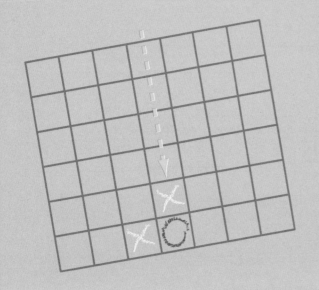

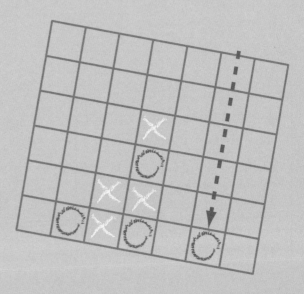

What you will need A sheet of paper and a pencil; a coloured pencil for each player

Tips for beginners
* If you imagine that the grid is governed by the law of gravity it will help you to understand that your marks must always be made in the bottom-most square of any one column.
* Be particularly wary of an opponent making a diagonal line.

Variation
* Draw a larger grid for a longer game.

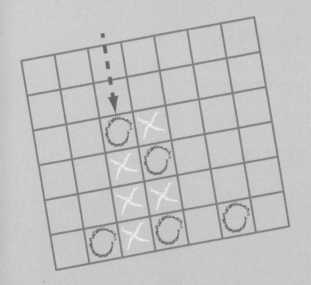

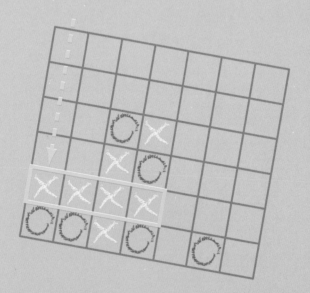

It all adds up

Age range 8+
Number of players One
What you will need A sheet of paper and a pencil

This is a basic number puzzle in which your child has to decode the symbols in a grid in order to produce their corresponding numbers. Your child will be surprised to find that the numbers in any one column or row make the same total when added together.

Preparation

Draw two 25-square grids – five across by five down – and erase the bottom-right-hand-corner square on each (see illustration, below). Above the two grids, write out a set of symbols representing the numbers 1 to 5. For example, the symbols might look like this:

1 = ●   2 = ✳   3 = ▲
4 = ∫   5 = □

For the left-hand grid copy the illustration given below, placing the right symbol in each of 16 squares, as shown.

✳	●	▲	▲	
∫	✳	✳	●	
●	□	✳	●	
✳	●	✳	∫	

How to play

Give the sheet of paper to your child and ask her to fill in the empty grid, using the code at the top to swap the symbols for numbers. When she has done this, ask her to add up each row across, writing the total in the square at the end of the row. Tell her to do the same with each column and watch her amazement as each total comes to 9!

2	1	3	3	9
4	2	2	1	9
1	5	2	1	9
2	1	2	4	9
9	9	9	9	

Variation

✳ Make your own version where the numbers all add up to different totals, in which case you can use symbols for every figure between 1 and 9.

Guess the gaps

Age range 9+
Number of players Any number
What you will need A sheet of paper and a pencil for each player; an extra sheet of paper; an egg timer or stopwatch

$$3 \times 3 = 9$$
$$5 \times 4 = 20$$
$$6 \times 7 = 42$$

This exercise can pose a real test of your child's mental agility. She has to figure out the pattern in a given sequence of numbers and fill in numbers where there are gaps. You can make the sequences more obvious for younger children.

Preparation

Cut the extra sheet of paper into six strips and write a sequence of numbers on each one, omitting every other number. Here are a few examples of sequences to try:

Consecutive numbers:
1, –, 3, –, 5, –, 7, –, 9
Alternate numbers: 2, –, 6, –, 10, –, 14
Adding 3: 1, –, 7, –, 13, –, 19, –, 25
3x table: 3, –, 9, –, 15, –, 21
4x table: –, 8, –, 16, –, 24
5x table: 5, –, 15, –, 25, –

How to play

Place a row of numbers on the table and give the children two minutes to copy out the list and add in the missing numbers. The players score points according to the number of people playing. For example, if there are three children playing, the first person to finish gets three points, the second two, and the third one. The winner is the player with the highest score at the end of the game.

Variations
* Instead of having the same gap each time, keep adding on one more number as you go up. For example,
  1, (2), 4, (7), 11, (16), 22.
* Start each sequence with a higher number rather than with 1. For example,
  46, (48), 50, (52), 54.

Tips for beginners
* Leave fewer blanks and keep them towards the end of each sequence.
* Give a clue if a child gets stuck: 'Think of your four times table', for example.

Battleships

Age range 8+
Number of players Two

Battleships has been a favourite seek-and-destroy game for many generations. Based on a simple grid formation, the idea is to discover your opponent's fleet of ships before he finds yours.

Preparation

Each player draws two 100-square grids, ten across by ten down. He writes the letters A to J above each square across the top of each grid, and the numbers 1 to 10 beside each square down the left-hand side. Each player then 'hides' his fleet of ships in one of the grids by colouring in the squares according to the key above right. The ships can run vertically or horizontally within the grid, but no two ships may touch. Each player's fleet contains: one battleship, two cruisers, three destroyers and four submarines.

Key to the fleet

Battleship = four adjacent squares in a row
Cruisers = three adjacent squares in a row
Destroyers = two adjacent squares in a row
Submarines = one separate square

Variation

* Invent your own alternatives for ships, such as vehicles, aliens, or monsters (for example, one Megamonster, two Maximonsters, three Minimonsters and four Micromonsters).

Tip for beginners

* Explain clearly to the players how to read the letters and numbers across and down to name the location.

What you will need Two sheets of
paper and a pencil for each player

How to play

It is important that neither player sees his
opponent's grids at any point during the game. The
idea is that each player has to guess where his
opponent has hidden his fleet. Players take it in
turns to ask about specific locations, quoting the
grid reference for a particular square each time. For
example, the first player may say 'B2'. If the square is
empty, his opponent answers 'miss'; if he does have
a ship there, he answers 'hit', but does not reveal
the type of ship that has been hit. The first player
puts a circle in the corresponding square of his
empty grid for a miss, or a cross

for a hit. A player who scores a hit may guess
another square immediately. Otherwise it is
his opponent's turn to guess. Play continues in
this way until a whole ship for either player is
discovered, at which point the person whose ship it
is shouts 'sunk!'. Since no two ships are allowed to
touch, all of the squares around the sunk ship can
be filled in with circles for water. The winner is the
first person to discover his opponent's entire fleet
of ships.

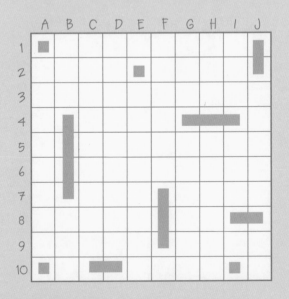

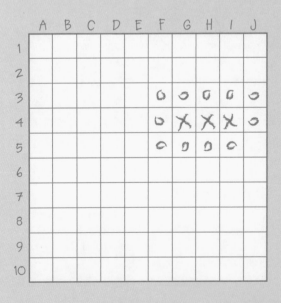

Stretch it

Age range 4+
Number of players Any number
What you will need Four sheets of paper and a pencil for each player; a die

Children love playing this game, tumbling over each other as they twist and bend to position themselves. It is a game that needs adult supervision: not only will you need to throw the die for the children, but you should also make sure the children do not slip about too much.

Preparation

Give each child four sheets of paper and ask her to write down four numbers between 1 and 6 on the separate pieces. Scatter the papers across the floor, number side up.

How to play

Throw the die for each player in turn. Whatever number you roll, that player must put her right foot on a sheet of paper with the same number. Play continues until all players have a right foot on a number. In the next round each of the players places her left foot on a sheet of paper with each roll of the die. In the third round, each player puts her right hand on a sheet of paper, and in the fourth round she places her left hand on a sheet of paper. Anyone who falls over during the game is out.

Variation

* If there are no available number sheets of paper left, you can throw the die again instead of the player having to try sharing a sheet of paper with someone else.

Tips for beginners

* Keep the pieces of paper close together.
* Play where each player simply jumps onto the right number with each roll of the die.

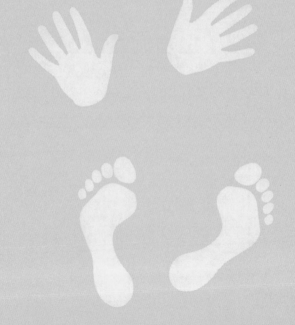

Magic square

Age range 10+
Number of players One
What you will need A sheet of paper and a pencil

Find out what your child makes of this challenging puzzle. It is a really good test of her mental arithmetic, although she can also find the solution through trial and error. Either way, she will enjoy testing her friends with the puzzle once she has mastered it herself.

Preparation
Draw a nine-square grid, three squares down by three squares across, with the numbers 1 to 9 written in a row above it.

How to play
Instruct your child to put one number from 1 to 9 in each of the squares (with no repetitions) so that each horizontal, vertical and diagonal row adds up to 15. See how long it takes her to work it out!

Tip for beginners
* Enter the figure for the centre square, or write in an entire column, before your child begins.

Variation
* Once your child has completed the puzzle, ask her to double all the numbers in it and see what happens when she adds up all the lines and diagonals now. (They should all add up to 30.)

See page 384 for the solution

Alphabet sentences

Age range 8+
Number of players Any number
What you will need A sheet of paper and a pencil

This is a game that gets harder as it progresses and will really test your child's verbal dexterity. The idea is to add a word to a sentence, where each word begins with a consecutive letter of the alphabet. There is always a very funny story to read out at the end of the game.

How to play

The first player starts writing a 'story' by putting down a word that begins with the letter 'a'. She could either use the article A, or find another word that begins with 'a', such as Alfred, Annie, armadillos, arms or angry. She then passes the paper to her left for the next person to write a word that begins with the letter 'b'. The paper moves to the left again and the third player writes a word that starts with 'c'. Play continues until the players have worked through the entire alphabet to make a reasonably coherent sentence.

Sample sentence

The type of sentence made could end up reading something like this:

Annie beheld Carol Drake eating four giant heavy iced jellied kippers, lips munching noisily, outside Peter's quarters round Swindon telling us very wittily, 'X-ray your zoo!'.

Variations

* Try a shorter version by opting for every other letter of the alphabet, for example, a, c, e, g, i, k ...; or b, d, f, h, j ...
* Make the game harder by telling everyone the 'story' must be on a particular theme, such as rock-climbing or disco dancing.
* Try making as long a sentence as possible using the same initial letter for every word of a sentence – for example, Bertie Bunny built bridges by breaking boulders.

Tip for beginners

* Improvise for the letter 'x' by allowing excite, exit or exist, or drop it altogether.

Missing letters

Age range 6+
Number of players One
What you will need A sheet of paper and a pencil; an extra sheet of paper; scissors; an egg timer or stopwatch

By showing familiar words to your child, but with certain letters missing, you are testing both her memory and her early spelling skills. This is a game you can play as your child's vocabulary increases, simply by using longer and more complicated words.

Preparation
Think of 20 words that you know your child can read. Write the words out, using large letters, on the extra sheet of paper, leaving enough room for you to cut each one out. As you write the words, replace the vowels with dashes. For example, if you had chosen 'dog', 'garden', 'book' and 'seaside', your cards would read: D_G, G_RD_N, B__K and S__S_D_. Also make some tiny cards with a single vowel written on each one (A, E, I, O and U), which can be placed over the dashes in your words.

How to play
Place the vowel cards face up on the table. Then shuffle the 20 word cards, place them face down on the table and ask your child to pick one. She then has one minute to work out what the missing letters might be, placing the vowel cards over the dashes to fill the gaps. You may find that she can make a different word to the one you intended. For instance, instead of DOG she might come up with DIG. If she completes a word within the minute she keeps the card. At the end of the game count up the cards your child has managed to collect.

Variations
* Try removing five consonants instead, such as H, R, M, S and F. So 'car', 'barn' and 'time' would be CA_, BA_N and TI_E.
* Try removing just the initial letters.

Tips for beginners
* Show your child how to experiment by placing the small vowel cards over the dashes to see if she can make a word.
* Use words with only one vowel missing.

Take away one

Age range 7+
Number of players One
What you will need A sheet of paper and a pencil

In this game your child has to study a word and see if, by taking away one letter, he can make a new word. Keep the words short until your child has a good understanding of how to play, then encourage him to come up with examples of his own.

Preparation
Think of a list of 10–20 short words at random. For example, your list might include: 'house', 'task', 'chair', 'lamp', 'break' and 'shape'.

How to play
Write out one word at a time and, together with your child, see if you can take away one letter and make a new word. Explain that it may be necessary to jumble up the letters that remain to make your new word.

Sample words

House – remove U to make Hose

Task – remove T to make Ask

Chair – remove C to make Hair

Lamp – remove L, jumble up the letters and make Map

Break – remove E, jumble up the letters and make Bark

Shape – remove H, jumble up the letters and make Peas

Variations
* Remove two letters – for example, ELBOW could lose E and L and become BOW, or CIGAR could lose I and G and become CAR.
* Add a letter to make a new word – for example RAIN could become TRAIN, or MALL become SMALL.

Tip for beginners
* Draw a picture for each of the words and talk through the images first with your child. Once he knows what the two words are, he can work backwards to work out which letter to lose.

Dot-to-dot letters

Age range 7+
Number of players One
What you will need A sheet of paper and a pencil

In this game of dot to dot, your child needs to move from one letter of the alphabet to the next in order to draw a picture. This is a very effective way of helping him to learn the alphabet.

Preparation

Lightly draw a picture outline of, say, a house, boat or teddy on the sheet of paper. Pick out 26 places to make a dot on the outline of the image, and then erase the faint line drawing. Write a letter of the alphabet beside each dot, working your way around the picture alphabetically, until you come back to the beginning.

How to play

Ask your child to make the picture by drawing a line from one letter of the alphabet to the next, starting at A and finishing at Z.

Variations

* Traditionally this game is played with numbers. Simply write the figures 1 to 26 instead of the letters A to Z.
* If your child has a reasonably long name, such as Christopher, and knows how to spell it, try connecting the letters of his name instead of those of the alphabet.

Tip for beginners

* It may help to print out the alphabet in a straight line above the picture.

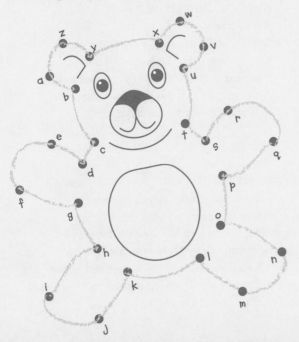

Unscramble the letters

Age range 7+
Number of players Any number
What you will need A sheet of paper and a pencil for each player; an egg timer or stopwatch (optional)

Give your child a series of anagrams to see if she can work out what you have written. The letters of the chosen words are rewritten in alphabetical order, and each list of words shares the same theme, so this should not be too difficult.

Preparation
Choose a few themes, such as girls' names, boys' names, flowers, fruit, trees, vegetables or the names of the planets, and think of a list of between five to ten words for each theme. Then rearrange the letters of each word in alphabetical order and write a new list on a sheet of paper with the theme title at the top. Copy the list for each player in the game.

Example of play
(Note that the answers are for reference only)

Vegetables
Acorrt (carrot)

Aooptt (potato)

Aabbceg (cabbage)

Eekls (leeks)

Abens (beans)

Aeps (peas)

Variations
* As players become more skilled, choose harder themes, longer words, or more of them.
* The words need not always be nouns — try verbs as well. For example, your theme could be exercising and your words could be 'run', 'jump', 'skip', 'hop', 'kick' and 'swim'.

Tips for beginners
* Play in teams.
* Younger children enjoy this more if you turn it into a 'story'. For instance, tell them that Joe loved vegetables and ate lots every day — can your child find out how many different vegetables he ate for lunch yesterday?

How to play
Give a list of rearranged words to each child and ask who can discover what all the different vegetables are by unscrambling the letters and putting them back in the right order. You can impose a time limit if you wish. When everyone has finished go through the lists to check the words are correct, and then bring out a new list.

Spelling bee

Age range 7+
Number of players Any number
What you will need A sheet of paper and a pencil for each team of players

Each child in a team takes a turn to spell a word correctly. The pressure is on, as she risks offering the chance of a bonus point to the opposition if she spells it wrongly.

Preparation
Draw up a list of some 50 or so words that you know the players can spell.

How to play
Divide the players into two teams: A and B (or some fun names of their choice). Read out a word from your list for the first player of Team A to write down on her team's sheet of paper. When she has written it, she passes the paper to the next player, who reads out the letters. If the word is spelt correctly, Team A scores one point. If it is spelt incorrectly, Team B has a chance to spell the same word for a bonus point. Play returns to the next player on Team A, who has to try to spell a new word. When each player in Team A has taken a turn, play passes to Team B. This time Team A can score bonus points for correctly spelling the words that Team B gets wrong. When everyone has had a go, all the points are added up to see which team has scored the most.

Tips for beginners
* Keep the words simple.
* Allow plenty of time.
* Remind children of tricky letters, such as the silent 'k' in 'knight' and the 'f' sound of 'ph' in 'photo'.

Variations
* Play this with your child on her own, giving her one word to spell at a time.
* Try spelling easy words backwards.

Beat the boat

Age range 8+
Number of players Two
What you will need A sheet of paper and a pencil for each player

This is a modern variation of the game known as Hangman. The idea is to guess an opponent's mystery word before he manages to draw a boat and sail away. There are ten chances for guessing, so children need to choose their letters very wisely.

How to play

The first player thinks of a word and draws a dash on his sheet of paper for each letter of that word. The second player starts play by guessing a letter that might be in the mystery word. If he guesses correctly, the letter is written over the corresponding dash. If the letter is not in the mystery word, it is written elsewhere on the page and the first line (the base) of the boat is drawn.

Play continues like this until either the word is guessed and all the letters are filled in correctly, or the boat is drawn with a wave underneath – which means it has sailed away. To draw the boat takes ten moves (see illustration, below left).

Variation
* Play a double-action game where both players choose a word and guess each other's letters simultaneously. Players should choose words of the same length, and the winner is the first player to guess his opponent's word.

Tips for beginners
* Younger children will need very simple words that they can read easily.
* If a child is struggling, fill in the first letter of the word for him, or give a clue.

Add a letter

Age range 9+
Number of players Any number
What you will need A sheet of paper and a pencil; magnetic letters (optional)

In this game your child has to make a new word by adding a single letter to the word that comes before it. This is quite a challenge, so it makes sense to start with easy words to begin with, to help your child grasp the rules of the game.

How to play

Start the game by writing a short word at the top of a sheet of paper. You need to think carefully what that word might be to make sure that it will work for the game. Ask the first player to add one letter to make a new word and to write the new word under the old one, lining up the matching letters. Play passes to the next player who adds another letter and so on, until no further words can be made. If you get beyond five letters you are doing very well, and the person who makes the last word scores one point.

Tips for beginners

* Score one point for every word made.
* Use magnetic letters so your child can experiment with different letters.

Example of play

PLAN

PLANE

PLANET

PLANETS

Variations

* An alternative method of scoring would be for the last person making a word to score a point for all previous words!
* You can also make new words from old by providing an 'inner' word and asking your child to add extra letters to either end. For example, 'add a letter to each end of "at" to make a word that means something you find in the middle of a fence' (gate); or 'add two letters to the end of "fir" to make something that comes at the beginning' (first).

Grid challenge

Age range 8+
Number of players Any number
What you will need A sheet of paper and a pencil for each player; a red felt-tipped pen; an egg timer or stopwatch

This game is great fun, and sets your child the challenge of making words from a given set of letters. Children enjoy competing with each other to see who can make the most words, and they are always amazed at how many words can be made using just nine letters.

Preparation
Draw a large nine-square grid, three squares across by three squares down. Write a vowel (a, e, i, o or u) in the middle square using a red felt-tipped pen. Add more letters at random in the other squares, including at least two extra vowels.

How to play
Explain that each player needs to write down as many words as he can think of using the letters in the grid. Each word can be of two or more letters and must include the red vowel in the centre of the grid. Players can use each letter only once in a word. Set a time limit of, say, five or ten minutes. At the end of this time compare all the words. You can either score a point for each word, with extra points for words of five letters or more, or score points only for words that no other players have written down.

an	air	sane	near	satin
as	ant	past	pear	paste
at	hat	pair	star	haste
ape	eat	part	rain	stair
ate	hair	rash	sari	stare
ash	pain	nape	shape	heart

Tips for beginners
* Choose letters carefully, with at least one 'e' and 'a', and a selection of letters that go together, such as 'th', 'ing', 'st' and 'wh'.

Variations
* Allow any letter in the grid to be used more than once when making a word.
* Omit the rule that the red vowel has to appear in each word.

Letter ladders

Age range 11
Number of players One
What you will need A sheet of paper and a pencil

This is quite a difficult game, requiring your child to work with a visual puzzle as well as a verbal one. Once he gets the idea, he will enjoy setting himself the greater challenge of using longer words, and testing his friends with the game.

How to play

Choose a four-letter word, such as 'gift', 'farm', 'arch' or 'word', and follow the illustration to write the word twice vertically on your sheet of paper – once with the letters in the correct order and once running backwards (1). Now try to make new words by building letter 'steps' of the same length between the two rows of letters. For example, if you had chosen the word 'term', your steps might look something like this (2):

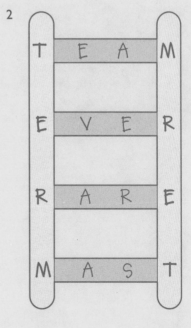

1
```
T        M
E        R
R        E
M        T
```

2

Variations

* Use five- or six-letter starter words.
* Try making the 'steps' of three or four letters, although this is hard.

Outdoor fun

Skip to my Lou

Age range 4+
Number of players Several pairs plus one extra child
Energy level 2
What you will need No props

If you want a group of children to learn to mix together or overcome shyness, try this game, which involves children constantly changing their partners. The aim is to 'Skip to my Lou' until everyone in the ring has had a chance to dance with someone new.

How to play

Players form a circle, and one child stands in the middle of the ring while the others choose partners. An adult helper can make a pair if necessary. During the first verse the player in the ring chooses someone's partner and takes her to dance around the outside of the circle. Then they both rejoin the circle.

Variation

* Another popular version of this song has these verses:

Flies in the buttermilk,
Shoo, shoo, shoo,
Flies in the buttermilk,
Shoo, shoo, shoo,
Flies in the buttermilk,
Shoo, shoo, shoo,
Skip to my Lou, my darlin'.

Cows in the cornfield,
What'll I do?
Cows in the cornfield,
What'll I do?
Cows in the cornfield,
What'll I do?
Skip to my Lou, my darlin'.

Lou, Lou, skip to my Lou,
Lou, Lou, skip to my Lou,
Lou, Lou, skip to my Lou,
Skip to my Lou, my darlin'.

Now the person who has lost his partner skips alone around the outside of the circle while the second verse is sung by all the children.

During the third verse he chooses a new partner from the circle and dances round the outside of the circle with her. Then they both rejoin the circle. And so the game goes on, with the new singleton in the middle and the children starting again at the first verse of the rhyme.

Lost my partner, what shall I do?
Lost my partner, what shall I do?
Lost my partner, what shall I do?
Skip to my Lou, my darlin'.

Find another one, just like you,
Find another one, just like you,
Find another one, just like you,
Skip to my Lou, my darlin'.

Ring-a-ring o' roses

Age range 3+
Number of players Two or more
Energy level 2
What you will need No props

This is one of the first – and most popular – dancing rhymes that children ever learn, resulting in everyone falling down in a happy heap at the end of the verse! Even the youngest child will enjoy it with a bit of adult help.

How to play

Hold hands in a circle – or facing each other, if there are only two of you. Then sing the rhyme below and follow the actions.

Ring-a-ring o' roses
(children walk round in a circle)

A pocket full of posies.
(children continue walking round in a circle)

A-tishoo, a-tishoo,
(children stand still and pretend to sneeze)

We all fall down!
(children fall down)

Tip for beginners
＊ Remind little ones to fall down gently – you don't want any bumped heads!

Variation
＊ Try this verse for getting up again:

The cows are in the meadow
(children pat the floor)

Eating all the grass.
(children continue patting the floor)

A–tishoo, a–tishoo,
(children sit still and pretend to sneeze)

Who's up last!
(children all jump up)

I sent a letter to my love

Age range 10+
Number of players Any number
Energy level 2
What you will need The letter in an envelope; an egg timer or a stopwatch

This is a sedate game for most of the time – but has a mad rush at the end of each verse when two children race each other for a single place in the circle. The aim is to keep your place if you receive the letter.

How to play

All the children sit in a circle apart from one. That one has the envelope – the 'letter' – and skips round the outside of the ring, dropping it behind one child as he gets to the end of the rhyme.

The child behind whom the letter has been dropped must now pick it up and, running in the opposite direction, race the first child round the outside of the circle to get back to his empty place and sit down again. If the first child beats him to it, then the other child gets to be the letter-bearer next time.

I sent a letter to my love
And on the way I dropped it.
One of you has picked it up
And put it in your pocket.
It wasn't you,
It wasn't you,
It wasn't you,
It was YOU!

Variation

* You can still play this game if you only have two children playing – simply mark out the missing players' spaces with pebbles or two crossed sticks around the playing circle. Young children may enjoy using dolls or soft toys as stand-ins, too.

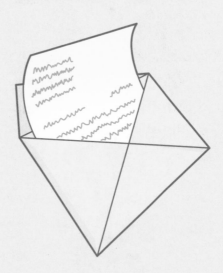

In and out the dusty bluebells

Age range 4+
Number of players A large group of children
Energy level 2
What you will need No props

This starts in a fairly sensible fashion – but ends up with a line of giggly children struggling under a single arch! They are trying to make as long a line as possible weaving through the 'bluebells'.

How to play

The children form a circle holding hands, with their arms raised, and one child is chosen to be the leader. The game then proceeds as follows:

1st verse: The leader weaves in and out of the circle – the 'bluebells' – while everyone sings the song. On reaching the word 'partner', the leader goes to stand behind whichever child she has naturally stopped at.

In and out the dusty bluebells,
In and out the dusty bluebells,
In and out the dusty bluebells,
Who shall be my partner?

2nd verse: The leader now puts her arms on the shoulders of the child she is standing behind and gently taps him while singing the second verse.

Tippy, tippy, tappy on your shoulder,
Tippy, tippy, tappy on your shoulder,
Tippy, tippy, tappy on your shoulder,
You shall be my partner.

At the end of this verse the tapped child comes out of the circle, stands behind the leader and puts his arms on her shoulder. Now the first verse is sung again and the two children weave through the bluebells together in a line of two.

As the game goes on and the verses are repeated, the line gets longer and longer, until there is only one arch left – at which point the two children making the arch choose a child to 'capture' and she becomes the new leader.

The farmer's in his den

Age range 3+
Number of players 12 or more
Energy level 2
What you will need No props

This is another favourite game with very young children, and is sometimes known as The Farmer's in the Dell. The aim is to choose all the members of the farmer's family one by one.

How to play
Choose a 'farmer' to stand in the middle of a circle. Holding hands, the children walk round him singing the song. At the end of the first verse, they stand still while the farmer chooses a 'wife' to join him in the centre.

After each subsequent verse the last person to join the group chooses the next person, until there are six children in the centre: the farmer, his wife, her child, his nurse, her dog, his 'bone'. When the final verse is being sung everyone stands still and claps, except the bone. The next time the game is played, the bone becomes the farmer and a new set of children is chosen.

Variation
* You can also play this game in the traditional way, where everyone pats the bone lightly, but this often gets too vigorous and you may end up with a rather tearful 'bone', so clapping is usually preferable.

The farmer's in his den.
The farmer's in his den.
E–ie, e–ie, e–ie,
The farmer's in his den.

The farmer wants a wife.
The farmer wants a wife.
E–ie, e–ie, e–ie,
The farmer wants a wife.

The wife wants a child.
The wife wants a child.
E–ie, e–ie, e–ie,
The wife wants a child.

The child wants a nurse.
The child wants a nurse.
E–ie, e–ie, e–ie,
The child wants a nurse.

The nurse wants a dog.
The nurse wants a dog.
E–ie, e–ie, e–ie,
The nurse wants a dog.

The dog wants a bone.
The dog wants a bone.
E–ie, e–ie, e–ie,
The dog wants a bone.

We all clap the bone.
We all clap the bone.
E–ie, e–ie, e–ie,
We all clap the bone.

Oranges and lemons

Age range 4+
Number of players Six or more
Energy level 2
What you will need No props

An update of the popular rhyme about the church bells of London, this version avoids the traditional 'chopping off' of the poor victim's head! The aim is to win the tug-of-war at the end.

How to play

Play this game on grass, so that no one hurts themselves in the final tug-of-war. Choose two tall children (or adults) to hold hands to make an arch. Privately, one of them chooses to be 'Oranges' and the other 'Lemons'.

All the other children line up in pairs in front of the arch, holding hands. As the song is sung they skip under the arch, then separate to go back down on either side of the arch-makers and skip back to the end of the line, where they join hands again to head towards the arch once more.

When the song gets to the final verse, 'Here comes a candle ... ', the two arch-makers draw their hands

down between each pair until finally one pair of children is caught on the last word 'OUT!'. The children then have to whisper either Oranges or Lemons to the arch-makers and go to stand behind the appropriate person.

At the very end of the game, when everyone is out and there are two long lines behind each arch-maker, there is a tug-of-war – which ends when one side falls over. The other side is then declared the winning team.

Variation

* If you want to avoid a boisterous tug-of-war, simply count how many children are behind each arch-maker at the end of the game. The one with the most children wins.

'Oranges and lemons,'
  Say the bells of St
  Clement's.
'I owe you five farthings,'
  Say the bells of St
  Martin's.
'When will you pay me?'
  Say the bells of Old Bailey.
'When I grow rich,'
  Say the bells of
  Shoreditch.

'When will that be?'
  Say the bells of Stepney.
'I do not know,'
  Says the great bell of Bow.
Here comes a candle to light
  you to bed.
Here comes a giant with a
  stomping tread.
Stomp, stomp, stomp, stomp
  – you're OUT!

Tip for beginners
✻ If it's hard to get a pair of children squeezing
  under the arch, arrange the players in single
  file instead.

Coming round the mountain

Age range 4+
Number of players Two or more
Energy level 3
What you will need No props

She'll be coming Round the Mountain is a well-known American folk song (reportedly either about a train or an early union organizer called 'Mother Jones'). It's become a campfire classic, so this action game is perfect for playing outside at any time.

How to play

Stand in a line or a circle and skip, while singing the song. When you get to 'Toot, toot!', mimic blowing a horn. Then stand with your hands on your hips and, moving from side to side, sing the chorus. Continue with different actions for each verse. All the players can break the circle and gallop around during the 'six white horses' verse, coming back together for the next chorus.

She'll be coming round the mountain
   when she comes!
She'll be coming round the mountain
   when she comes!
She'll be coming round the mountain
Coming round the mountain
Coming round the mountain
When she comes!
Toot, toot!

Chorus:
Singing ai–ai–yippee–yippee–ai
Singing ai–ai–yippee–yippee–ai
Singing ai–ai–yippee
Ai–ai–yippee
Ai–ai–yippee–yippee–ai.

Continue with the following verses:
She'll be riding six white horses
   when she comes ... 'Whoa back!'
(pull on reins)

We'll all go out to meet her
   when she comes ... 'Hiya Babe!'
(wave)

We'll all have chicken and dumplings
   when she comes ... 'Yum, yum!'
(rub your tummy)

She'll be wearing pink pyjamas
   when she comes ... 'Night night!'
(pretend to sleep)

The grand old Duke of York

Age range 3+
Number of players One or more
Energy level 2
What you will need No props

Even the youngest child will love this first marching game, which has lots of energetic variations to try. If several children are playing, they can all march in a line.

How to play
Sing the song and do the actions suggested.

The grand old Duke of York
(march on the spot)

He had ten thousand men,
(continue marching on the spot)

He marched them up to the top of the hill, (march one way)

And then he marched them down again. (turn round and march the other way)

And when they were up, they were up. (march the original way)

And when they were down, they were down. (march the other way again)

And when they were only halfway up, (march on the spot)

They were neither up nor down!
(continue marching on the spot)

Variations
If you want to add more verses, change the third line with these suggestions:
* He skipped them up to the top of the hill
* He hopped them up to ...
* He walked them up to ...
* He danced them up to ...
* They beat their drums to ...
* They tooted their trumpets to ...
* They blew their trombones to ...

Mission impossible

Age range 5+
Number of players One or more
Energy level 3

This game uses lots of physical skills as children wriggle, jump, balance and run. It's designed to enable them to create and enjoy a mini-obstacle course, of which they can do one circuit or several. Before starting the game, make sure any items the players will stand on are sturdy and can take the child's weight. Check also for any sharp edges on boxes or flowerpots and clear the ground of twigs or stones that may cause scrapes.

Preparation

Arrange your equipment around the garden to create a circuit. For example, two open cardboard boxes that a child has to wriggle through like a tunnel, then a row of upright plastic bottles she must jump over without knocking them down, a sheet to crawl under, flowerpots to step across carefully, and a long, thin strip of newspaper to walk along, balancing so that she doesn't touch the ground on either side. Mark the start and finish lines clearly with a strip of newspaper or a flag.

How to play

Make sure the children are wearing loose, comfortable clothing that's suitable for wriggling along the ground! Then line the first one up at the starting post. When you say 'Go!' she has to set off and complete the circuit as quickly as possible. Use a stopwatch if she enjoys the challenge of improving her time on subsequent circuits.

What you will need A selection of sturdy, everyday household items, such as cardboard boxes, empty plastic bottles, an old sheet or groundsheet, upturned flowerpots; newspaper (or flag); stopwatch (optional)

Variations

* If you've made a complicated course, mark each stage with a number, written clearly on a piece of paper.
* To extend the game, include some running within the course – for example, complete the circuit once, then run twice round the outside, then do another circuit.

Tips for beginners

* Arrange the obstacles in an obvious order – a circle or straight line – so that there's no confusion about which part of the course to tackle next.
* 'Walk' the course together, so that the child knows exactly where to go.

Snake race

Age range 3+
Number of players One or more
Energy level 2
What you will need A ball of string or wool; scissors; a child's bike, tricycle or toy car

This simple game can be adapted to any outdoor space where there's room to manoeuvre wheels, adding spice to a child's favourite ride-on toy – whether that's a bicycle, tricycle or toy car.

Preparation
Unravel the ball of string or wool and lay it down in a random pattern around the garden, ending back where you began. Cut the wool, then repeat the pattern with a parallel line, so that you've created a race track.

How to play
Get the child onto his bike or car and set him off along the race track, making sure that he stays on the 'road'.

Variations
* Start the ride with ten points. The child can gain extra points for completing the track without riding outside the marked area, or can lose them for straying off the road.
* Make the track more twisty and complicated for a more advanced rider.

Tip for beginners
* To build confidence in a very young rider, set the track down where the child usually rides around, so that it's already familiar.

Age range 4+
Number of players One or more
Energy level 2
What you will need No props

Count me in

Adults can help with this game by counting along with the child and practising the steps together, before she goes it alone. It encourages counting skills as well as getting children moving.

Preparation
Go over the steps you'll be using in the game. These could include:

• Jumps
• Skips
• Hops
• Big steps
• Little steps
• Ballet leaps
• Sliding steps
• Star jumps

Variations
* Ask the child to count aloud as she does each of the actions.
* Extend the game by including other instructions, such as: run to the fence and back; turn around; touch your toes. Older children might manage sit-ups or even press-ups as part of the routine.

Tips for beginners
* Use a maximum of three instructions so that the child doesn't get confused.
* Help by counting along with her as she does each of the steps.

How to play
Start by asking the child to do one, two or more of any of the steps. Gradually build up the number and variety. There are three things to remember: **which** step, **how many** to do and **which order** they go in.

For example, you could start by saying:
'Do two big steps.'
Then move on to:
'Do two little steps and one jump.'
Then:
'Do one hop, three skips and one big step.'
Then:
'Do six jumps, two star jumps and one little step.'
And so on.

If she makes a mistake, she loses a point. If she gets them all right, she gains a point. You might need to write down the instructions to remember the order in which you've asked them.

Then it's her turn to ask **you** to have a go!

Yo, heave-ho

Age range 5+
Number of players Possible with one, but best with two or more
Energy level 2
What you will need No props

Yo, Heave-ho is suitable for any weather, although a blustery day is best, as the wind will give realistic on-board effects. And, even if your outdoor space is small, children's imagination can furnish lots of action in this adventure game.

Preparation

Get everyone to imagine they're about to set sail on a magnificent ship, with white sails billowing and the open seas ahead. Encourage children to talk about what the ship looks like: how the cabins might be furnished; the colour of the wood; how many ladders and masts there are on board; the oarsmen beneath the deck; and how the captain stands in command, turning the big wheel to steer his vessel.

Once everyone has a clear picture of the ship, you can start the game.

How to play

Tell the children they're hard-working sailors on board the ship. They have to do the actions for all the events that happen on board. For example, they must:

- **Swab the deck**
  (pretend cleaning with buckets and mops from side to side all over the garden)

- **Climb the rigging**
  (hand-over-hand actions, as if climbing a rope)

- **Bail out the boat, which has taken in water and is sinking**
  (pretend to empty lots of buckets overboard)

- **Help with the rowing**
  (sit down in a line and row in unison, counting each stroke)

- **Assist the captain in steering**
  (haul the wheel round in one direction, then the other)

You could also send them running up and down the deck to fetch ropes, jumping into the sea to rescue a man overboard, and so on.

Finally, night falls and the sailors can lie in their bunks for a rest!

Age range 5+
Number of players One or more
Energy level I
What you will need A washing line or similar; a selection of hoops; string; a beanbag

Bowled over

The aim of this game is to get a beanbag through a variety of different-sized hoops, which challenges children's accuracy and throwing skills. There are some variations that can make the game more difficult for accurate throwers.

Preparation

Put up a line at roughly eye level. It could be a washing line; or hang a skipping rope or some strong string between two supports.

Collect a selection of hoops: spinning rings, hoops from a stacking game or hula hoops; or cut out shapes from cardboard packets or boxes. You could even bend a wire coat hanger into a circular shape (don't let a child attempt this). Tie a string to each of the hoops and suspend them in a row along the line.

Mark a line at a reasonable distance from the row of hoops, behind which the child has to stand.

How to play

Ask the child to throw the beanbag, aiming to get it through the largest of the hoops. Count how many goes it takes before she's successful. Next, ask her to get the beanbag through each of the smaller hoops in succession. Keep a tally of the total number of goes it takes before all the hoops have been completed.

For the next round, see if the child can beat her last record.

Tip for beginners
* Let the child stand right in front of the biggest hoop to begin with, gradually moving a step further back to make it a little harder after each successful throw.

Variations
* If a child's throws are very accurate, give her a handicap, such as throwing with her left hand if she's right-handed.
* Adjust the height of each hoop so that they aren't all at the same level.
* Tie other smaller targets to the line, such as a small toy or tightly screwed-up ball of newspaper, for precision practice.

Animal Olympics

Age range 3+
Number of players One or more
Energy level 3

In this game children pretend to be a variety of strong, flexible or bouncy animals that are undoubted masters of their sporting abilities! It's a great opportunity for children to practise all sorts of physical skills.

Preparation

Cut out six pieces of paper or card and write an animal's name on each one. The child could do a picture on each card too, if he enjoys drawing. Decide on an event that would be suitable for each animal, such as:

• **Bunny**
  Hops over hurdles with ease

• **Monkey**
  Does astonishing gymnastics displays

• **Cheetah**
  Sprints into the lead in a short-distance race

• **Cat**
  Amazing balancing on the beam

Variations

* Make more animal cards and ask the child to act out each one. See if you can guess which it is without being told. Then pick a picture yourself and do the same.

* Use a stopwatch and time some of the events, such as the sprint or long-distance race, to see if a child can improve his time.

What you will need Animal picture cards, or name cards; a few props, such as short bamboo canes, beanbags or other items that are to hand; stopwatch (optional)

• **Gorilla**
  The strongest weight-lifter

• **Horse**
  The best long-distance runner.

Put all the name cards into a bag. Have some simple props to hand so that you can set up the appropriate items for whichever activity is picked.

How to play

The child chooses one of the cards from the bag (without peeking). If he chooses the powerful gorilla, you could put down a bamboo cane with a beanbag tied to each end to act as his weight-lifting challenge. He then has to raise it above his head to be declared the winner.

For the cheetah, mark a start and finish line. The bunny can hop over bamboo canes (raise them on flowerpots for more of a challenge) or pieces of string on the ground. Mark the four corners of the monkey's performing space – this is the child's chance to show off leaps, roly-polys, jumps and any other gymnastic skills. For the cat, set down two parallel lines of bamboo canes (or string), which the cat must stay inside while on the beam. Set the horse off on a steady trot, two, three, four or more times round the garden.

Once the child has completed one animal challenge, he chooses another until all six events are done.

Tip for beginners
* Keep the activities very simple; for example, the bunny could simply hop ten times.

Dizzy snail trail

Age range 5+
Number of players One or more
Energy level 1
What you will need A ball of wool or string; a pebble or other weight; scissors (optional)

Challenge children's coordination skills and concentration with this game. It's lots of fun, and very easy to set up and put away too, which makes it useful when you need a diversion in a hurry.

Preparation

Secure the end of the ball of wool or string by putting a pebble (or similar) on it to make sure it doesn't move. Then gradually feed out the string in a large spiral shape, like a snail shell. Keep going round and round, making the spiral bigger, until you've made at least five or more rotations. Either cut off the string or put the ball down on the ground to mark the end of the course.

How to play

Get the child to start in the centre of the 'shell' and walk along the length of the string, without allowing his feet to step off on either side. He must follow the spiral round steadily until he reaches the end.

Tips for beginners

* Younger children can walk along the spiral pathway between the lines of string, rather than having to walk on it.
* If a child doesn't like feeling dizzy, make the string into a random wiggly pattern instead of a spiral. This way he can still enjoy following the line and challenging his balancing skills.

Variations

* Once he's reached the outside of the snail shell, the child has to turn round and carefully come back again, finishing the game at the centre.
* Try this as a speed race for an older child – how fast can he get along the spiral string without losing his balance and stepping off?
* Make the gaps between each spiral narrower, so that there are more of them – and a greater risk of getting dizzy and falling off!

Age range 5+
Number of players One or more
Energy level 1
What you will need Plastic cups; two plastic jugs; food colouring (optional); pencil and paper (optional)

Fetch the water

Skill and a steady hand will prove essential in this game, the aim being to transport a jug full of water from one end of the garden to the other using a beaker – and spilling as little as possible.

Preparation
Mark a start and finish line, placing a jug full of water at the beginning and an empty jug at the end.

How to play
Fill a plastic cup or beaker with water and give it to the child. She has to walk or run to the finish line holding her cup of water, attempting to spill as little as possible. She pours it into the plastic jug, then runs back to you for a top-up. When she's emptied the full water jug, measure how much she's managed to pour into the jug at the finish line.

Variations
* The child can walk or run in zigzag lines.
* Make the course more complicated by setting out a longer circuit that goes all round the various parts of the garden. Mark the route with twig arrows or numbers written on pieces of paper.
* Time how long it takes her to transfer all the water from one jug to the next.

Tips for beginners
* Use a couple of drops of food colouring in the water so that it's easy for the child to see how much she's collected.
* Only fill the plastic cup half or three-quarters full, so that she's less likely to spill it en route.

Trail blazer

Age range 5+
Number of players One or more
Energy level 2
What you will need Pen and paper;
scissors; an envelope; a small prize

This is a great problem-solving game and
gives children a good run around, too!
They have to solve an intriguing treasure
hunt, which can be made harder or
easier, depending on their ages.

Preparation

Cut out five or six pieces of paper and write a
clue on each one. You may want to number them,
as you need to make sure that each clue leads
directly to the next one. For example, your first
clue might read:

1. Look behind the big tree!

Down the path, behind the tree,
That's where your next clue will be!

Then hide clue two behind the tree, ready for your
child to find. Continue laying down clues all over
the garden, until the final clue leads to the hiding
place of the prize – perhaps a small toy or some
wrapped sweets.

How to play

Put the first clue into the envelope, which you can
deliver to the child; or write his name on the front
and pretend it's just been delivered through the
letterbox. When he opens it, help him decipher the
clues and get going on the treasure trail. If outdoor
space is limited, spread the clues through both
house and garden, so that he gets a good run
around as he chases after the trail.

Variations

* An older child may enjoy decoding more
  complicated clues, such as codes, anagrams or
  riddles. For example, 'Roll up to the top, then
  roll me back down' could be a clue hidden in
  a rolled-up curtain or blind at the top of the
  house.
* This game can encourage a very young child
  to read the clues himself, so keep them
  simple, such as, 'On top of the table' or 'Next
  to the bench'.

Crocodile hop

Age range 4+
Number of players One or more
Energy level 2
What you will need Sheets of old newspaper

An imaginative game that is easy to set up and bursting with energy. Children have to escape safely from the snapping crocs in a river by hopping over stepping stones to the security of an island.

Preparation

Tear the newspaper into sheets and arrange them at random around the garden. They represent the stepping stones in the river. In the centre, make a small 'island' with several sheets of newspaper. This will be 'home'.

How to play

The child is an intrepid explorer, investigating the river. Any area around the newspaper sheets is crocodile-infested water. The child starts off on the island, but then has to hop all over the stepping stones without falling into the 'water'. When you call out 'Crocodile!' she must jump back over the stones to the island as quickly as possible, to take refuge until you call out 'Crocodile clear!', when she can set off again.

Tip for beginners

* Keep the newspaper stepping stones close to each other, so that it's easy for the child to move from one to the next.

Variation

* Write big black numbers on each stepping stone, then call out numbers for the child to jump to.

Feeling hot, hot, hot

Age range 3+
Number of players One or more
Energy level 2
What you will need A small toy (perhaps a dog or a teddy) or a coin to hide

This very simple hide-and-seek game is especially popular with younger children, who can be encouraged with tips on how close they are to the prize and then rewarded with it, once they find it.

Preparation
While the child is not looking, hide a little toy or a coin in the garden.

How to play
Ask the child to look for the prize. If he finds it quickly, hide it again in a less obvious place. Once he starts having difficulty locating it, give clues such as 'You're getting hotter' as he gets nearer; or 'You're getting colder' as he moves further away.

If he's very close, say, 'You're boiling hot!'

Getting hotter

Boiling hot!!!

Tip for beginners
* Before the game, make the toy have a little 'conversation' with the child, explaining that he's off to hide outside and hopes the child will find him soon.

Variation
* For older children, explain that you're going to give 'opposite' clues. So if you say he's getting *hotter*, it actually means *colder*.

Beanbag bowls

Age range 4+
Number of players Two or more
Energy level 2
What you will need Sticks, chalks or flowerpots; a small ball (the 'jack'); a beanbag for each player

To play this game successfully requires an accurate aim, though younger children will simply enjoy the fun of learning to throw underarm and trying to hit the jack. The aim is to score the most points at the end of an agreed number of rounds by getting the beanbag as close as possible to the jack.

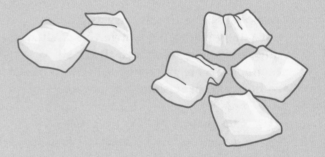

Preparation

Mark out a rough rectangle with sticks, chalks or corner markers, such as upturned flowerpots. Standing at one end, throw the small ball so that it lands within the rectangle.

How to play

Each person takes a turn to throw their beanbag at the jack, to try to get as close to it as they can. If the small ball is hit or moved, it is its final position at the end of the round that counts.

After the round is finished (when all the players have thrown their beanbags), the person with the beanbag closest to the jack scores one point and throws the ball for the next round, which is then played from the opposite end of the rectangle. The overall winner is the person with the most points at the end of an agreed number of rounds.

Variations
* Give each child more than one beanbag, so that he can throw two or more when it is his turn. But make sure you know which beanbags belong to which child!
* Instead of beanbags, try rolling soft balls towards the jack.

Tip for beginners
* Rather than throwing the jack, place it down on the ground not too far away from the throwers, to make it an easier target.

First hopping fun

Age range 4+
Number of players One or more
Energy level 2
What you will need Tape measure; scissors; string; a small object such as a ring, ball or small toy; some plastic stacking beakers

Hopping isn't quite as easy as it looks – but young children will love the challenge once they have mastered the basic technique. This game teaches them how to hop with precision and control.

How to play

Explain that to hop, the child needs to take a little step, with one foot on the ground and the other foot in the air; then build up a series of steps on one foot. Once a child has got the knack of this, these easy games will help her gain confidence:

- Measure the child's height, then cut a piece of string to that length and lay it flat along the ground. Then ask her if she can 'hop her height' by hopping from one end of the string to the other. Then ask if she can hop twice her height/your height/the length of the garden fence.
- Mark a starting line with a horizontal stick and place your chosen object a few feet away (not too far or the challenge will be exhausting). From the starting line, ask the child to hop on one foot to the object, pick it up and then hop back on the other foot. If she puts her foot down on the ground, she has to go back to the starting line and begin again.
- Lay out a few upturned stacking beakers in a zigzag line and see if the child can weave her way around them while hopping.

Tip for beginners

* If a child has never hopped before, begin by holding her hand gently to steady her. Then show her how to use her arms to help her balance herself.

Skipping without a rope

Age range 4+
Number of players One or more
Energy level 3
What you will need No props

Skipping is a great form of exercise for children and has a definite 'feel-good' factor. The aim of skipping without a rope is to practise the basic skill so that children can go on to skipping with a rope (see page 208) and other more advanced versions.

How to play

Explain that to skip, the child needs to take a little step and bounce on the foot she has down on the ground, then repeat this on the other foot until she builds up a rhythm. Practise maintaining a rhythm with her by chanting a rhyme while she skips, such as 'Lou, Lou, skip to my Lou' (see page 180). As with hopping, once a child can skip a few steps, a series of small challenges like the ones below will improve her technique:

- Develop control by playing 'Red, Amber, Green'. When you shout 'Red', the child must stop; when you shout 'Amber', she must walk; and when you shout 'Green', she must skip.
- Improve her concentration by mixing skipping with other physical skills, such as hopping, running, walking and jumping. In the park, get her to play some simple races, either with you or with another child, such as skipping to the tree and running back; hopping to a bench, skipping round it and jumping back; walking with giant steps to the end of the path, then skipping on the spot until you catch up.

Variation

* Combine skipping with an imaginative game, such as pretending she is a bee fluttering from flower to flower, or a fairy escaping from a fearsome giant.

Hopscotch

Age range 7+
Number of players One or more
Energy level 2

This traditional and well-loved game is played in many different ways across the world. The aim is to complete the course (following the squares' numerical order) without stepping on the lines, falling over or putting your non-hopping foot down. If the marker is not thrown into the correct square, it must be thrown again.

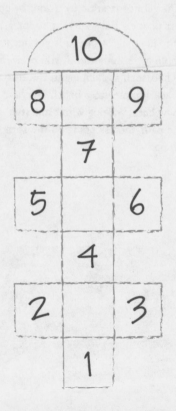

Preparation

Mark out the pavement (or other flat surface) following the diagram, below left. Number the boxes 1–10, with 1 being the nearest and 10 the semicircle.

How to play

Standing outside the square numbered 1, the player throws the marker into the first square and hops to 10 and back like this:

- Avoiding square 1 (where the marker is), she jumps over it and lands with one foot in square 2 and the other foot in square 3
- Then she hops onto square 4
- And jumps with both feet onto squares 5 and 6
- Now she hops onto square 7
- Then jumps with both feet onto squares 8 and 9
- And hops onto semicircle 10, where she turns around without putting her foot down
- Then she hops and jumps her way back to squares 2 and 3 – where she can bend down to pick up her marker from square 1
- And finally she hops into the now-empty square 1 and out of the grid entirely.

She then continues, each time throwing the marker into the next square up and avoiding landing in that square. She carries on in this way until she has thrown her marker into every square up to 10 and has hopscotched her way up and down the grid each time.

What you will need A marker (such as a flat stone); some chalk; an even surface that you are allowed to mark with the chalk

Variations

* Hop up – and into – the squares in turn, starting at 1, then pick up the marker, turn round and hopscotch back to the beginning from that square. For instance, if the marker has landed in square 5, the child will hop up and into square 5, stoop and pick up the marker, turn round, then hopscotch back to square 1 and out. In this version she only reaches square 10 on the very last go.
* Grids can be laid out in many different ways. Some may have diagonals dividing one large square into four triangles for the numbers 4, 5, 6 and 7 (see below right). Or they might run in a spiral rather than a straight line (see above right). Experiment with devising your own layout.

Tips for beginners

* Instead of hopping, get children to jump into each square using both feet.
* Tell them to put both feet down in square 10 to make turning round easier.

Skipping with a rope

Age range 6+
Number of players One
Energy level 2

Here's how to teach a child to skip with a rope, so that she can then go on to skip on her own or play some of the skipping rhyme games that children often play together in the school playground (see the ideas on pages 210–217).

How to play

Get the child to hold the rope in a loop behind her, standing straight and with her arms outstretched. The rope should just skim the ground behind her – if it's too long, wind the rope round her hands until it's the right length.

Then explain that to begin skipping, she needs to swing the rope over her head and jump over it in a small jump, with both feet off the ground. Get her to keep practising this until she has developed a steady rhythm.

What you will need A skipping rope

Then try these ideas:

• Add a little hopping jump when the rope is overhead (double bounce)
• Jump on one foot
• Jump on alternate feet
• Skip forwards by taking steps on alternate feet
• Jump with the rope turning from front to back
• Go slower when you call 'Salt!' and faster when you call 'Pepper!'

Variations
* Try tapping first one foot, then the other one behind the opposite leg when the rope is overhead.
* Tap alternate heels in front instead.
* Jump the feet apart a little when the rope is overhead.
* Try crossing the arms in front as the rope comes down.

Tips for beginners
* Skip on a clear, flat surface.
* Make sure there is plenty of room.
* Perfect one skill before introducing a new one.

Skipping with friends

Age range 8+
Number of players Three or more
Energy level 3
What you will need A skipping rope long enough to share

If skipping alone is fun, skipping in a group is even more so ... And there are endless variations on the theme, using different rhymes, varied formations and different numbers of children.

How to play

Two people stand opposite each other and turn the rope. The third person skips in the middle. He may do this in two ways: either by skipping facing the rope (as he would if he were skipping alone) or by skipping parallel to it (that is, facing one of the rope-turners).

When skipping parallel to the rope, it's best to start with one child standing beside the rope before it starts to turn. As the skipper becomes more proficient, he will soon learn how to run into the rope while it is turning (best done when the rope touches the ground). Both running in and running out take some practice, but when it's mastered a whole line of children can run in and out without the rope stopping turning at all. Here's a rhyme to practise this:

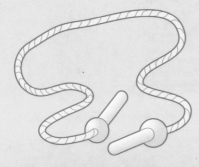

Variation

* If, rather than replacing each other at the rope, several children want to skip together in a long line, get them reciting a rhyme that gradually introduces a new child:

I love the river, I love the sea,
(first child sings and skips)

I love Naomi skipping with me.
(second child comes in)

I love the river, I love the sea,
(Naomi now sings and skips)

I love Barney skipping with me
(third child comes in)

Mother's in the kitchen
(child skips)

Doing all the stitching
(child skips)

In comes the pussycat
(child points to or names the next person)

And shoos her OUT
(new person comes in and original child goes out)

Age range 7+
Number of players Three
Energy level 3
What you will need A long skipping rope

Bubble car

Children can practise stopping the rope with this 'round the corner' game, in which the aim is to skip out and then back in again – and bring the rope to a standstill.

How to play

Two people turn the rope for the skipper, who sings the rhyme below and follows the actions.

I'm a little bubble car, Number 48
(child skips over the rope)

I whizz round the cooooorner
(child runs out of the rope, around one of the rope-turners and back in on the other side)

And slam on the brakes!
(child raises only one foot as the rope comes round, then stamps that foot down so the rope is trapped between his feet)

Variation

* Rather than the skipper being a car, get him to try being an aeroplane (with his arms held out as 'wings') or a bicycle (make cycling movements with his arms).

Tips for beginners

* Get children to practise stopping the rope a couple of times before chanting the whole rhyme.
* Remind them not to run too fast when they are 'whizzing round the corner' in case they fall over.

Teddy bear, teddy bear

Age range 6+
Number of players Three
Energy level 3
What you will need A long skipping rope

This nursery rhyme is better known as a skipping game in which the players do all the actions and then complete as many continuous skips as possible.

How to play

Two people turn the rope, while the third skips in the middle. The two rope-turners chant the rhyme while the skipper follows the suggested actions. If she successfully completes the whole verse, the skipper does as many continuous skips as she can (without bouncing in between) while the rope-turners count them. As soon as there is a stumble, a new game begins and the rope-turners become skippers.

Teddy Bear, Teddy Bear
(skip with bounces in between)

Turn around,
(turn in a circle)

Teddy Bear, Teddy Bear
(skip with bounces in between)

Touch the ground,
(bend down to touch the ground)

Teddy Bear, Teddy Bear
(skip with bounces in between)

Climb the stairs,
(lift knees to mime climbing the stairs)

Teddy Bear, Teddy Bear
(skip with bounces in between)

Say your prayers.
(bend head and put hands together)

Teddy Bear, Teddy Bear
(skip with bounces in between)

Turn off the light,
(mime pulling a light cord)

Teddy Bear, Teddy Bear
(skip with bounces in between)

Say 'Goodnight!'
(children all shout GOODNIGHT)

Variation
* If there are several children playing, start with a single child skipping, then begin the rhyme again with a second person running in to join her, then a third, and so on.

All in together

Age range 8+
Number of players At least six
Energy level 2
What you will need A very long skipping rope

This is a great game if a large number of children are playing together. They are trying to get to 'December' with everybody skipping in a line and without the rope ever having stopped turning.

How to play
Two people turn the rope. The others all stand in a line to one side, in the order of the month of their birth, with January at the head. As the rope-turners chant the rhyme below, the others gradually run in to skip, as the appropriate month of their birth is called out.

Variations
* If just boys are playing, replace 'girls' with 'boys'; if both boys and girls are playing, replace 'girls' with 'mates'.
* Play the game using children's names instead of birthdays – just swap 'birthday' with 'letter' and the months of the year with letters of the alphabet.

All in together, girls.
Never mind the weather, girls.
When I say your birthday,
   please run in.
January... February... March...
April... May... June... July...
August... September...
October... November...
DECEMBER!

Who will I marry?

Age range 10+
Number of players Three
Energy level 3
What you will need A skipping rope

This game is intended to predict the name of the boy or girl whom the skipper will marry in the future. It's often a cause of great hilarity and speculation among the children playing it.

How to play

Two children turn the rope while the third skips. As the rope-turners turn, they chant the rhyme below. When the skipper eventually stumbles, the letter being chanted as she stops becomes the initial of her boyfriend's name, which is then chosen by the other two children – usually amid much giggling.

Variations

* If boys are playing, replace 'her boyfriend' with 'his girlfriend'.
* If you don't feel K-I-S-S-I-N-G is appropriate, change it to H-U-G-G-I-N-G or even T-A-L-K-I-N-G.

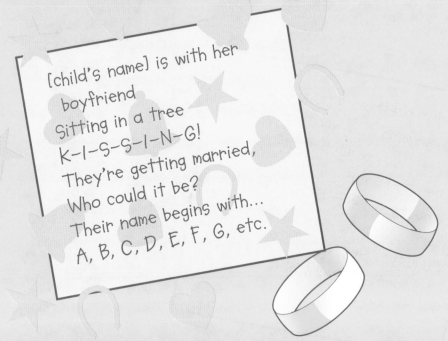

[child's name] is with her
   boyfriend
Sitting in a tree
K-I-S-S-I-N-G!
They're getting married,
Who could it be?
Their name begins with...
A, B, C, D, E, F, G, etc.

Age range 8+
Number of players Three or more
Energy level 3
What you will need A circular elastic rope (or similar, made by looping large elastic bands together and tying them in a knot at the end to create a circle of elastic)

French skipping

Rather than using an ordinary skipping rope, this game uses a stretchy 'rope', which is held in place around the rope-holders' ankles. The aim is for the skipper to do the moves and chant a rhyme, while the stretchy rope is held at a low level.

How to play
The two rope-holders stand inside the circular rope with their feet apart. Holding it behind their ankles, they pull the rope into a rectangular shape. The skipper starts with both feet on the outside of the rope and, chanting a rhyme of his choice, jumps in and out of the rectangle in time with the rhyme. The steps get more complex as the skipper gets more skilled.

Variations
* The skipper begins with both feet inside the rectangle, then jumps over the outside of the rope with either one foot or both, and back in again.
* Standing with both feet outside, the skipper jumps and loops the near-side rope over the far-side rope, tapping his foot, then jumps back to the start.
* The rope-holders move the rope higher up their legs to make the game harder.

Tip for beginners
* Get novices to jump behind someone who already knows the moves and copy them.

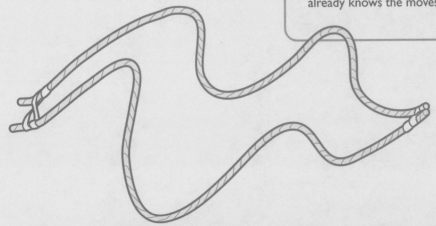

Double Dutch

Age range 10+
Number of players Three
Energy level 3
What you will need Two long skipping ropes of the same length

A highly skilled skipping game, this uses two ropes and requires precision timing – both from the skipper and from those turning the rope. It's likely to take a lot of practice, but the sense of achievement will be great.

How to play

The two rope-holders have a rope in each hand and turn one clockwise and the other anticlockwise, so that one rope is in the air while the other is on the ground. This isn't easy, and it will take considerable practice to establish a regular rhythm.

Once the ropes are turning evenly, the skipper runs in from one end and, hopping from one foot to another, quickly skips over one rope and then the other. To leave the ropes, she runs out past a rope-holder.

Tip for beginners
* Make sure that any child who tries this is totally confident skipping with a single rope.

Variation
* Experienced Double Dutch skippers can try adapting their favourite single rope moves to the double ropes.

Cinderella

Age range 7+
Number of players One or more
Energy level 3
What you will need A skipping rope

Cinderella is a very popular skipping game that is played in many school playgrounds. Players count the highest number of 'disgusted people' they can! There are many variations, with different numbers of players, actions and rhymes.

How to play
Skip to the rhyme below with double bounces. Then, when the number section is reached, change to single bounces and try to count as high as possible without stumbling.

Cinderella dressed in yella
Went to town to meet a fella.
On the way her girdle busted –
How many people were disgusted?
1, 2, 3, 4, 5, etc.

Variations
* Play this as a group skipping game by adding new people into the line when the counting section starts (stick to double bounces in this case).
* This game can also be played as a clapping game. Facing a partner, clap first with one hand, then with the other and then with both. Skilled clappers can add in their own moves, too.
* There are many alternative rhymes for this game. Here is one of them:

Cinderella dressed in yella
Went to town to meet a fella.
By mistake she kissed a snake,
How many doctors did it take?
1, 2, 3, 4, 5, etc.

Tip for beginners
* Novice skippers will find it easier to stick to double bounces for the counting section, rather than attempting fast single bounces.

Hot potato

Age range 8+
Number of players Two or more
Energy level I
What you will need A tennis ball

Players need to be pretty confident about their catching skills for this game, as it involves throwing, catching and keeping in the air a 'hot potato' while on the run, without dropping it.

How to play

The first player picks up the ball – the 'hot potato' – and throws it up and down. He then throws it to another player, who must catch it, but isn't allowed to hold it for more than a second at a time. He then throws it to another player, and so on, until one player drops the hot potato or holds it for too long.

Tip for beginners

∗ The player with the hot potato calls out the name of the player he's going to throw it to, to give her time to prepare for a catch.

Variations

∗ To make the game more challenging, the players all have to run around as they throw and catch the hot potato.
∗ Use a chestnut or a small bouncy ball instead of a tennis ball.

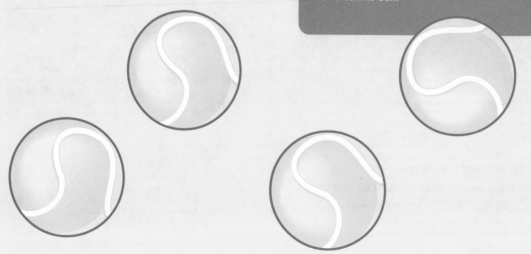

Age range 7+
Number of players One or more
Energy level 2
What you will need Football coaching markers, or a selection of twigs or stones to act as markers; a stopwatch or watch with a second hand

Weaving wonders

This game encourages physical coordination and speed – the aim being to weave in and out of a series of markers placed on the ground as accurately and speedily as possible, in the style of slalom skiing.

Preparation
Lay down the markers in a long row, allowing 90 cm (3 ft) or so between each one.

How to play
Start the stopwatch and the first player sets off, weaving in and out of the markers, working from left to right. At the end of the row she turns around and runs back in a straight line alongside the markers to the finish.

Any remaining players take turns to do the course, and make a note of their times. When everyone has had a rest, they do the course again and see if any players have improved their times. If there is only one player, she will be competing against her own previous times.

Tips for beginners
* Leave a bigger space between the markers to make it easier for younger players.
* Use fewer markers.

Variations
* Devise a more complicated pattern for the players to follow – for example, weaving in and out of one marker, then leaving two, then one again, and so on.
* If players aren't too dizzy, they can weave in and out of the markers on the return journey as well.

Dodge that ball

Age range 8+
Number of players Six or more
Energy level 2
What you will need A soft ball; watch

A favourite of school sports teachers, this game translates easily into the park – and is great for larger groups. Players try to hit the other team's members with the ball and get them out.

Preparation

Divide the players into teams. Each team lines up in a row, and the teams then face each other. There should be a space of at least 2–3 m (7–10 ft) between teams, with a dividing line between them (this can be imaginary, or can be marked out with leaves or twigs if necessary).

How to play

One person on the first team throws the ball underarm towards the opposing team, trying to hit a member of that team below the knees.

If he scores a valid hit below the knee, that player is captured and has to cross the line and stand behind the first team.

Then the second team has a turn at throwing the ball. They can try to hit it over the team, so that their captured player catches it and is allowed to escape, or they can try to hit members of the opposing team and take their own prisoners.

The winning team is the first to capture all the other team members, or the team with the most prisoners after a time limit.

Tip for beginners

* Use a larger – but still soft – ball to make the game easier.

Stuck in the mud

Age range 4+
Number of players Four or more
Energy level 3
What you will need No props

This energetic game requires lots of cooperation for it to continue! Players try to keep moving and at the same time help their team-mates escape from being stuck fast in the mud.

How to play

One player is the 'baddie' while all the others are on the same team.

The players all run away from the baddie, who has to try to touch as many of them as possible. Any player he touches has to stand still with his legs wide apart – stuck in the mud.

He is not allowed to move again until one of his team-mates crawls through his legs to free him. If someone is caught trying to rescue a team-mate, then that player must also stand stuck in the mud.

The game continues until all the players are stuck in the mud – or until the baddie can no longer catch any of them!

Tip for beginners
* The baddie can allow stuck players to escape after being in the mud for 30 seconds, if no one is able to rescue them.

Variations
* To make it harder, the rescuer has to crawl in a figure of eight around the stuck player's legs before that player is rescued from the mud.
* If the ground you're playing on is too hard or wet for crawling, devise another method for releasing stuck players, such as the rescuer holding their hands and the pair swinging round in a full circle together, or jumping up and down together holding hands three times.

Colourful croc

Age range 3+
Number of players Two or more
Energy level I
What you will need No props

This is a simple game with an element of danger that the youngest players can enjoy. They are attempting to travel safely to the fairy's castle on the far side of the river, without Mr Croc getting his teeth into them.

How to play

One player, chosen as the crocodile, stands on one side of an imaginary line, guarding a fairy castle (a tree or bush), while the other players line up on the opposite side.

The players who want to visit the fairy who lives on the other side of the river all chant together:

Swim across the water
To see the fairy daughter.
Which colour will she wear?

The crocodile then takes a good look at all the players and calls out a colour, such as 'Pink!'.

Any player who is wearing pink must then try to cross to the other side of the river without being caught by the crocodile. Anyone who is caught becomes the next crocodile.

Variation
* For players who don't find fairies appealing, change the rhyme to:

Swim across the water
A knight upon his charger.
What colour will he wear?

Tip for beginners
* If all the players are wearing similar colours, the crocodile can pick out one particular player by saying, 'He'll wear the same blue shirt as ... [name of player]!' Then that person has to try to cross the river.

Age range 7+
Number of players One or more
Energy level 2
What you will need A selection of football coaching markers or other items to act as markers and obstacles; a bike or skateboard

Rally cross

Setting up an obstacle course is easy in a wide open space and can give even experienced riders or skaters a fresh challenge. The intention is to get round the course accurately – and without falling over!

Preparation
Set up an obstacle course using the markers, for the players to cycle or skate around.

How to play
Players have to complete the course successfully. Try these ideas:

• Weaving in and out of the markers
• Riding around a group of trees
• Riding along a straight line
• Riding to make 'shapes', such as a triangle, square or rectangle.

Variation
* If players are confident riders, set up your obstacle course on an area where there's a slight slope, to add extra interest.

Follow my leader

Age range 3+
Number of players Two or more
Energy level 2
What you will need No props necessary, but you may like to include a few, such as a ball or ribbons

This copying game can be as energetic as you like. Players have to follow their leader's actions, and then think of their own when they get a turn as leader.

How to play
Players line up behind a leader. The leader then sets off at a jogging pace and the players follow in a line behind, singing this song:

We're following the leader
The leader, the leader,
We're following the leader
Wherever she may go.

Then the leader begins an action. For example, she might start to hop like a frog, or run madly in a zigzag line. The other players imitate the action, still following behind.

After a while the leader stops the action and goes back to an ordinary jog again. Then the followers begin the song again and wait for the next action.

This might be something along the lines of:
• Flying like a plane, running along fast with arms outstretched
• Zooming along like a car, holding an imaginary steering wheel
• Chuffing along in a train, with wheel-like arms.

Variation
* After each action has finished, the leader goes to the back of the line, allowing the next in line to be leader.

Tips for beginners
* To make it easier, the leader can face the players to show them the action and make sure they understand how to do it, before turning round and leading them on.
* The leader can ask the players if they can guess what the action is meant to be, before they begin it themselves.

Please, Mr Policeman

Age range 4+
Number of players Three or more
Energy level 2
What you will need Twigs as markers

Most children will love this game, where Mr Policeman gets to be the boss and makes all the decisions – but keep an eye out to make sure that no child is being unfairly penalized!

Preparation

With a few twigs, mark out a starting line and a finishing line some way apart.

How to play

Players choose one person to be Mr Policeman, who then stands behind the finishing line. The others all stand in a row behind the starting line.

The first person – say, Fiona – starts the game by saying,

Please, Mr Policeman, may I take two big hops?

(or some other choice).

Mr Policeman then answers in one of the following ways:

Yes, Fiona, you may take two big hops

No, Fiona, you may not take two big hops

No, Fiona, you may not take two big hops – but you may take one long stride

(or some other choice).

Fiona then has to say, 'Thank you, Mr Policeman', and do whatever movement Mr Policeman has said she may do. If she forgets to say 'Thank you', or does the wrong movement, she has to go back behind the starting line.

The play moves on to the next person, who asks her request. The game continues in this way until one person eventually crosses the finishing line and becomes the new Mr Policeman.

Tips for beginners

* Very young children will need an adult to be Mr Policeman.
* If they are finding it hard to think of different ways of moving, give the children some suggestions to pick from: hops, skips, jumps, fairy steps, sideways crab steps, leaps, giant strides or tippytoes steps.

Snake chase

Age range 6+
Number of players Five or more
Energy level 3
What you will need No props

In this game children switch from being free runners to being part of a long catching 'snake'. If several children are playing, the snake can get rather unwieldy, so for safety, play the game on soft grass. The aim is to be the last person to be caught.

How to play

The children choose who will be It. He then covers his eyes and counts to ten, while all the other players run away. Once It has finished his countdown, he chases everyone else until he eventually catches someone.

This person now join hands with It and runs with him to catch a third person, who then joins the line. As more and more people are caught, the line becomes a long 'snake'. The last player left uncaught wins the game and becomes the new It.

Tip for beginners
* Tell the children that the players at both ends of the snake can catch a new person, which makes it easier to tag them.

Variation
* Add another element to the game by allowing anyone who is touching wood, such as a tree, fence or bench, to be safe from being caught by the snake. They may only touch wood for a count of three, though, after which they must run around again.

Tree, bench, home

Age range 4+
Number of players Four or more
Energy level 3
What you will need A few trees and a park bench; something to mark 'home'

This game needs an adult to call out the instructions, as well as to judge who is in and who is out, as players try to stay in the game for as long as possible without being called 'out'.

Preparation
Choose a place in the park that has some trees and at least one bench. Then mark out a spot as 'home' – using a picnic rug, a log or a pile of sweaters – a little way from the trees or bench.

How to play
When you call out 'Run!' everyone runs around until you shout out another instruction: 'Tree!', 'Bench!' or 'Home!'.

• Tree
Everyone has to run and find a tree to touch (one person per tree). If a player fails to find a tree before you count to three, he is out.

• Bench
Everyone has to run to a bench and sit on it with their feet off the ground (sitting on laps is allowed). If they don't get to the bench before you count to three, or there is no room on it or their feet touch the ground, they are out.

• Home
Everyone has to run to home and touch it. If they cannot reach it before you count to three, they are out.

You then shout 'Run!' once more and the game begins again. The last person in is the winner.

Variation
* Adapt the instructions to suit the environment. For instance, if there isn't a bench, choose another landmark, such as a wall ('Wall!') or tennis-court net ('Net!').

Tips for beginners
* Count up to three more slowly if you sense that a younger child is having difficulty getting to a target.
* Allow more than one person per tree.
* For safety, set a clear boundary, beyond which no one is allowed to run – such as 'up to the path, but no further'.

Home corner

Age range 6+
Number of players Four or more
Energy level 3
What you will need Several trees, bushes or park benches that are well spaced apart – these are the 'home corners'

This game is an outdoor version of musical chairs – on a much bigger scale. Players try to get back to one of the home corners before the other players beat them to it.

Preparation

Decide which trees, bushes or benches are going to be your 'home corners'. If there are four players, there should be three home corners – that is, one fewer than the number of players. Make sure they are all at roughly the same distance from the players' starting area.

How to play

The players all gather and hold hands, dancing round in a circle together. Alternatively, they can jump on the spot or jog round in a circle. As long as they are all together, no one player has an unfair advantage.

You should either sing or beat time with a stick on the ground, to act as the music. When you stop, the players all have to dash to reach the safety of a home corner. This means that one player will be left without a home and is called out. The other players come back to the centre and the game begins again, this time minus one home corner.

The last round will be between two players aiming for the final home corner – whoever gets there first wins!

Variations

* To be scrupulously fair about distances, you can position your own markers at, say, 30 paces from the centre.
* If two players reach a home corner simultaneously, they have to run back to the starting point – whoever gets back first is the winner of that home corner.

Tip for beginners

* You can handicap older or faster players by making them stay in the centre of the playing area for a few seconds, while younger ones get a head-start once the music has stopped.

Splashing sponges

Age range 7+
Number of players Three or more
Energy level 2
What you will need A plastic bucket of water; one or more cheap bath sponges

This is a very silly game that's strictly for hot days only – when it has a refreshing, cooling effect! The aim is to get your opponent wet and to remain dry yourself, though usually everyone gets soaked by the end.

How to play

One player is the baddie, armed with a wet sponge. She chases the other players and has to hit one of them with the soaking sponge. The wet player then becomes the baddie and tries to hit another player, topping up the sponge with cold water from the bucket as necessary.

Variation

* Older players may enjoy making this a 'paintball'-style game, with all players armed with wet sponges and creeping up on each other to strike from hidden positions.

Tips for beginners

* Use small sponges or small, soft sponge balls for younger players, so the 'impact' isn't as strong.
* Warm water makes it a gentler game, too.

Dog and bone

Age range 7+
Number of players Six or more
Energy level 2
What you will need An object such as a beanbag, sponge ball or soft toy to act as the bone

All children love 'tag' games, and this one can be played wherever there is some open space. An even number of children is best.

Preparation
Pick the object to be the 'bone'. Divide the children into two teams, each of which allocates all its members a different number, starting with 1, 2, 3, etc. This must be done in secret so that the members of each team don't find out who on the opposite team has the same number as them.

How to play
The teams line up at opposite ends of the playing area. Place the bone equidistant between them and call out a number.

The child with that number from each team has to run out, grab the bone and return it to his side. The player who manages to do this first gains a point for his team. While the child is carrying the bone, his opponent is free to try and tag him; if he succeeds, his own team wins the point.

You then put the bone back into play and call the other numbers out until they have all been called, when the points are added up and the winning team is announced.

Variations
* Players who are tagged have to drop the bone immediately. Neither player can tag the other until one of them has picked the bone up again, and the first player back to his team with the bone wins the point.
* After a few goes, the referee can call two or more numbers together, or call out some mental arithmetic, such as '6 minus 4, then add 1'.

Tip for beginners
* Another member of the team, whose number has not been called, might pretend to run forward, tricking the opposition and allowing his own player to perform a surprise tag.

Hen and eggs

Age range 3+
Number of players Three or more
Energy level 2
What you will need A basket or box; different coloured balls or other small objects

This game for younger children is guaranteed to produce lots of screams and excitement. It's a good way to teach them colours and will help to improve their coordination and throwing skills.

How to play

One player is the hen and covers her eyes some distance away from the other players, who each steal an 'egg' from the basket.

When everyone has chosen, the hen calls out a colour. All those holding eggs of that colour have to return them to the basket without being tagged by the hen.

Anyone who is tagged is out of the game. The last person to be caught is the winner.

Variation

∗ Players can try throwing their eggs into the basket without being tagged by the hen.

Tip for beginners

∗ Younger players will find it easier to start with just one egg. Once they have got the hang of the game, they can progress to picking several, which can be stuffed into pockets while they run.

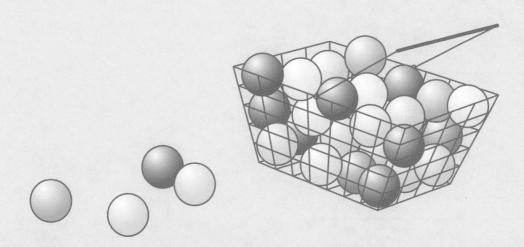

Pass it round

Age range 5+
Number of players Two or more
Energy level I
What you will need A cricket bat (a light plastic one is best for young players); a small soft ball

This simple version of a park favourite (also known as French Cricket) can be played by a twosome, though it's more fun as a team game. The aim is to score runs and not get caught out.

How to play

One player is chosen to be the batter, the other to be the bowler. If there are several players, they can be divided into two teams. The batter holds the cricket bat in front of his legs. The bowler then throws the soft ball underarm, trying to hit the batter's shins.

If the batter hits the ball, the bowler (or fielders, if there are other team members) runs to get it. Meanwhile, the batter passes the bat round his tummy, scoring a 'run' each time.

The batter is out if:

- The bowler catches the ball after the batter has hit it, without it bouncing
- The bowler manages to hit the batter's shins while bowling the ball.

Variations
* Decide on boundaries – if the batter hits the ball beyond the agreed boundary, he scores six runs.
* Allow the bowler to use false starts to try to trick the other player into lifting the bat and exposing his shins.

Tip for beginners
* Novices can play the game simply as a 'hit your legs' challenge without runs, until they are really confident about batting and bowling the ball.

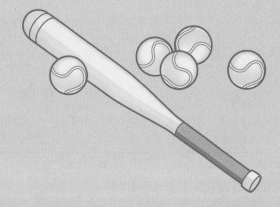

Roll around

Age range 3+
Number of players Four or more
Energy level I
What you will need A large soft ball

This is a very simple game that is ideal for pre-schoolers and their parents. Play should continue until everyone has had a turn at catching the ball and calling out the name of the next person to receive it.

How to play

Get everyone to sit in a circle and give the ball to one person (a grown-up may be best to begin with). She chooses someone else in the circle, calls out his name and then rolls the ball gently towards him. When the child whose name was called out has received the ball, he chooses a new child, calls out her name and rolls the ball towards her. The game continues like this until everyone has had at least one go of calling and rolling the ball.

Tip for beginners
* Little ones are not always great at aiming the ball correctly, so get them to look directly at the child who is going to receive the ball before they actually begin rolling it.

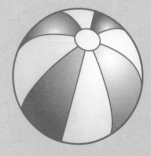

Variations
* Older children can stand in a ring and throw the ball to each other.
* Speed up the time between throws.
* To make the game harder, don't call out the names to give warning who you're throwing to next.

The aim game

Age range 3+
Number of players One or more
Energy level 1
What you will need A bucket and a collection of small balls, such as tennis balls, bouncy balls or table-tennis balls

Young children will love this simple target-practice game, while older children can enjoy a more demanding variation. Players are trying to get as many balls into the bucket as they can.

How to play

Place the bucket upright on the ground, then let the child stand by it and take five steps backwards. Give her as many small balls as you have and ask her to try to throw them – one at a time – into the bucket. For each ball that she successfully gets in, she scores one point.

When all the balls have gone, it's your turn (or another child's turn). If anyone manages to get all the balls into the bucket in one go, she takes another step backwards for the next round of the game.

The player with the most points at the end wins. Try playing 'best of' three or five rounds.

Variations

* If you are playing with children of different ages, handicap the older ones by positioning them further away from the bucket, or by telling them to throw with one hand behind their back.
* For more competitive older children, mark out a line with set points along the way. Starting from the point nearest the bucket, each child takes turns to throw a ball into it. When they get one in, they move back down the line to the next point. The first person to get to the end of the line is the winner.
* Turn the bucket on its side and roll the balls into it, rather than throwing them. Allow a point for every ball that goes in, even if it rolls out again.

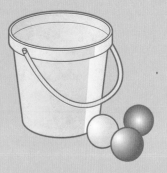

Tips for beginners

* Stand younger children even closer to the bucket.
* Give little ones juggling balls or beanbags to throw with, because they are easier to aim accurately.

Age range 7+
Number of players Two or more
Energy level |
What you will need Cardboard
boxes; three soft, small balls; pencil and a
score-sheet

Box drop

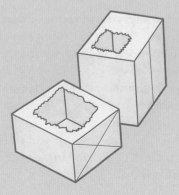

Although similar to The Aim Game (see opposite), this game is more demanding because it requires accuracy and scoring skills. Players have to try and throw their balls into the highest-scoring boxes to win the greatest number of points.

Preparation

Collect as many cardboard boxes as you can (at least three) and seal them shut. Then cut out different-sized holes in each one, going from large to small. Now write the score points on the boxes, with the largest hole having the lowest score (1) and the smallest hole having the highest.

Line up the boxes with the higher-scoring ones in the middle and the lower-scoring ones at the edge. Mark out a line behind which the throwers must stand.

How to play

Taking turns, each player throws three balls at the boxes. Any ball that lands inside a box scores the number of points written on that box. Scores are recorded on the scorecard at the end of each go.

At the end of an agreed number of turns, the total scores are added up and the winner is the one with the most points.

Tips for beginners
* When there are children of different ages and abilities playing, have several lines behind which they must stand, to even up the competition.
* Make sure the ball can definitely fit through the smallest hole!

Variation
* If you have several cardboard boxes, rather than lining them up in a row, arrange them in a cluster so that they are two (or even three) layers deep.

Piggy in the middle

Age range 4+
Number of players Three
Energy level 2
What you will need A medium-sized ball

A favourite playground game – but watch to make sure that no one gets left in the middle for too long, or there'll be tears! Players need to be fair in giving the 'piggy' a chance to catch the ball, by not throwing it too high. This game is ideal for any outside play, including the beach, and can even be enjoyed in the shallows or at the swimming pool, under adult supervision.

Variations
* Try rolling the ball along the ground instead of throwing it.
* If there are several children, play the game standing in a circle with a couple of 'piggies' in the middle.

How to play
The three players line up in a row. The two outside players throw the ball to each other, while the middle one – the 'piggy' – tries to intercept it. If he does intercept it successfully, he then swaps places with the person who threw it, and that person then becomes the piggy in the middle.

The game is open-ended and finishes when everyone has had a turn at being the piggy.

Tip for beginners
* Throw the ball quite low down, so that it's easier for shorter children to intercept it.

Age range 5+
Number of players Three or more
Energy level 2
What you will need A plastic bat (any kind will do); a foam ball

Bat that!

This first bat-and-ball game has easy-to-learn rules, making it a good starter ball game for young children. The aim is for players to win the right to be the batter as often as possible.

Tip for beginners
* Use big bats and balls for young children.

How to play
Choose one player to be the batter – all the others are fielders. The batter hits the ball towards the fielders, then places the bat on the ground and stands still. Meanwhile the fielders try to catch the ball.

If someone catches the ball without it dropping on the ground, she automatically swaps places with the batter. If someone catches the ball after it has bounced, or just picks it up from the ground, she has to roll it back towards the bat.

If the rolling ball hits the bat, the person who rolled it swaps places with the batter. If it doesn't hit the bat, the original batter has a second go.

Simon says

Age range 6+
Number of players Four or more
Energy level 2

You can adapt this well-known action game to focus on improving ball skills. As in the traditional version, players have to do what Simon says – and *not* do anything he doesn't say!

How to play

Give each child a ball and choose one to be 'Simon'. Simon then tells the children an action that they should do with their balls and demonstrates it himself. Usually he prefaces his commands with 'Simon says ...' – but sometimes he doesn't. The

'Simon says throw the ball up in
the air and catch it with one hand'

What you will need A small ball for
every child playing

children must listen carefully and only do the
actions that begin with 'Simon says ...'

Any command that isn't prefaced with 'Simon
says ...' should be ignored and the children should
just stand still. Those who forget to do so are out.
The last one left in is the winner.

Actions to try

Not sure what actions to suggest? Try these:

* Throw the ball from one hand to the other
* Throw the ball up in the air and catch it with
  both hands
* Throw the ball up in the air and catch it with
  one hand
* Throw the ball up in the air and catch it with
  the other hand
* Throw the ball up in the air and clap before
  catching it
* Throw the ball up in the air and clap twice
  before catching it
* Throw the ball under one leg and catch it
* Bounce it on the ground while standing still
* Bounce the ball on the ground while moving
* Pass the ball around your body
* Roll the ball along the ground
* Dribble it along the ground with your foot.

Tips for beginners

* If there are children who haven't played
  'Simon says' before, have a warm-up game of
  the traditional version first. (This is where
  Simon just gives simple actions to do, such as
  jumping, hopping, turning around, touching
  their nose or waving their hands in the air.)
* If you haven't enough balls, team the children
  into pairs, with one ball between two, and let
  them throw to each other.

Queen-i-o

Age range 7+
Number of players Four or more
Energy level 2

This game of bluff works best with several children, but smaller groups will still enjoy it. The aim is to guess who is hiding the ball, so as to enjoy more time as 'Queen-i-o'.

How to play

One person is given the ball and goes to stand a little way off from all the other players. Facing away from them and calling, 'Ready, Steady, *Throw!*', she throws the ball backwards over her shoulder for one of the children to catch.

The child who catches the ball must quickly hide it behind his back. Then all the other children put their hands behind their backs in a similar way, stand in a line and chant the rhyme on page 241.

When they have finished chanting, the thrower must turn round and select the person she thinks has the ball. If she's wrong, that person then becomes Queen-i-o, and the thrower goes back to join the other children. If she's right, she continues being Queen-i-o for the next round.

Variations

* When it's a boy's turn to be the thrower, change the name to 'King-i-o'.
* Instead of players hiding the ball in their hands behind their back, they can hide it elsewhere – up a jumper, tucked into the back of a sock or squeezed between the knees – and do the following actions while chanting the rhyme:

Queen-i-o,
(point towards the thrower once)
Queen-i-o,
(point towards the thrower a second time)
Who's got the ball-i-o?
(make a ball-shaped circle with their hands)
I haven't got it,
(point to themselves)
It isn't in my pocket,
(mime emptying out pockets)
So Queen-i-o,
(point towards the thrower)
Queen-i-o,
(point towards the thrower again)
Who's got the ball-i-o?
(make a ball-shaped circle with their hands)

What you will need A small ball

Queen-i-o, Queen-i-o,
Who's got the ball-i-o?
I haven't got it,
It isn't in my pocket.
So Queen-i-o, Queen-i-o,
Who's got the ball-i-o?

Tip for beginners
* Young children may find it hard to throw the
ball very far over their shoulders, so keep
the others quite close behind.

Upsy-downsy

Age range 5+
Number of players Two or more
Energy level 1
What you will need A small ball

This throw-and-catch game of forfeits is best played on a grassy surface to protect the children's knees. They're trying to catch the ball without dropping it and, in doing so, avoid the forfeits.

How to play

Position the children so that there is a reasonable space between them. Give the ball to one child and ask him to throw it to the other – or at random, if there are more than two children playing. If the other child catches the ball, he then throws it back to the original player – or on to someone new, if there are several children.

If anyone fails to catch the ball, he must suffer a forfeit (see above right) and then the throwing continues. Forfeits for dropped balls can be reversed if the player catches the ball on the next go. If he misses again, another forfeit is added on. Finally if a ball is dropped while the child is lying down, he is out. The last person still in the game is the winner.

Forfeits

Penalties for missed catches go in the following order:

* Go down on one knee
* Go down on two knees
* Put one hand behind the back
* Lie down flat on the grass.

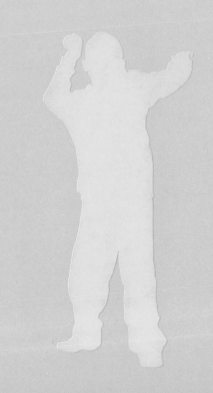

Tips for beginners

* Make sure the distance between the children is smaller with younger ones.
* Throw the ball in a circle, not at random.

Age range 7+
Number of players Four or more
Energy level 3
What you will need A large foam ball

Spot

In this high-energy ball game, also known as Spud, players work hard to avoid turning into a 'spot' by collecting the four letters of the name, and try to be the last person left in.

How to play
Play starts with one person holding the ball and the others surrounding her. She then shouts out a name, throws the ball high up into the air and runs away. The player whose name has been called tries to catch the ball – all the others run away.

If the person whose name has been called catches the ball without it bouncing, he can then call out another player's name and throw to them.

If he misses, or the ball bounces, he shouts 'Spot!' and everyone must freeze. He then picks a player, takes three steps towards her, and throws the ball to try and hit her body or legs. If he's successful, the person who is hit 'collects' the S of Spot. If he misses, or the person catches the ball, the thrower himself collects the S. Then it's the throwee's turn to throw the ball.

Play continues like this until someone has collected all four letters of 'Spot' – and is out. More players will gradually fall out until the last person left in is the winner.

Variation
* Adapt this game for younger children by playing it in a circle, throwing randomly across to each other. If someone drops the ball, he collects the first letter of a three-letter word, such as 'cat'. As soon as he has collected all three letters, he is out.

Tip for beginners
* Establish a boundary, beyond which no player is allowed to run.

Web ball

Age range 10+
Number of players Six or more
Energy level 1
What you will need Several small balls; a sheet of paper and pencil; a stopwatch

Web Ball starts out fairly simply, but quickly becomes very tricky – it's great for encouraging concentration and cooperation. The intention is to add as many balls into the game as possible without dropping any of them.

How to play

Ask the children to stand in a circle with a decent amount of space between them. Explain that during the game everyone will need to remember two people: the person who throws the ball to them, and the person to whom they throw the ball.

Give the first ball to one child, who calls out the name of the person she is going to throw to and then throws the ball. The child who receives the ball calls out the name of another child and throws the ball on to them, and so on.

When everyone has got used to the ball circulating in the same way each time, a second ball is then introduced and play continues, with everyone calling out names, throwing and catching in the same order.

Once this is established, a third ball is added, and so on, until a ball is finally dropped. Record the most number of balls used and how long each game takes, to find the best.

Tips for beginners
* Use larger balls.
* Throw them more slowly.
* Throw around the circle rather than across it.

Stage one

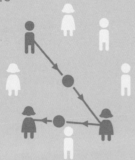

Stage two

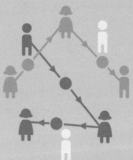

Ball against the wall

Age range 9+
Number of players One
Energy level 1
What you will need A bouncy ball, such as a tennis ball; a brick wall without windows

This countdown game is a great way for children to have fun with a ball on their own, by trying to get through all ten of the countdown tasks without dropping the ball. It's challenging, but practice makes perfect!

How to play
Throw the ball against the wall, completing the following challenges:

- Ten sets of throwing the ball, allowing it to bounce once and catching it
- Nine sets of throwing the ball, allowing it to bounce once, clapping once and catching it
- Eight sets of throwing the ball, allowing it to bounce once, clapping twice and catching it
- Seven sets of throwing the ball under the leg, allowing it to bounce once and catching it
- Six sets of throwing the ball with the best hand, allowing it to bounce once and catching it
- Five sets of throwing the ball with the worst hand, allowing it to bounce once and catching it
- Four sets of throwing the ball, without any bouncing, and catching it
- Three sets of throwing the ball, without any bouncing, clapping once and catching it
- Two sets of throwing the ball, without any bouncing, clapping twice and catching it
- One set of throwing the ball, spinning around and catching it.

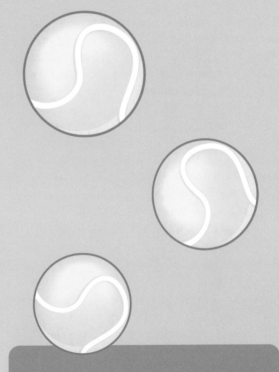

Variations
* You can add new challenges, such as: a third clap; allowing the ball to bounce twice; throwing it under the other leg; bending down to touch the ground; touching both elbows and the nose; and so on.
* Children could try playing this by simply throwing the ball into the air, rather than against a wall – but it will be harder.

Sixty-six

Age range 9+
Number of players Three or more
Energy level 2
What you will need A football; a whistle; a goal (or equivalent)

This football-based game can be played with just a few children – but they do need to work as a team! The aim is to score as many goals as possible before the goalkeeper reaches a count of 66.

How to play

One child is the goalkeeper, the others are the opposing team. When the whistle blows, the goalkeeper begins to count to 66, while the team players pass the ball to each other and try to score goals. The catch is that goals can only be scored with a volley (that is, the ball must be passed by another player and not touch the ground before being shot into goal).

If the team manages to score a goal, the goalkeeper has to revert to counting from one again. But next time around the team will need to score two goals before the goalkeeper goes back to counting from one again. Then it will be three goals, four goals, and so on.

However, if the goalkeeper saves the ball, he swaps places with the player who scored the goal. And once he has managed to count up to 66, he automatically swaps places with the last person to touch the ball.

Tip for beginners

* This game works best when players cooperate with each other, so remind the children to work together to score as many goals as they can.

First to 100!

Age range 9+
Number of players Three or more
Energy level 3
What you will need A ball

This is a good game for honing children's adding skills, since they are trying to be the first person to reach 100 points. The arithmetic can be made more challenging for older children (see the variations below).

Variations

* Use larger number units (say 25s) and collect points up to 500.
* Alternatively, rather than calling out numbers at random, award fixed points for different types of catching: 20 points for catching the ball without dropping it; 15 points for catching it with one bounce; 10 points for two bounces; and 5 points for claiming it from the ground.

Tip for beginners

* For younger children, count only up to ten and award them one point for every catch they get, regardless of whether or not the ball bounced.

How to play

The first player throws the ball in the air and calls out a number between 10 and 50 in units of tens (10, 20, 30, 40, 50). If another player catches the ball without it bouncing, he 'collects' that score. If he catches it with one bounce, he collects half the score. If he almost catches it, but subsequently drops it, he deducts the score from any points that he's already collected (he remains at zero if he didn't have any points to begin with). If no one catches the ball, no points are collected.

The player who now has the ball is the next to throw it and calls out a new number. Play continues like this, with each person collecting his scores until one person reaches 100 – and wins the game.

Rounders

Age range 7+
Number of players Minimum of eight (four per team)
Energy level 2
What you will need Four markers; a bat; a soft ball

This classic playground game works best with a big group of players in an open space. Players strive to score as many rounders as possible during their team's turn at batting, by hitting the ball as far as they can without it being caught.

Tip for beginners

* Make sure an adult helper is the bowler. Underarm bowling makes it as easy as possible for the batters to hit the ball.

Preparation

Divide the players into two teams, Team A and Team B, each with an adult helper. Set up a marker to form a stump at each corner of a square playing area.

How to play

Team A bat first. Team B have a fielder guarding each of the four stumps.

Team B's bowler bowls the ball to Team A's first batter. Once she's hit the ball, she drops the bat and runs off towards the first stump. If no one has caught the ball yet, she can continue to the second, third and fourth stumps. If she makes it all the way round, she scores a full rounder. If,

however, she sees that the ball has been caught, she waits at whichever stump she's reached. If the fielders catch the ball and touch the stump before the running batter reaches it, she is caught out. No stump can have more than one player at a time waiting there.

If a batter has hit the ball, but has to wait at the second or third stump for fear of being caught out, she can set off again once the next batter has hit the ball and started to run. If she reaches the fourth stump safely, she scores half a rounder.

The game continues until all the batters have been caught out, when the teams swap sides. The team with the most rounders is the winner.

Variation
* For older, faster players, set the stumps further apart to make running between them harder. This gives other players who are fielding a better chance of catching them out between stumps.

Get back!

Age range 7+
Number of players Four or more
Energy level 3
What you will need A landmark to act as 'home'

This chasing game tests all the players' nerves – and speed. It's best played in a big open space with some potential hiding areas. The aim is for players to get back 'home' without being caught.

Preparation

Everyone agrees on which landmark is home – it could be a jumper on the grass, a garden chair or a picnic table.

How to play

All the players gather at home. One player is chosen to be the chaser and counts to at least 20 to give the others a chance to run and hide. Then he calls out 'Ready' and starts to look for the other players. They must emerge from hiding, or sneak into another hiding place nearer home, while the chaser looks for them.

When the chaser sees another player attempting to make it home, he runs to catch her – if he touches her, the other player joins his team and has to chase the hidden players, too.

Eventually all the players will either be back at home or caught and on the chaser's team. Another person is then chosen to be the chaser.

Variations

* The game can start again with the chaser's expanded team all counting to 20 and then trying to catch the remaining players, until everyone has been caught and is on the chaser's team. The last person to be caught becomes the chaser for a new game.
* When a player has been caught by the chaser, she is out (instead of joining the chaser's team). So the winner is the last player who hasn't yet been caught, as long as she gets back to home safely.
* Try adding different characters to the game, such as knights chasing dragons, dogs chasing cats or cats chasing mice.
* If there aren't many good hiding places, the players can simply spread out and try to run back home by dodging the chaser.

Tip for beginners

* Give younger players an extra 'life' or two, so that they have a second chance to escape if they're caught too quickly.

Tail end

Age range 6+
Number of players Six or more
Energy level 3
What you will need Enough socks in two different colours for each player to be given a 'tail'

Based on the same principle as Tag Rugby, which is often played in primary schools, this fun game is a great way for children to burn off energy trying to capture the 'tails' of the opposing team.

Variations
* Handicap stronger or faster players by making their team have fewer members, or by making them walk fast rather than run.
* Use shorter socks to make them a trickier target to grab.
* The referee can be strict about cheating – giving anyone who touches another player 'time out' for a few minutes.
* Players who have captured tails have to tuck them into their own waistband, giving the other team a chance to win them back.
* Set a time limit to the game. The team with most tails is the winner.

Tip for beginners
* Use tights rather than socks to make it easier to catch a tail.

Preparation
The players divide into two teams. Each team chooses a sock colour – for example, grey for Team A, black for Team B. Each team member is given a sock in his team's colour, and has to tuck it into his waistband at the back. Now all the players have a tail.

If playing in an open area, decide where the boundaries of the 'pitch' are and make this clear to all the players.

How to play
The players spread out around the pitch. When an adult helper says 'GO!' they run around trying to capture the tails of the opposing team.

They are not allowed to touch or hold other players in any way – they must snatch the tails by skilful running and dodging alone!

Players remain in the game even if they have lost their tail. The winning team is the first to capture all the other team's tails.

Fire and ice

Age range 6+
Number of players Six or more
Energy level 3
What you will need No props

This catching game has a rescue element, too, the aim being to avoid being frozen by the ICE players or melted by the FIRE players, or to rescue other FIRE or ICE players! It's similar to Stuck in the Mud (see page 221), but involves two teams and is suited to slightly older players.

How to play

The players divide into two teams. One team is FIRE, the other ICE.

The ICE players have to try and touch the FIRE players as they run around. If an ICE player succeeds in touching a FIRE player, the latter has to freeze straight away in whatever position he's in. He isn't allowed to move again until one of his FIRE team companions touches him to warm him up. Then he unfreezes and can run off again.

The game continues until the ICE players have succeeded in freezing all the FIRE players. Then it is the FIRE team's turn to catch the ICE players, who have to melt into a heap on the ground when they are touched, until they are refrozen by another ICE player.

Variation
* If you don't have enough players for two full teams, make the fastest player ICE, while all the others are FIRE.

Tip for beginners
* Practise making 'ice statue' shapes before the game, so that the players understand they have to stop running once a member of the ICE team has touched them.

What's the time, Mr Wolf?

Age range 3+
Number of players Two or more
Energy level 2
What you will need No props

This classic childhood game has a scary build-up of tension that's just right for younger players, who will love trying to escape from the clutches of big, bad, hungry Mr Wolf.

How to play

The children line up together at a distance from the 'wolf' – usually the adult – who has his back to them. The children then call out together,

'What's the time, Mr Wolf?'

The wolf turns round slowly and replies,

'Two o'clock.'

The children then take two steps towards the wolf, and ask again,

'What's the time, Mr Wolf?'

They take steps nearer to him each go, depending on what time Mr Wolf says it is. Once they are almost on a level with the wolf, they ask again,

'What's the time, Mr Wolf?'

He turns round and roars, **'Dinner time!'** and chases them all back to the starting line.

Whichever child he catches then becomes Mr Wolf for the next game.

Variation
* The wolf can pretend to be asleep as the children creep up on him. When they're almost there, he wakes up with a start and chases them all back to the starting line.

Tip for beginners
* For very young players, it's best if the wolf allows them all to escape back to the starting line. He can then huff and puff crossly about still being hungry, and begin the game again.

Age range 8+
Number of players Four or more
Energy level I
What you will need A tennis ball

Pat ball

Another playground favourite, this game adapts well to the garden or any playing area where there's a wall. Players must attempt to keep the ball bouncing against the wall for as long as possible, using only their hands as rackets.

How to play

The players stand in a row next to each other, a few feet away from the wall. The first player bounces the ball on the ground, then 'pats' it with his hand to make it bounce against the wall. The next player has to let it bounce, then 'pat' it again so that it hits the wall. Play continues along the team, until one of the players either:

• Fails to hit the ball, or
• Hits the ball on the volley, instead of letting it bounce first.

If this happens, the player is out.

If the ball bounces and is hit, but strikes the bottom of the wall where it meets the ground, this is known as 'mids'. Like a 'let' in tennis, that player is allowed another turn.

The player who keeps going longest without dropping the ball is the winner.

Variation
* Try using a small, bouncy rubber ball for a real challenge.

Tips for beginners
* Use a bigger ball.
* Allow more bounces between players to keep the game going.

Red Rover

Age range 9+
Number of players Ten or more
Energy level 2
What you will need No props

This very robust game is best kept for older players who don't mind some rough and tumble – in fact, they'll probably love it! The plan is to break through the other team's defences and capture their players.

How to play

The players divide into two teams. Each team lines up on either side of the playing area and links arms.

One team then gathers in a 'huddle' and secretly decides which player they will pick from the other team. If they've chosen a boy called Peter, they would then line up, linking arms, and call out:

Red Rover, Red Rover,
Send PETER right over.

Peter then has to run from the other side and try to break through the team's linked arms. If he breaks through successfully, he returns to his own team, taking a player of his choice back with him. If he can't break through, he has to join the opposite team.

Then it's the other team's turn to pick a player to try to break through the opposing defences. The winning team is the one with the most players once everyone's name has been called.

Variation
* To make a break-through easier, the team can hold hands instead of linking arms.

Tip for beginners
* Make sure there's plenty of room behind each team, as it may take a while for the Red Rover to come to a standstill once he's broken through the line!

Age range 6+
Number of players Minimum of four
Energy level 3
What you will need A baton or ball
for team members to pass

Relay race

This game is great for kids who don't like being chased, but enjoy the excitement of competitive running and team spirit. They're attempting to be part of the first team to complete the race.

How to play

Divide the players into teams and establish the boundaries of the race clearly.

Both teams start from the same place. The first runner is given a ball or baton. On the command 'Go!' she runs as fast as possible to a given point at some distance – for example, a tree. She has to touch it with the ball, then run back to the start, where she hands the ball on to the next player, who runs off to the tree again.

The relay race continues until all the players on each team have run the course and one team has got back to the start first.

Variation
* Handicap faster players by making them run round the tree, or bounce the ball off it three times before being allowed to set off back to the starting line.

Tip for beginners
* You can plan the race around a circuit, where players start from a set position around the course. They have to take the ball or baton from the previous player as she runs up to them.

Three-legged race

Age range 5+
Number of players Four or more, but there must be even numbers to pair up
Energy level 2
What you will need Scarves or strips of soft cloth to tie the legs together

The three-legged race looks much more straightforward than it actually is, and demands good coordination with a partner to avoid tumbles. The aim is for the three-legged partnership to get to the finishing line first – without either (or probably both) of them falling over.

Preparation
Each player finds a partner and they stand together side by side while an adult helper ties their inside legs together with a scarf or strip of cloth at ankle level – so that, in effect, each pair of players has three legs.

How to play
Each pair lines up at the starting line. When you call out 'Go!' they set off, trying to walk or run together by moving their joined-together legs forward, followed by their own 'free' legs in unison. The winners are is the pair who reach the finish line first.

Tips for beginners

* Match players who are roughly the same size and weight, so that it's easier for them to coordinate their steps.

* If the players put their arms around each other's waists, it's much easier to balance.

Variation

* Try playing individually by tying players ankles together so that they have to hop to the finish line as fast as possible without falling over.

Hot rocks

Age range 5+
Number of players Three or more
Energy level 1
What you will need Several dessertspoons or tablespoons; the same number of large pebbles or small potatoes

In this 'Egg and spoon' standby of school sports days – where players try to be the first over the finishing line without dropping their 'egg' from its spoon – it's much easier and less wasteful to use pebbles instead of the real thing!

How to play

Each player is given a spoon, plus a pebble or potato to balance on it.

The players line up behind the starting line, all holding their spoons and 'rocks' carefully in front of them. On the word 'Go!' they all set off as speedily as possible towards the finish line.

If players drop their rocks, they must go back to the beginning and start again.

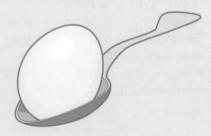

Variation

* The classic version of this game is 'Egg and spoon', using hard-boiled eggs instead of potatoes, with players eating their eggs at the end of the race.

Tip for beginners

* Younger players can be allowed to put their pebbles back on the spoons, instead of having to go back to the beginning.

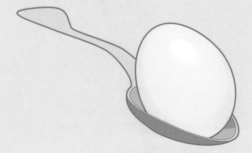

Wheelbarrow race

Age range 6+
Number of players At least four
Energy level 3
What you will need No props

This is a game for strong arms and straight legs, otherwise the partnership will end up in a tangled heap as it attempts to be the first 'wheelbarrow' to cross the finishing line.

Preparation
Each player chooses a partner. One player lies on the ground and puts his arms out straight, while the other holds his legs by the ankles, to form a 'wheelbarrow'.

How to play
On the word 'Go!' the wheelbarrows set off towards the finish line. If any of the wheelbarrows collapse – either arms or legs – they are out, or have to start again. The winning wheelbarrow is the one that crosses the line first.

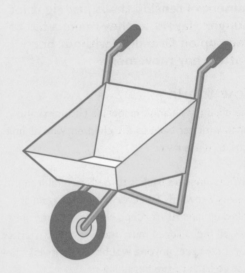

Tips for beginners
* Allow younger players to continue even if they collapse on the way to the finish, instead of going back to the beginning.
* Try to ensure that wheelbarrow partners are evenly matched in terms of strength and body weight.

Variations
* Three players can form a wheelbarrow, if two players hold one leg each. This is helpful if the player lying down is much heavier than the others.
* The wheelbarrow player can wear gloves if the ground is hard.

Grandma's footsteps

Age range 3+
Number of players Four or more
Energy level 1
What you will need No props

This game is very easy to play, yet has an element of tension that's just right for younger players, as they make a bid to creep up on Grandma without her spotting any movement.

How to play

One child (or an adult helper) is Grandma and stands with her back to the children, who all line up some distance away.

While Grandma's back is turned, the children creep up slowly towards her. Every now and again she 'wakes up' and turns round suddenly. When she does, all the children must stand as still as statues. If Grandma sees anyone wobbling or moving, they must go back to the beginning.

She then turns back and the players start to creep towards her again. The game continues like this as the children creep ever closer to her. The first person to touch Grandma's back, without her spotting him moving, is the winner.

Variation
* Handicap players by making them jump or hop instead of walking up to Grandma. This makes it much harder to keep still when she looks round!

Tip for beginners
* Give younger players a second chance if Grandma sees them wobbling, so they can stay in the game longer.

Red letter day

Age range 7+
Number of players Six or more
Energy level 3
What you will need A sheet of paper
and a pencil (optional)

This game encourages spelling skills, as well as expending lots of children's energy. They have to guess the other team's word by catching each player and finding out what his letters are.

Preparation

The players divide into two teams. Each team chooses a word made up of the same number of letters as there are children in the team. For example, if there are three children in each team, both teams secretly choose a three-letter word, such as FOX or CAT.

Four-letter words could be LEAF or TWIG.

Five-letter words could be GRASS or RIVER. And so on.

Each child in the team is assigned one of the letters that makes up the whole word.

How to play

The first team are given a few seconds to run away, before the second team chases after them. If they catch anyone, the player who is caught has to reveal his letter. The second team carry on catching the other team's players until they've discovered enough letters to guess the word.

Then the teams swap roles, and the first team try to discover the other team's word.

Variations

* The word has to be a certain subject, such as animals or types of food.
* In small teams, each player can have more than one letter, so that longer words can be used.
* The guessing team are only allowed to guess one word per letter found.

Tip for beginners

* Each player can carry the letter written on a small piece of paper in his hand, so that it doesn't get forgotten.

Number plates

Age range 6+
Number of players 2–4
Good for Keeping passengers occupied on long car journeys
What you will need To show support and interest during those periods when the game seems to stall

This is a cooperative game to keep passengers alert and interested on a long journey. If everyone works together, there is shared satisfaction if you succeed in the task.

How to play

The object is to work through the alphabet from A to Z by mentally ticking off the letters as they are spotted on car number plates. Only the letters that appear at either end of the whole number plate count, and they must be spotted in the correct order. Therefore, the first thing to find is a car with an A at the beginning or end of its number plate. When A has been found, you then search for B.

The letters must be spotted in the correct sequence. If you are looking for M and you see N, you cannot keep the N 'in reserve' and count M and N when you later see M. It can be frustrating, but it's better than the perpetual 'Are we nearly there yet?' every five minutes.

Variation

∗ If you want a quicker game, you can allow any letter in the car number plate to be eligible, not just those at each end. In this case, if you are looking for C, for example, and a car number plate has C and D, you count both.

Age range 9–12
Number of players 2–4
Good for Passing a bit of time on long car journeys
What you will need A willingness to smooth over arguments about whether somebody has taken too long, for example

Next letter

This is a simple, competitive game where players get knocked out if they cannot go.

How to play

A subject is chosen – countries, for example. The first player must name a country beginning with the letter A. The next player names a country beginning with B, and so on down the alphabet, the turn going round from player to player. A player who cannot produce a country beginning with the appropriate letter within, say, five seconds, is eliminated, and the last player remaining is the winner.

Suggested subjects
* Countries
* Towns
* Animals
* Football teams
* Boys' names
* Girls' names
* Capital cities
* Recording artists
* Parts of the body
* Sportsmen's surnames
* Celebrities' surnames

The postman's dog

Age range 9–12
Number of players 2–4
Good for Taking the minds of 9–12-year-olds off a tedious journey
What you will need To provide encouragement by praising good efforts

This is a competitive game, where young passengers might get eliminated first. The last surviving player is the winner.

How to play

Each player has to describe and name the postman's dog, the first with words beginning with A, the second B and so on. If a player cannot do it in within, say, five seconds, then he drops out.

For example, the first player could say 'The postman's dog is an angry dog and its name is Arthur'. The second player has B, and might say 'The postman's dog is a brown dog and its name is Bruno'. And so on.

Tips for beginners

* For younger players, you might decide to leave out the more difficult letters Q, Z and X.
* Allow younger players or beginners to have their go first, so that they are less likely to run out of ideas.

I'll take my Auntie Pam's dog

Age range 8+
Number of players 2–4
Good for Otherwise boring car journeys
What you will need A readiness to get involved and to suggest the end-of-sentence requirements for successive games

This is a competitive game, but not to be taken too seriously. It's object, after all, is to provide some entertainment on a long car journey, so the more weird and wonderful items players can dream up to take to the cinema the more laughs there will be.

How to play

This is another game where players are eliminated if they do not come up with a correct item quickly enough when it is their turn.

Each player in turn must supply an end to the sentence: 'Tonight I'm going to the cinema, and I'm taking my ...'. The missing word or words must agree to a formula. For example, they could be a word beginning with a certain letter. If it were W, successive players could take a wig, water pistol, watch or wheelbarrow. The item taken need not be relevant, so players can dream up the funniest items they like.

The end-of-sentence requirement could be any two-word item, so players could take a mobile phone, Wellington boots, toilet paper and so on.

You could make it quite difficult (where the items taken might get outlandish) such as stipulating the sentence must end with a 'three-word item beginning with A'. You could say 'Tonight I'm going to the cinema and I'm taking my Auntie Pam's dog' or 'my anti-tetanus pills' or 'my arty suede shoes'.

Other requirements could be you must take an item beginning with the last letter of the previous player's item, so the sequence might go: harp, pyjamas, socks, saucepan, newspaper, rabbit, teeth, hairspray, yogurt and so on.

Or the items taken must be items of six letters, so my canary, eyelid, carrot, kitten and so on.

A player failing to provide a suitable sentence within ten seconds on his turn is eliminated.

Age range 7+
Number of players 2–4
Good for Keeping the back-seat passengers occupied when travelling, especially if there's nothing much to see through the window
What you will need A willingness to join in if interest seems to be waning

Food store

This is a game that can be played by any number at any time, but is suitable for this specialized travelling use. It is a sort of I-spy (see page 299) of the mind.

How to play

The player who agrees to start says 'My father runs a food store and in it he sells something beginning with...'. And she names the first letter of the item she is thinking of. The other players then try to guess what the item is. For instance, if the letter was P, the item might be potatoes, plums, pies or peppermints.

The first to guess what the item is then becomes the one whose father runs the shop, and sets a puzzle for the others. When the subject of food seems exhausted, the father's shop could become a newsagent.

Variation

* Players take turns to make the statement 'My father runs a food store...'. The first player must think of something beginning with A, and end the sentence accordingly. When the item is guessed, the next player must make the statement and the object must begin with B. And so on. Each player on her turn must be given a minute or two to think of an object beginning with the appropriate letter. By agreement, and if you get that far, the letters Q, X and Z can be omitted.

Age range 7+
Number of players 2–4
Good for Providing entertainment for tedious journeys
What you will need A certain amount of patience as you listen to lists endlessly repeated; remember – it's keeping them occupied

One omelette

This game is another that can actually be played at a party with any number of players, but since it requires nothing but imagination it is particularly suitable for whiling away the time sitting in the car.

How to play

Players in this game take turns to name objects according to the rules of the game, and a player who fails is eliminated.

The first player must name an object beginning with the letter O, as O is the first letter of 'One'. She might say 'One omelette'. Each player in turn repeats 'One Omelette', including the first player to say it. The second player now says 'One omelette and two...', adding something beginning with T, for 'Two'. He might say 'One omelette and two toffees'. All in turn repeat this until the third player comes in again, and she says 'One omelette, two toffees and three ...'. And so on.

Notice that 'Three' also begins with T, so two things beginning with T get into the list. Also, of course, 'Four' and 'Five' each start with F, 'Six' and 'Seven' with S, and when 'Ten' is reached, a third item beginning with T gets into the list.

Players are eliminated if they forget the order of the items already listed. Any hesitation and a player automatically is out.

One omelette

Two toffees

Ending the game
* It is unlikely that this game will last beyond the 20s and 30s because every new object (20 altogether) must begin with the letter T, and it will be difficult for players to recall which object beginning with T fitted, for example, 'twenty-three' and which fitted 'twenty-four'. In fact by then the game is likely to disintegrate in argument, and you must gently suggest a new one.

I love my love

Age range 8+
Number of players 2–4
Good for Car journeys, when impatience creeps in among the younger travellers
What you will need The ability to join in occasionally to keep things going

In this game, players have a chance to show off a little by using rather outlandish words.

How to play

Players in turn take a successive letter of the alphabet and complete the following sentence by filling in the spaces with a name, an adjective, a place name and a present, all beginning with the relevant letter in the alphabet.

The first player starts with the letter A and says 'I love my love with an A, because her name is A..., she is a..., she comes from A... and I shall give her a...'.

The second player then does the same with the letter B, and so on. Any player who cannot complete the sentence on his letter leaves the game, and the last remaining player wins.

Examples for D, L and M are:

'I love my love with a D, because his name is David, he is dashing, he comes from Denmark and I shall give him a Dalmatian.'

'I love my love with an L, because her name is Lydia, she is lovely, she comes from London and I shall give her a locket.'

'I love my love with an M, because his name is Mike, he is manly, he comes from Massachusetts and I shall give him a motorbike.'

... and I shall give him a dalmatian

Age range 6+
Number of players 2–4
Good for Keeping youngsters awake, alert and happy on a daytime car journey
What you will need Refereeing skills, as disputes will always arise as to who saw which car first, or whether it is actually green or more like blue

Colour collecting

This game will keep back-seat children entertained as they try to be the first to spot certain cars on the road.

How to play

Choose a colour. Players have to watch out for cars of that colour and shout out when they see one. A player scores a point each time he is the first to see a car of the chosen colour, and the first to 20 points is the winner.

It is best to choose a colour that is not too common, or players will be shouting out all the time and the game will end quite quickly. Thus black and white are colours to be avoided.

Similarly, if you choose a rare colour such as purple, the game might never end. Good choices are colours like red or blue.

Variation

* You could make the game more interesting by having two colours, one, such as red, which scores one point for the first to see it, and another rarer one, such as orange or yellow, which will score two points. Different types of vehicle could also be incorporated, so a lorry, bus and motorbike are all worth extra points in the game.

Overtaking

* If you overtake a point-scoring car, and later that same car overtakes you, the player who spots it overtaking scores a point. This avoids any arguments beginning 'You cannot have that, we've seen it before'.

Where's the treasure?

Age range 5+
Number of players One or more
Energy level I
What you will need Some 'treasure' (a few coins will do, especially if they come to about the cost of an ice-cream); a plastic bag

Can a child find the hidden treasure in the sand? If she can, she can keep it! This game, which is reminiscent of tales of pirates and hidden treasure troves, will delight children and is particularly appropriate for the beach, where the 'treasure' can be hidden easily.

Preparation

Put the treasure inside a plastic bag and seal it tightly. Then tell the child to turn her back and cover her eyes – no peeping – while you bury it, quite deeply, in the sand. Mark the spot with a particular stone that you would recognize, so that you know where to find it again; but disguise it by placing other stones around it.

How to play

Draw a large circle in the sand around the spot, then tell the child that the treasure is buried within that circle. It's her job to find it!

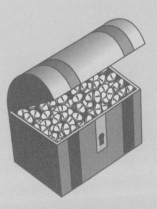

Variations

* Give some clues to help locate the treasure, such as: start at the entrance to the cave; face the sea and take three big steps forwards; turn right towards the large rock; go behind the rock and start digging!
* Describe the route in paces, such as: ten paces left, turn right and take five paces; turn left and take three paces; and so on.

Tips for beginners

* Adjust the size of the searching circle according to the age of the children playing – smaller for younger ones, larger for older children.
* Play 'Where are my feet?' instead. Just get your little one to bury your feet in sand and then pretend not to know where they are – they'll find it endlessly amusing.

Up, up and away

Age range 4+
Number of players One or more
Energy level 2
What you will need A paper bag; a hole punch; ring reinforcements; wool; tissue paper; glue

Help a child make his own kite and fly it along the beach. There's something very exhilarating about seeing your own creation dip and weave like a bird in the air, and the satisfaction of flying your own kite is immense.

Preparation

Open the paper bag slightly and punch two holes on each side. Strengthen them with paper ring reinforcements. Then, on each side, tie a 'handle' of wool and join the two handles with another long length of wool. Glue some thin tissue-paper streamers to the bottom of the bag.

How to play

Now open out the bag fully and run! It should fill with wind and fly.

Tip for beginners

∗ For safety's sake only fly kites in wide-open spaces away from roads and overhead wires. Never fly a kite in stormy weather in case lightning strikes.

Variation

∗ The sky is the limit with kite-making! Older children can experiment with different shapes and decorate their creations. For a traditional shape use bamboo canes tied together to make a cross, then join the tips with string to form a frame and cover with polythene. Join brightly coloured strips of polythene cut from old plastic bags to form a tail.

Castle magic

Age range 5+
Number of players Two or more
Energy level 2

A flat expanse of untouched sand just cries out for a sandcastle competition. In this game each team tries to make a beautiful, individual sandcastle within an agreed time limit; the results are then judged to decide the best one.

How to play

If there are more than two children, divide them into two teams. Mark out an area of sand where each team is to build their sandcastle. Then tell them they have an hour (half an hour for younger children) to each build a sandcastle as *different* from

What you will need A bucket and spade for each child; lots of shells and pebbles; packs of sandcastle flags (or other suitable items) for prizes

the other team as they can. Build excitement by calling out how much time they have left at certain intervals: half an hour, ten minutes, five minutes, one minute.

At the end of the hour, judge their efforts – and award prizes! Of course all the castles get praised for their own specialities and all the teams get a prize: sandcastle flags with which to decorate their creation.

Tricks of the trade

To help children get started, you could ask the following questions:

* Do they want a round or a square castle?
* Do they want a moat? Or two moats surrounding the castle?
* How about a drawbridge? Large, flat pebbles usually work well for this.
* Would they like a symmetrical or asymmetrical castle?
* Do they want corner towers?
* Could they make towers of different sizes? They could use buckets, picnic cups, disposable drinks cups, yogurt/fromage-frais pots or other containers.
* Would a spiral path up to the top be a good idea?
* What will they use for decoration? Perhaps shells, small pebbles, twigs or seaweed.
* Have they tried the dribbling technique (where very wet sand is dribbled into mini-mounds)?
* Who lives in their castle: soldiers, kings and queens, wizards, witches, fairies, and so on?

Tips for beginners

* Pair a child with an adult. Get a third adult to judge.
* Make the time limit flexible, and end the game when you feel the child is losing interest or getting tired.

Castle destroyer

Age range 5+
Number of players Two or more
Energy level 1
What you will need A bucket and spade; a small soft ball

This is similar to the classic bowling-alley game of Skittles, but has five sandcastle targets to aim at rather than skittles. Players have to knock down as many castles as they can.

Preparation

Using the bucket, make six sandcastles, laying them out in one row of three, with one row of two behind and then a row of one. Alternatively, lay them out in row. Draw lines in the sand down each side of the run-up, to make a bowling 'alley'.

How to play

Players take turns to throw the ball and try to knock the sandcastles down. Each person can have three goes at throwing in their turn. Then the castles are built up again for the next player. The winner is the one with the most hits after three rounds.

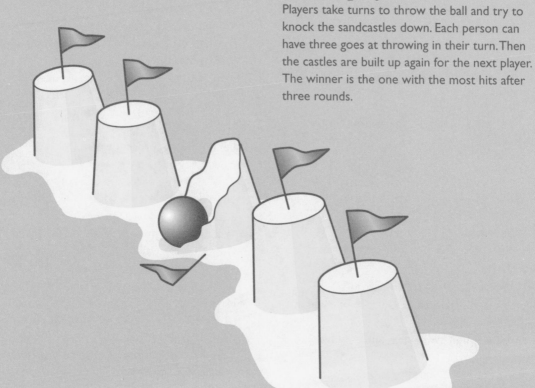

Age range 5+
Number of players Two or more
Energy level I
What you will need A flat area of wet sand; a stick; some small pebbles

Tot it up

This throw-and-count target game is a bit like Tiddlywinks, only on a larger scale and played on the beach. The aim is to score as many points as possible by throwing pebbles onto numbered circles in the sand.

Preparation
Draw five concentric circles in the wet sand with a stick. Write the number 5 in the smallest middle circle, 4 in the next one, 3 in the next one, 2 in the next one and 1 in the last and largest circle.

How to play
Give each child three small pebbles and get her to stand behind a starting line in the sand. Then tell the players to take turns to throw their pebbles into the circles to score as many points as they can. If a pebble lands on a line, the lower of the two numbers is taken. The person with the most points at the end of three rounds is the winner.

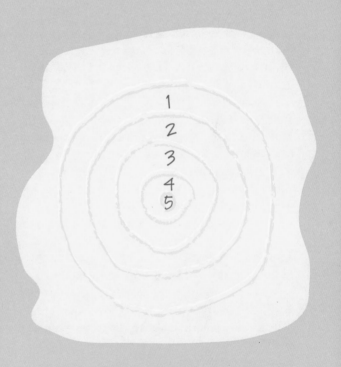

Variations
* Up the challenge by marking each circle with higher scores, such as 50, 25, 15, 10, 5.
* Mark different starting lines for different ages of players.

Tip for beginners
* Play in pairs, matching up younger children with older ones.

Boat races

Age range 7+
Number of players Two or more
Energy level I
What you will need Bits and pieces to improvise a boat (see the suggestions below)

Get children to use their ingenuity to make improvised boats, then build their own watercourse, so that they can race their boats down a rivulet and see who gets to the finish first.

Preparation

First get the children to make their boats. These can be anything from a raft made of twigs to a more fancy creation made from cut-down plastic bottles, with a mast made from a plastic straw and a sail from a paper bag. They can make it any way they like – the only essential is that it floats.

How to play

Now find a fairly wet bit of sand with some shallow pools, or get them to dig a mini-trench to act as the 'river'. Children will probably have lots of fun building dams in various places to direct the water flow. Then, placing the boats in the water at the same time, let the race begin!

Tip

* If children are using man-made items to make their boats, make sure that you collect all the bits at the end, to avoid causing environmental damage.

Variation

* A timeless game that can be played wherever there's water flowing under a bridge is to follow the progress of a favourite stick from one side of a bridge to the other, just as Winnie-the-Pooh and friends did in the game of Poohsticks.

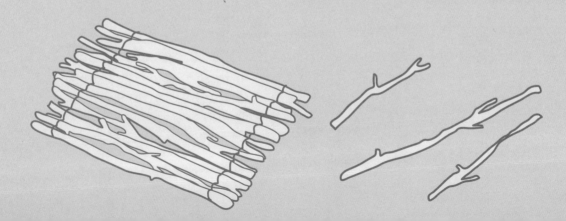

Age range 3+
Number of players One or more;
with adult helper
Energy levels 1–3
What you will need No props, except
perhaps a beach ball or body board

In the swim

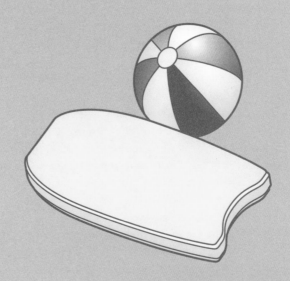

Paddling and swimming in the sea are a
real treat and a great form of exercise,
but need to be approached with caution
because of tides and currents. However,
with adult supervision, children can have
tremendous fun in the shallows.

How to play
Here are some ways for children to enjoy the water
safely:

- Very young children will enjoy playing 'wave chase',
  where they stand at the water's edge, holding your
  hand and running away from an incoming wave
  onto the beach. They've 'won' if the wave doesn't
  touch their feet – but 'losing' is probably more
  exciting!
- Slightly older children will enjoy 'leapsies' – a
  paddling game where they have to leap over
  an incoming wave.
- Beginner swimmers will enjoy being in the water
  with you and 'swimming', parallel to the shore,
  with you standing in front and holding their hands
  to guide them along.
- Older children who are confident swimmers
  can play swimming races, or Piggy in the Middle
  (see page 236) with a beach ball. But they *must*
  know how to stay safe in the water (see Sea
  safety, right).
- Teenagers will probably love using a body board
  or surfboard.

Sea safety
* Read all beach safety notices.
* Children must only swim between the safe
  range of the flags.
* They should always swim parallel to the
  shore, not out to sea.
* Make sure children stay within their depth.
* They must always have an adult nearby in the
  water with them.

Hit the hole

Age range 7+
Number of players Two or more
Energy level 1
What you will need Plastic golf clubs (or other bats); small soft balls; a spade

This is a golf-type game that is played in a circle instead of a straight line. Players are trying to be the first person to get right round the circuit and back to the beginning again.

Preparation
First, dig a hole in the sand a little larger than the size of the largest ball. Then draw a very big circle around the hole (as big as you can make it in the space available) and mark several points off along the circumference (at least one pace apart).

How to play
Starting at the top of the circle, players take turns to hit their balls into the hole. Once a ball is in, the player can collect it and move on to the next point in the circle. The first person to get back to the beginning is the winner.

Variation
* Create a crazy golf course around the circuit making 'bunkers', mounds and channels in the sand that players have to negotiate on their way to the hole.

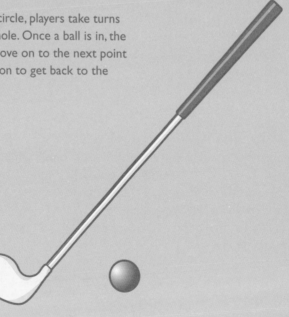

Big fish, little fish

Age range 4+
Number of players Four or more
Energy level 3
What you will need No props

This is a great game to play on the beach if the weather isn't too hot. As it involves running around, you will need a fair bit of clear space in which to play. The purpose is for the Big Fish to catch the Little Fish within a set time limit.

Preparation

With a stick or stone, draw two largish circles in the sand, one inside the other.

How to play

Select one player to be the Big Fish, and ask everyone else to stand with him inside the inner circle. Then choose another player to be the Little Fish, and ask him to stand alone on the sand in the outer circle.

The Big Fish now has to try to escape from the inner circle – while the other players do their best to stop him – and catch the Little Fish, who can only run within the boundary of the outer circle (that is, he can't cross into the inner circle or go outside the outer circle). A time limit is set and the game begins.

If the Big Fish catches the Little Fish within the time limit, the Little Fish becomes the Big Fish and a new Little Fish is chosen. If the Big Fish fails to catch the Little Fish within the time limit, he is out of the game altogether. The Little Fish then becomes the Big Fish, and a new Little Fish is chosen, as before.

It's categorical

Age range 7+
Number of players One or more
Energy level I
What you will need A sheet of paper and a pencil for each player

This is a nature-walk version of the classic pencil-and-paper game of Categories. It's also a variation of the spotting game Can You Find It?, with the objects sorted into groups this time.

Preparation

Each player draws a row of columns on her paper. At the top of each column she writes the name of a different category, such as:

• Animal
• Bird
• Flower
• Tree

How to play

As you walk through the park or woods, each player has to write down at least five of each category that she has seen. The winner is the first to complete her sheet.

Variations

* For older players, make the categories more specific, such as the names of trees: pine, oak, maple, beech, yew, and so on.
* Or try the classic *animal, vegetable, mineral,* with ten things to find in each category.

Tip for beginners

* For younger players, you can take away the competitive element of the game and simply enjoy finding one of each category.

What am I like?

Age range 5+
Number of players One or more
Energy level |
What you will need No props

This game is great for youngsters, who can have fun identifying the characteristics of the things seen on walks and discovering exactly what makes each creature or thing the way it is.

How to play

Go for a walk outdoors – it doesn't have to be in a wide open space; an urban area works just as well. The first player (usually the adult) spots something, such as a bird or squirrel, and asks if the other player can identify its characteristics.

For example, if it's a bird, the questions for a young player might be:

- Can it *swim* or does it *fly?*
- Does it have *fur* or *feathers?*
- Do its babies come from *eggs?*
- Does it live in a *nest* or in a *burrow?*

Tips for beginners
* Keep the questions very simple, such as: 'Is it alive?'
* Young players will enjoy acting out the thing they've identified, such as a bird flying or a tree swaying in the wind.

Variation
* Turn the game into a '20 questions' format, where the first player decides on a thing or object, and the other player has to guess what it is by asking 20 questions about it, which can only be answered 'Yes' or 'No'.

Secret trails

Age range 4+
Number of players Two or more
Energy level 2
What you will need A selection of twigs and pebbles; small prizes

The aim of this game is to follow the trail left by secret symbols to the end of the route, where a small prize is hidden. It is best played in a woodland or park with lots of shrubs and pathways.

Preparation

Collect a group of twigs and pebbles, ideally all of a similar shape and colour. The players all need to know what the clues will look like: for example, the twigs will be arranged in arrows, while the pebbles will be set out in a row of three.

How to play

The players hide their eyes while you lay a trail of twig arrows and pebble rows, which they must spot. Each clue leads them in a new direction, until finally they reach the last stage of the trail, where a small prize is hidden for each player or team to find.

Variation

* If you know the playing area well – for example, if it's your local park – plan ahead by preparing some written clues that can be found along the way, to make the game into more of a treasure hunt.

Tip for beginners

* Keep the trail clues close to each other so that they're easy to spot.

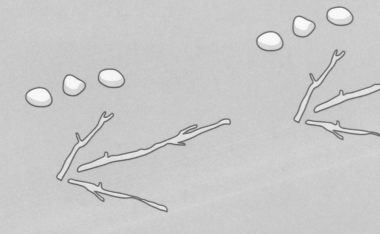

Age range 4+
Number of players One or more
Energy level 2
What you will need A sheet of paper and a pencil for each player; clear plastic jar (optional)

Insect hunt

Encourage an interest in the tiniest and busiest creatures in the open with this game, which has the players exploring far and wide to spot and record as many different insects as possible within a set time limit.

Preparation
All the players write the names of several different insects along the top of a sheet of paper. These might include:

• Ant
• Bee
• Woodlouse
• Fly
• Beetle
• Ladybird
• Butterfly

Younger players can familiarize themselves by doing the actions for each one – for example, fluttering like a butterfly or buzzing like a bee.

How to play
Players have ten minutes to search the local habitat for the insects. Each time they see one, they can put a tick on their paper in the column under the insect's name.

The winner is the player who has recorded the most finds once the time is up.

Variations
* Put one or two ants or beetles in a clear plastic jar so that children can look at them closely before releasing them again.
* If players find an ants' nest, or see lots of ants, mark the papers with a cross for each ten ants seen. Warn the children not to touch an anthill.

Tips for beginners
* Limit the number of insects to three or four.
* Draw pictures of the insects instead of writing the names, so that it's easier for younger players to spot them.

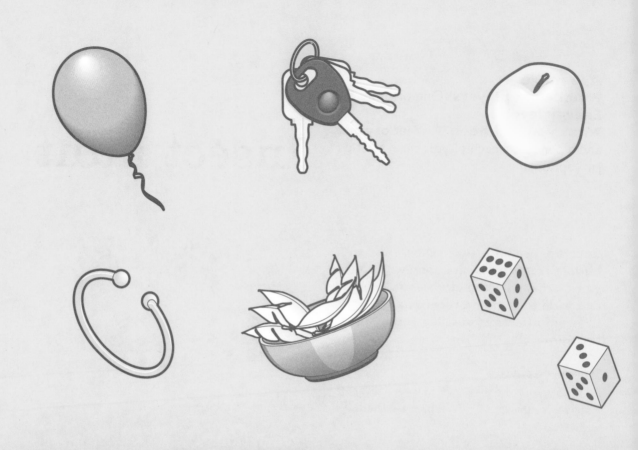

Party time

Hunt the thimble

Age range 3+
Number of players Any number
Good for Parties of young children who need a simple game to occupy them
What you will need A small object, traditionally a thimble

This is a very simple game that, nevertheless, needs to be supervised by an adult or two, especially when very young children are involved, since even some 3-year-olds have not yet grasped the principle of hiding things. Traditionally, the object to be hidden is a thimble, but any other small, distinctive object such as a brightly coloured button or a cork from a wine bottle will suffice.

How to play
There are two ways to play the game.

1. One child is chosen to be first to hide the thimble. The other children leave the room while she hides it. When the thimble is hidden, the other children come into the room and wander about trying to find the thimble. The first to succeed then has the job of hiding the thimble for the next game.

2. One child is chosen to go out of the room while one of the remaining children who stay in the room hides the thimble. The seeker is then let in to search. If she starts a long way from the thimble the children call out that she's 'cold', as she approaches it they call 'getting warmer', and so on through 'warm', 'hot', 'very hot' and 'boiling' until she actually finds it. The finder then has the role of hiding the thimble while the next seeker leaves the room.

Warning
* Tell the children – and ensure that it is true – that the thimble is always 'hidden' where it can be seen, so there is no need to open drawers or cupboards or look underneath ornaments. You do not want any breakages!

Age range 3+
Number of players 4–7
Good for Entertaining young children
What you will need A large house
with, ideally, many places to hide

Sardines

**This is a hiding game that will need two
or three adults to supervise as it entails
children wandering around your house.**

How to play

In this game a certain amount of darkness adds to
the pleasure, but the age and disposition of the
children will decide how much darkness you think
will be desirable.

One child is chosen to be the 'sardine' and to go
away and hide while the other children are kept in a
separate room. The sardine must hide in a space
where other children can join him, such as under a
bed, in a large cupboard or under the stairs. For this
reason, it is best for an adult to help find a suitable
hiding place.

When the sardine is safely hidden, the other
children are let loose to find him. Adults should
encourage them to split up and go their separate
ways all over the house.

When a seeker finds the sardine, she joins the
sardine in the hiding place, and gradually the hiding
place gets tightly packed, hence the game's name.

The last child to find the hiding place becomes the
sardine for the next game.

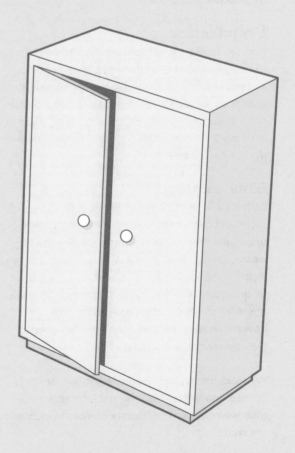

What's in the bag?

Age range 3+
Number of players 4–6
Good for Small family gatherings or parties
What you will need Ten plastic bags and items to fill them; a pencil and a sheet of paper for each player

This is an easy game to play, but adults might need to help any very young children unable to write. Children enjoy trying to guess what is in the bags in the same way that they like feeling presents at Christmas time.

Preparation

Find ten familiar objects the children should be able to recognize by feeling them through a plastic bag, and put one into each bag. Tie the bag so that it is impossible to see inside, and attach a label to each bag numbered 1 to 10. Prepare a sheet of paper for each child with the numbers 1 to 10 written down the left-hand side.

How to play

Each child is given one of the bags, with a sheet of paper and pencil with which he writes his name on the sheet. He is asked to guess by feeling the bag what is inside. He then writes his guess against the appropriate number on the sheet (or he whispers to an adult who writes it down for him). When all the children have made their guesses, they are handed the next bag until each child has guessed the contents of each bag.

When all the guesses are made, the bags are opened one by one and the contents shown. The child who guessed the identity of most objects is the winner.

Some suggested items

* Grandad's slipper
* Teddy bear
* Orange
* Potty
* Hairbrush
* Plastic cup
* Tube of toothpaste
* Rubber duck
* Wellington boot
* Toy car
* Old sock

Warning

* When opening the plastic bags, make sure they are collected up, as they can be dangerous around young children.

Pin the tail on the donkey

Age range 3+
Number of players Any number
Good for Small children's gatherings
What you will need Coloured pencils and paper; a good-sized pinboard; drawing pins; a piece of cardboard; wool (optional), a blindfold

This is a quiet game that nevertheless provides plenty of amusement for young children.

Preparation

Draw a large donkey without its tail on a sheet of paper and pin it to the pinboard. Unless you are a good artist, it's best to copy a drawing of a donkey from a book. Colour in the donkey and mark a black spot at the point where the tail should hang. Make a donkey's tail from cardboard, coloured as the donkey. Otherwise a circular piece of cardboard with lengths of wool stuck on makes a good donkey's tail. The top end of the tail should have a drawing pin piercing the cardboard so that the tail can be pinned to the drawing.

How to play

The pinboard with the donkey is propped upright, and in turn the children stand a few paces away from the donkey, are handed the tail and then blindfolded. They then have to step forward and pin the tail on the donkey, trying to place it in its correct position. Their efforts will usually cause laughter among the others.

When the tail is pinned, the blindfold is removed and the child surveys his handiwork. An adult then removes the tail and draws a circle round the pinhole, writing against it the name of the child.

When all children have had a turn, the child whose pinhole is nearest to the black spot is declared the winner of the game.

Musical chairs

Age range 5+
Number of players 6–12
Ideal for Entertaining a group of active children

This is a boisterous game that children love, but you must be prepared for an occasional argument, somebody falling over and possibly even a tantrum. Just keep your fingers crossed that there's no damage to the chairs.

Preparation

You need one fewer chairs than there are children taking part. There are two main ways to arrange the chairs. One is in a circle, with the backs of the chairs facing inwards and spaces between the chairs, say roughly the width of two chair-spaces.

The other is to arrange the chairs in a row, with alternate chairs facing in opposite directions. Both arrangements are illustrated.

How to play

The children spread themselves out around the chairs, as shown. An adult switches on some music, which is the signal for the children to begin dancing round the chairs. It is best that the person playing the music is out of sight, because at intervals he must stop the music without warning, and it would spoil the game if the children could see when this takes place.

Variation

* If you can rustle up enough of them, hats make a good addition to the game. They need not fit the children's heads; in fact, the funnier they look the better. Each hat is put onto one of the chairs, and before sitting on the chair the child must grab the hat off it and sit down putting the hat on. If one child grabs the hat while another sits on the chair, you must give preference to the child with the hat, since the hat must have been taken before the chair was sat upon.

Musical bumps

* This is a variation that does not require chairs. The children skip in little jumps to the music and when it stops they must immediately flop to the floor and sit cross-legged. The last to do so is out. This, of course, requires impartial and keen-eyed refereeing, and you will be lucky if there isn't a sulk or two.

What you will need A number of
chairs; a means of playing music (a record,
tape or CD player)

When the music stops, each child sits down on the
nearest chair. As there is one more child than there
are chairs, one child will be left standing. This is
where there must be adult supervision since there
will often be arguments with two children sitting on
the same chair, and an umpire's decisions will be
necessary for the game to continue.

The child left standing is eliminated from the game,
one chair is removed and the music is restarted.
The game continues until eventually only one child
is left, and she is the winner.

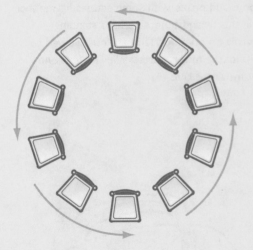

The chairs can be
arranged in a circle.

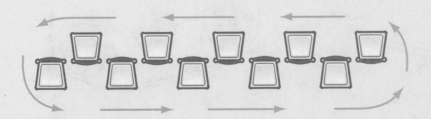

As a variation, you
could also arrange
the chairs in two
lines.

Musical statues

Age range 5+
Number of players Any number
Good for Parties with a number of over-energetic children

This is a game where you can take your time eliminating the children, as you do not need to eliminate somebody on every round. It is a game that can follow Musical Chairs (see page 292), and you might be able to engineer a different winner and allow some of the younger children to stay in the game longer than perhaps they should.

How to play

As with Musical Chairs, an adult, preferably not in the line of vision of the children, plays music to which the children dance. You should encourage them to dance flamboyantly, throwing their arms about. Praise the energetic dancers.

When the music stops, each child must stand still like a statue in whatever pose they are in. You will get some odd poses, with some statues having their arms in the air and others perhaps standing awkwardly on one foot. They are not allowed to move until the music starts again. The first one caught moving is out.

What you will need A means of playing music (a record, tape or CD player)

You should be the judge of who moves first. However, do not hold up the music for more than a few seconds, and if there isn't any obvious early movement, say 'Very good, I did not spot anyone moving'. At this, the person playing the music should begin it again, and the children continue their dance. Eventually only one child will remain and that child is the winner.

Variation

* In this variation, best played if the children are at least 7 or 8 years old, you, as the judge, actually try to make one or more of the children move or giggle. Once the music stops and they are frozen in their poses, you move amongst them trying to provoke a reaction. You do this by imitating their stance, staring at them, pulling a funny face, or saying 'Did I see you move?' The children, of course, being statues, must ignore you completely. If one does move or laugh you say 'Sorry, you're out, go and stand over there and help me be a judge in the next round'. You should not be too harsh in your judging at this stage and not spend too long at it, since a child caught in an awkward pose, like standing on one leg, cannot be expected to maintain it for long. As soon as all the children have resisted your efforts for a few seconds, ask for the music to start again.

Keeping them all interested

* One way to keep the children involved once they've been knocked out is to invite them to join you as judges. If little Isobel is knocked out first, you can prevent her throwing a fit by saying 'Never mind, Isobel, you can come and stand with me and help me be a judge because I cannot keep my eyes on everybody at once'. When you eliminate the next person, make Isobel feel she is part of it by saying 'I think Sammy moved then don't you, Isobel? Sorry Sammy, you're out, but you can come over here and join Isobel and me as judges'.
* When you have a few fellow judges, ask them if they saw anybody move. You do not necessarily have to follow the advice. You can always say 'No, I was watching him. I don't think he moved. Let's carry on with the music'. With luck, all the children will participate until the end.

Pass the parcel

Age range 5+
Number of players Any number
Good for Entertaining young children, with the prospect of a prize
What you will need A record, tape or CD player; three or four sheets of wrapping paper; a small prize

This is a traditional game that many of the children will know already.

Preparation

Take the prize, which may be a small box of sweets and wrap it in a piece of the wrapping paper, using just enough paper to wrap it adequately. Seal the package with something easily removed, such as one piece of sticky tape, or if the shape of the package allows, two elastic bands. The idea is that one layer of packaging can be removed by the children without tearing any layers below.

Continue to re-wrap the package, alternating the patterns of wrapping paper and sealing each layer until the prize has been wrapped up at least a dozen times.

How to play

The children sit around in a circle and one is given the package. When the music starts, the parcel is passed, usually to the right, from child to child. When the music stops, the child holding the parcel unwraps the first layer of wrapping. The music resumes, the parcel is passed again and each time the music stops, the child holding the package unwraps one layer.

Eventually the last layer is unwrapped to reveal the prize, which the child who unwrapped it keeps.

Give all a chance

* In this game, it helps if the adult operating the music can see the children so can continue to give as many of them as possible a chance to unwrap a layer. Another supervising adult will need to see that nobody holds the parcel too long, and also to decide who unwraps it when the music stops in mid-hand-over.
* A variation is sometimes adopted where each layer contains a small prize, say a small packet of sweets, while the final unwrapping reveals a bigger prize.

Age range 5+
Number of players Seven or more
Good for A mixed age group
What you will need A banana; a means of playing music (a record, tape or CD player)

Banana relay

This game requires bluffing and children will enjoy fooling the 'piggy in the middle', but the game can be played by all ages, including adults.

How to play

Somebody is selected by any means (drawing straws, volunteering or being told) to be the first piggy in the middle, while the others sit round him shoulder to shoulder in a circle or semicircle, with their hands behind their backs. The more in the circle the better: six is about the minimum. One of the players is handed the banana in front of the others.

The person operating the music begins. When the music starts, the player with the banana passes it behind his back to the next player. She in turn passes it on. However, at any stage the player passing the banana on needn't do so. He can fake to pass it on. Of course, the next player must pretend to pass it on, even if he didn't receive it.

The player in the middle cannot see behind the backs of the others, and must try to guess by their movements who actually has the banana.

Any player who has had the banana passed to him (whether he has it or not) can pass it (or pretend to) one way and then pass it (or pretend to) the other way. The player in the middle must decide whether the movement is genuine or fake.

When the music ends, the player in the middle must decide who has the banana. If he is right, he changes places with the player with the banana. If he is wrong, the player with the banana shows it and the music starts again.

If the player in the middle gets it wrong three times, he still changes with the player holding the banana.

Hide and seek

Age range 6+
Number of players Any number
Good for Parties of young children
What you will need A house with lots of potential hiding places; a watchful eye to make sure children don't wander where they shouldn't; the game can also be played outside

Hide and Seek is a game that hardly merits description, since all children know it from a young age. However, it is surprising how old some children get before they grasp the idea of hiding themselves. Even when they have 'got it', they often cannot stay hidden long – they need to be in the action.

How to play

One child is the seeker. She stands in a corner facing the wall with her eyes shut and counts to 50 while the others hide about the house. On reaching 50, she calls 'I'm coming' and goes off to seek. Anyone found retires from the game, and the game ends when all are found. The first to be found becomes the seeker for the next game. If before being found a hider can slip back to the starting corner without being seen and call out 'I'm home', the game ends and the seeker has to be the seeker once more.

One, two, three, four ... fifty!

I'm coming!

Warning
* There might be places where you do not want young children to hide, such as wardrobes containing expensive clothes. You should make sure the players know of any 'out of bounds' places before they set off.

Variation
* One person can hide, while all the others become seekers. The seekers remain in the room and count up to 50 while the 'fugitive' hides. The seekers then split up and hunt for the fugitive. The seeker who finds the fugitive becomes the fugitive next time round.

Age range 6–10
Number of players Any number
Good for A party of youngsters where a quiet interlude would be welcomed
What you will need A room containing plenty of objects

I-spy

This is a game in which children need to know how to spell. If any participants are not able to spell, the sound of the first letter can be given to the children rather than the letter itself.

How to play

The children sit in a room together. One of them chooses any object in the room that is visible to all, and cries out 'I spy with my little eye, something beginning with ...' And she names a letter.

The other children look round and name things they can see beginning with that letter. The first to guess the chosen object becomes the chooser for the next round.

If the game goes on too long, a supervising adult should suggest that a clue be given, and ask questions intended to narrow the field. These could include 'Is it hanging on the wall?' 'Is it on the floor?' 'Is it on a cabinet?' 'Could you tell us its colour?' or 'Is it make of wood?'

If the object still remains unguessed, there is the possibility that the child has made a mistake and that the object doesn't begin with the letter announced at all, so the supervisor should suggest that everybody gives in.

The chooser then announces the object and is allowed to choose another. If a mistake has been made, it can be tactfully pointed out (and any derision of the other children halted) and the chooser can still have another turn.

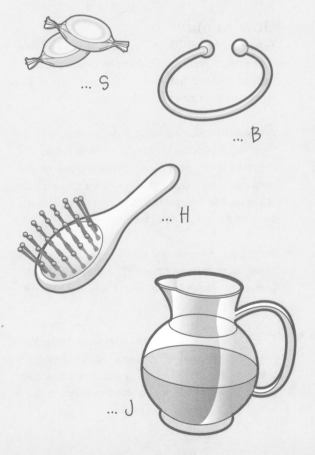

... S

... B

... H

... J

Department store

Age range 8+
Number of players Eight or more (in teams)
Good for A game for all ages that promotes fun and cooperation
What you will need The cooperation of players who might need to take off their socks or bracelets; a pencil and paper

This is based on an adult game where players have to supply the customer from their own resources, no matter how intimate the required items might be. Children can collect items from anybody present, as they will not be expected to have them all.

How to play

Two teams are chosen, one positioned at one side of the room, one at the other. The teams should each contain old and young, males and females. They represent department store assistants.

A customer (you or another adult) enters with a shopping list (which for convenience could be prepared in advance). He sits halfway between the teams and reads out the things he wants, one item at a time. The first person to bring the item to the customer scores a point for her side.

Items could be what the teams might have on them (a pair of shoes, a wristwatch) or they could be something that will have to be found and brought from within the house.

Only those under a certain age (you must decide what it is, with your players in mind) can bring things to the customer, so if a watch is demanded, an adult must give it to a child to deliver.

Tick off the shopping list with ticks for one side and crosses for the other. The team with the most points wins. An odd number of items on the shopping list will ensure a winner.

Some suggested items
* A pair of children's shoes
* A pair of white or red socks
* A lady's wristwatch
* A bunch of keys
* A patterned tea towel
* A knife, fork and spoon (all rush to the kitchen)
* A bracelet
* A magazine
* A child's hairclip
* An apple
* A man's belt
* A chocolate

Age range 8–12
Number of players Any number
Good for A quiet interlude, where the only noise made is sniffing
What you will need Ten plastic or paper bags with holes in them; ten strongly smelling objects; a sheet of paper and a pencil for each player

Bloodhounds

This is called a hunting game because the players pretend to be bloodhounds, identifying items by their smell.

Preparation

Find ten quite small but strongly smelling objects such as a sprig of lavender or a piece of smelly cheese, and put each into a bag with small holes to release the smell. Tie the bags and place them at intervals around the edge of a table, numbering them by means of a piece of paper 1 to 10. Draw up sheets of paper with the numbers 1 to 10 written down the left-hand side.

How to play

Give each player a prepared sheet of paper and a pencil. The players walk round the table attempting to identify each smell and writing what it is on their sheets. They are not allowed to touch the bags. When everyone has been round the table, open the bags and show everybody the contents. The player with the most correct guesses is the winner.

Some suggested items

* Lavender
* Curry powder
* A strong-smelling cheese
* A bar of soap
* A cut onion
* A piece of rag or cotton wool soaked in vinegar
* A cut orange, or some peel
* A very smelly sock
* Some chocolate sweets
* A few strong peppermint sweets

Find the other half

Age range 6+
Number of players Any number
Good for Getting people at a party to get to know each other
What you will need The pictures from some of your old Christmas cards

This is a game that will help your guests get to know each other as they have to mingle. It will eventually provide two 'winners'.

Preparation

In a way, this needs planning well in advance because you need a stock of old Christmas cards. Take those of a more or less equal shape and size, cut off the front (containing the picture) and cut each picture in half. Each guest at the party will need half a card, so you can estimate how many cards to cut up.

How to play

Each player is given half of a Christmas card. If you have an even number of players, you must ensure that two of those halves will not match up with another half. All the players then mingle and try to find the player with the other half of their card. When they do, they bring both halves to you and go into the next round. When all cards are matched up, there will be left the two players who had the unmatched cards. They are eliminated. You then shuffle the cards, remove one and repeat the exercise for those still playing, remembering to ensure that two halves of cards are unmatched. Change the two unmatched half-cards each round. Two players get eliminated each round, and the last pair are the winners.

Odd number of players

* If you start with an odd number of players, you will want to eliminate one only on the first round, so distribute just one half-card that cannot be matched. After the first round, proceed as above, eliminating two players each round.

Hunt the shoe

Age range 4–6
Number of players Eight or more
Good for Young children to take part in a simple guessing game
What you will need A child's shoe

If you are hosting a party for very young children, you can get them together into a manageable state with this game.

How to play

All but one of the children sit in a circle as close as possible to each other, the odd one sitting in the centre. The child in the centre is given a shoe. All the children (including the one in the centre) recite the following rhyme:

'Cobbler, cobbler, mend my shoe,
Have it done by half past two.'

While this is being recited, the child in the centre hands the shoe to one of the children in the circle. She then closes her eyes and covers them with her hands.

The children now start passing the shoe from one to another behind their backs round the circle. As they are doing this, all recite:

'Cobbler, cobbler, tell me true,
Which of you has got my shoe?'

Whoever is holding the shoe when the word 'shoe' is reached keeps hold of the shoe behind her back. The centre child then opens her eyes and guesses from the expressions and giggles which child has the shoe. She is allowed two guesses. If she gets it right, she stays in the centre. If not, she changes places with whoever is holding the shoe.

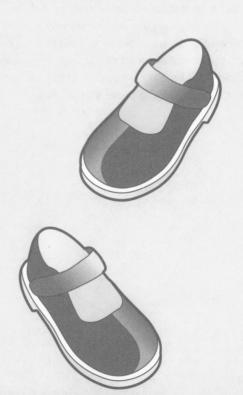

Card for card

Age range 8–12
Number of players Any number
Good for A party of children who can recognize playing cards
What you will need Two packs of playing cards; a score-sheet and a pencil

In this game each child has a playing card from one pack of cards and he goes round the house searching for the identical card from another pack, which you have hidden.

Preparation

One pack of playing cards, or as many cards as you think necessary for the number of children (about four cards per child) should be placed around the house in easily visible positions. It might be best to restrict the cards to one or two rooms that the children would not go in without invitation, otherwise all the cards will be spotted before you begin the game. Keep a list of the cards distributed and put aside from the other pack of playing cards the equivalent cards to those lying around.

How to play

Give each player a playing card from the second pack and, on the command 'Go', send the children off to find the matching card from those that you have spread around. When a player finds a match to his card, he brings both cards to you and you write his name against that card on your checklist. You then give him another card to try and match.

When all cards are found and returned to you, add up each score and announce the winner.

Age range 8–12
Number of players Any number
Good for Entertaining children in a quiet manner
What you will need About six lengths of wool of different colours; scissors; a tape measure; prizes (optional)

Gathering wool

This game has the benefit of allowing you to get rid of all those odd lengths of different coloured wool that you've kept for several years and that are never going to be used for anything except this simple children's game.

Preparation

The pieces of wool must be cut into lengths, but not necessarily all the same length – anything between 15–30 cm (6–12 in). There should be perhaps six to ten lengths for every child you expect to be playing. These lengths are hidden about the house, where part or all of them can be plainly seen. Locations could include poking out from under a curtain or rug, sticking out from the pages of a book or magazine, hanging from a drawer, curled up on the floor or hanging from a door-knob. Remember they must all be seen (it is unnecessary for anyone to open drawers) and they must be reachable by all.

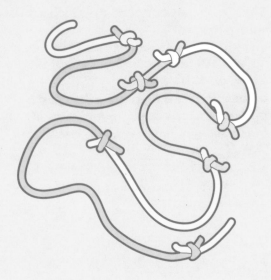

How to play

Get all the players together (if you have more than eight you might divide them into pairs) and, on the command 'Go', they must go and search for the wool. When they have two pieces, they must immediately be tied together and every subsequent piece must also be tied on. The object is to get the longest piece of wool, so the knots should be as small as they can be made.

At a given time, call a halt and measure each length of wool to find the winner. If you are giving prizes, there could be a secondary prize for the player who has collected most pieces of the same colour.

Memory game

Age range 7+
Number of players Any number
Good for Providing a quiet period in parties where players must concentrate

This game tests players' memories. If all your players are of a similar age, you can play the game as individuals. If the players are of differing ages – and it is assumed older people (up to a limit) will be better at it – then the game can be played in teams of two or three, with an older and younger person in each.

Preparation
On a tray, spread out up to 20 small objects and cover them with a cloth.

Variation
* Later in the party, when the items on the tray have been dispersed, you can assemble the teams, hand out pencils and paper, and ask them how many of the original items on the tray they can remember.

Some suggested items
* A watch
* A shoe lace
* A corkscrew
* A pair of nail scissors
* An elastic band
* A screw
* A ball-point pen
* A small photograph
* A key
* A ring
* A coin
* A tube of toothpaste
* A matchstick
* A tin of shoe polish
* A piece of chocolate
* A biscuit
* A walnut
* A marble
* A small piece of string
* A feather

What you will need A large tray; a cloth to cover it; about 20 small objects; a sheet of paper and a pencil for each player or team; a stopwatch or watch with a second hand

How to play

Arrange teams if required. Give each individual or team paper and pencil. Produce the covered tray and tell them that you have a tray on which there are a number of objects. Tell them you propose to remove the cloth for 45 seconds, during which time they must remember as many objects as they can. You will then cover the tray again, and they will have four minutes to write down every item they can remember. There is to be no writing down during the memorizing period.

Look at your watch and, at a time suitable to you, uncover the tray. After 45 seconds, cover the tray again, and ask them to write down all the items they can remember. Call time after four minutes and make sure nobody adds to the list after that.

Uncover the tray. The winners are those who have correctly remembered most objects.

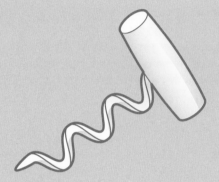

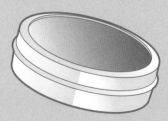

Follow-up game

* Collect all the sheets of paper.
* Tell your audience you are going to take the tray into the other room for a minute. Do so, and remove about five of the items.
* Return with the covered tray. Hand out to each team or individual a fresh sheet of paper. Tell them that you have removed five objects and that when you uncover the tray they have four minutes to write down what they are.
* After four minutes, cover the tray and ask if anyone has got all five. If not, ask if anyone has four, then three and so on. The winning team or individual is the one that has correctly remembered most.

What is it?

Age range 9+
Number of players Any number (in teams)
Good for Entertaining a group of children over the age of about 9, as well as adults – all can compete together

This game's success depends mostly on the things that you put in the bowls. At best these can inspire bewilderment, squeamishness or horror, but with luck all the players will be fascinated at the denouement.

Preparation

It is best if you can prepare the bowls before the party begins and keep them out of sight of the players. You should at least have all the items for the bowls ready.

Fill the bowls with things that players can identify by touch. Some can be fairly straightforward: a bowl of paperclips, for example, is easy to identify. Other bowls could have things a bit more difficult, such as unusual breakfast cereal or some blades of grass. Some could contain liquids, pure orange juice, for example, which could be identified by smelling the fingers dipped in it; a bowl might have something slimy in it, like cold custard. If you knew your guests well, you could put a couple of earthworms in a bowl. This should induce some shrieks from some, but of course you'd have to watch that they (the worms) don't escape.

How to play

You will need three or four adults not in the game to help supervise, since the players themselves will be blindfolded.

Set the bowls, each covered with a cloth, around three sides of a table. Tell the players you are going to blindfold them, remove the covers from the bowls, and that they are going to go round the table feeling the contents of each bowl, deciding what is in them, and remembering them. Tell them that as some of the bowls might contain wet or sticky objects you are going to give each a piece of kitchen roll for wiping their fingers. Tell them that also smelling their fingers might help after feeling some of the items.

Explain that at the end, when all the players have been round, you are going to cover the bowls again and remove their blindfolds. Then they have to write down the contents of as many of the bowls as they can remember.

The player who remembers correctly the contents of most bowls wins. After the game, you can show the contents of the bowls to the players.

What you will need A number of fruit bowls, basins, dessert dishes or the like (preferably a couple or so more than the number of players); various items to fill them (see below) and cloths to cover them with; blindfolds; a sheet of paper; a pencil; and a piece of kitchen roll or similar for each player

Some suggested items

* Breadcrumbs
* Holly leaves (prickly)
* Feathers
* Rice pudding (sticky)
* Cut up rubber bands
* Used tea leaves
* Baked beans (slimy)
* Small toy furry mouse
* Nails
* Cherry tomatoes
* Shredded paper
* Sand

Twenty questions

Age range 9+
Number of players Any number (in teams)
Good for A party of brainy types

This is a game that ran for many years on the radio and made one or two people quite famous. It is sometimes called Animal, Vegetable or Mineral.

How to play

Players are divided into two teams (they need not be exactly equal as an extra person on a team doesn't matter). The two teams sit roughly facing each other.

One team is the team setting the puzzle and the other team is the questioning team. The first decides amongst itself on some subject, which can be a person (living or dead, real or fictional), an object or a place. This can be general, for instance 'a shop', or it can be specific, such as the name of an actual shop local to you.

They tell the questioning team whether the subject is animal, vegetable or mineral, or sometimes a combination. Most things come under one of these categories (see right). It makes it easier if other abstract things are not chosen.

It is also helpful to say how many words there are in the subject to be guessed, and if any are the definite article (the) or indefinite article (a, an). For example if the subject is 'a black cat', you would say 'Animal, three words including the indefinite article'.

Categories
* **Animal** This covers all animal life, from insects to human beings, and anything that derives from it. Examples: a racehorse, a slug, Britney Spears, milk, a cat's paw, a toe nail, Lassie, a boiled egg, leather shoes.
* **Vegetable** This covers everything in the realm of plants and trees and things that derive from them. Examples: a chestnut, breakfast cereal, a Christmas tree, mistletoe, carrots.
* **Mineral** This covers inorganic, inanimate things such as stone, iron, glass and anything made of them. Examples: a Ferrari, the Eiffel Tower, a diamond ring, a horseshoe, the Golden Gate Bridge.
* **Combination** Sometimes a subject can best be described as a combination, thus Nelson's Column might be said to be 'mineral, with animal connections'.

What you will need An authoritative manner (or authoritative friend) to cool down disputes over misleading answers to questions

The guessing team have 20 questions in which to find the subject. Each question must be of the kind that can be answered either 'Yes' or 'No'.

Any of the questioning team can ask a question. A usual line of questioning, if the subject is animal, might take the form:

'Is it human?'	*'Yes, one'.*
'Male?'	*'No, two'.*
'Female?'	*'Yes, three'.*
'Living?'	*'No, four'.*
'A particular person?'	*'Yes, five'.*
'Famous?'	*'Yes, six'.*
'In show business?'	*'Yes, seven'.*

And so on. In seven questions, the team will know they are looking for a dead woman or girl who was famous in show business.

If the questioning team fails to discover the subject within its 20 questions, the posing team thinks of another subject. If the questioning team succeeds, however, the roles are reversed.

Spoof

Age range 10+
Number of players 3–8
Good for A relaxing interval between more exacting games, for instance while taking a drink
What you will need Three identical small objects for each player such as coins, counters, draughtsmen or pebbles

This is a game in which each player guesses how many objects are concealed in the fists of all the players, himself included. Guesses can be high or low, based on other players' guesses, but remember everybody is free to indulge in a bit of bluff.

How to play

All players are given three coins each.

Each player conceals in his fist as many of his three coins as he wishes: the number could be 0, 1, 2 or 3. The object is to guess the total number of coins hidden in the fists of the players.

Any player can volunteer to be first guesser on the first round, after which the privilege of being first guesser passes to the left. All the players then conceal a number of coins in whichever fist they prefer and hold that fist out over the table. Any coins not being held in the fist are held in the other hand under the table. The first player then states how many coins he thinks are held collectively by all the fists on the table. If there are five players, this could be between 0 (all fists holding no coins) and 15 (all holding three). The second player guesses a different number (it is not allowed for two players to guess the same number) and so on until all have guessed. The fists are then opened, and the correct guesser scores a point. If nobody is correct, no points are scored. The first person to reach an agreed number of points is the winner.

Players will tend to call higher or lower according to the number of coins in their own hand, but it sometimes pays to bluff.

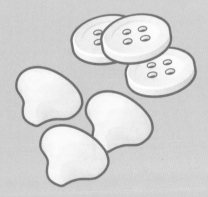

Variation
* The game can be played to find a loser rather than a winner. When a player guesses correctly, he drops out. The last player remaining is the loser.

Age range 8+
Number of players Six, eight or ten
(in two teams)
Good for Entertaining a group of
boisterous children
What you will need A long table to
seat three, four or five on each side; a
small object such as a marble or coin

Up Jenkins!

This is an old-established game requiring a little dexterity and bluffing. It can be quite hilarious.

How to play

Two teams sit on opposite sides of the table. Team captains toss for who is first to bluff. The winning side has the 'tippit' – a small object such as a marble.

The tippit is shown to the guessing side and is then passed by the bluffing side from hand to hand under the table, while they try to confuse the other side as to the whereabouts of the tippit. The captain of the guessing side eventually calls 'Up Jenkins!' and all the bluffing side raise their fists into the air. Then the guessing captain calls 'Down Jenkins!' and the fists are dropped to the table, with the back of the hand upwards. The hands are then spread flat, with palms on the table, beneath one of which is, of course, the tippit.

The guessing side now has to guess which hand conceals the tippit. First, half the hands are eliminated by each member of the guessing side pointing in turn to one of the hands he thinks doesn't hide the tippit, and saying 'Take that hand away'. If a hand is chosen that does contain the tippit, then the guessing side has lost. If, however, all goes well, and half the hands are removed, then the captain must choose, after consultation with his team, which remaining hand does hide the tippit.

If the guessing side finds the tippit, it wins and scores a point. It takes over the tippit and becomes the bluffing side. If it fails, the bluffing side scores a point and retains the tippit for the next round. The winning side is the first to an agreed number of points, usually one more than the number of players taking part.

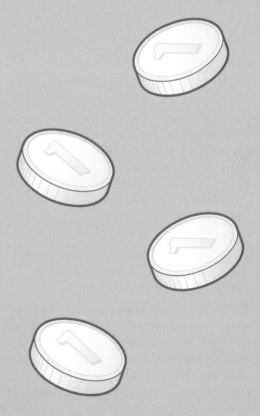

What's in the sock?

Age range 6+
Number of players Any number
(in teams)
Good for Family parties
What you will need Two large socks
(which cannot be seen through); a number
of objects to fill them; a sheet of paper
and a pencil for each team; a stopwatch

This is a little like the racing game
Emptying the Sock, but it is not a race –
it is designed to test how well players can
identify things, and then how good their
memory is.

Preparation
Fill the large socks with the same number of objects
– at least twice as many as there are players. Avoid
sharp objects.

How to play
Divide the players into two teams (they do not have
to be exactly equal). Each team must appoint a
captain. Hand a sock to each captain. Each team has
five minutes to try to identify and remember as
many objects as they can by feel. They can either all
feel the sock together and discuss their guesses, or
hand the sock round.

After five minutes, tell the teams to keep
remembering the objects, and change the socks
over. Teams have another five minutes to identify as
many objects as they can in the other sock.

When the time is up, take the socks and hand out
to the captains a pencil and paper. The teams have
another five minutes to recall as many objects as
possible. It is not necessary to specify which sock
the objects were in. The team with the most
correct items wins the game.

Some suggested items
* A ring
* A pebble
* A watch
* A piece of string
* A toothbrush
* A lipstick case
* A roll of sticky tape
* A coin
* A door key
* A bulldog clip
* A jar of jam
* An orange
* A comb
* A birthday card
* A beer bottle top
* A shoe polish tin
* A cork
* A nail brush
* A glasses case
* A plastic cup

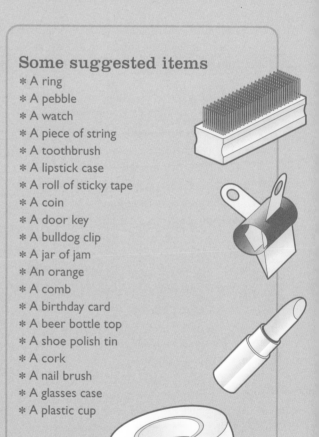

Age range 6–8
Number of players Any number
Good for Sitting children together quietly for a few minutes
What you will need A long piece of string; a ring

Ring on a string

This is a quiet, sitting-down game in which the child in the middle must guess which of the other children is holding a ring. The other children try to make it as difficult as possible, of course.

Preparation

A ring is threaded onto a piece of string and the two ends of the string are tied. Make sure the knot isn't too large to allow the ring to pass over it.

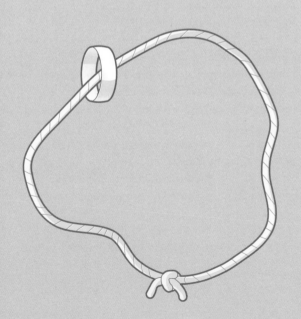

How to play

The string holding the ring is spread in a circle on the floor. One child is chosen to sit in the middle, while the others sit round her, taking the string that passes through all their hands. One of the children takes the ring in her fist. The child in the middle knows where the ring is.

On the word 'Go' from a supervising adult, the child holding the ring passes it (or pretends to) to the child next to her, who passes it from one hand to another before passing it on (or pretending to). It can be passed either way, and go backwards or forwards. The child in the centre must try to keep track of the ring, and decide whether any of the passes was faked.

After a few passes, the adult says 'Stop' and the child in the middle must guess who is now holding the ring. If she is correct, she changes place with the ring holder; if wrong, she stays in the middle for another turn. After three unsuccessful turns, another player can volunteer to change places.

Who am I?

Age range 12+
Number of players Any number
Good for Mixed-age family parties when the younger children have gone to bed

This is an interesting game that can prove very frustrating. Each player is given an identity which he has to discover by asking questions. It is amazing how difficult it is to guess your own identity when everybody else's seems so easy.

How to play

There is no preparation needed beforehand. Each player is given a sticky note upon which he writes the identity of a well-known character, either real or fictional, alive or dead. The character need not be human – it could be, say, Lassie, or a cartoon character like Bugs Bunny.

Each player places his sticky note on the forehead of another player so that eventually everybody has the name of a character of some sort stuck on their forehead. Each player, of course, knows the identity of every other player, but not his own.

Players arrange themselves roughly in a circle (they usually stay in the chair they were already sitting in).

One player starts by asking questions of the others with a view to finding out who he is. The questions can only be of the sort to be answered 'Yes' or 'No'. Occasionally, though, the answer is not clear-cut, and the other players must answer as best they can. They must be helpful to the questioner and not deliberately deceive.

While the questioner gets 'Yes' for an answer he continues questioning. If he gets a 'No', his turn passes, and the player on his left begins to ask questions likewise.

Eventually a player feels confident enough to name who he thinks he is, and if he is right he unpeels his sticker and enjoys the admiration of the others. If wrong, his turn passes to the left as usual.

The sort of questions to ask are: 'Am I human?', 'Am I alive?', 'Am I a man?' or 'Am I a celebrity?'

Madonna

What you will need A sticky note and
a pencil for each player

Some suggested identities
* Harry Potter
* Elizabeth Taylor
* William Shakespeare
* Robin Hood
* Mickey Mouse
* Tony Blair
* Gandhi
* Napoleon
* Woody Allen
* Marge Simpson
* Justin Timberlake
* Charlie Chaplin
* George W. Bush
* Lance Armstrong
* Fred Flintstone
* Pelé

The killer wink

Age range 8+
Number of players Any number
Good for Mixed parties of adults and older children, including dinner parties
What you will need A pack of cards

This game is best played during a lull, such as if the table has to be cleared or if it's time to pass round a box of chocolates. It can also be played while another game is being prepared or while everybody is talking around the dinner table after a meal.

How to play

The host takes a number of cards from a pack, to equal the number of players. One of the cards must be the Ace of spades, the card of death.

The cards are shuffled and one is handed face down to each player. The players secretly look at their cards, without letting anybody else see which card they have, and pass the cards back to the host. One of them will have received the Ace of spades. She is the killer.

As normal activity resumes (such as passing the chocolates or the resumption of chatting), the killer sets about her murders. To commit a murder, the

killer must wink at a victim as surreptitiously as possible, hoping nobody else notices. The victim waits a few seconds (so as not to make the identity of the killer obvious) and then, with suitable yells, moans, gurgles, throat clutching or other histrionics, sinks to the floor (or slumps back on his chair) dead. Would-be actors or other exhibitionists will like this part.

The job of the killer is to kill as many as possible without being caught. The killer is caught when another player thinks he has spotted the killer wink at her victim. The spotter announces he knows the killer, at which point all those not dead must close their eyes. The accused then touches the person he thinks is the killer and returns to his place, when everyone can open their eyes. If he is right, the game ends with the killer apprehended, but if he is wrong, he takes no further part in the game and the killer seeks out more victims.

Age range 6+
Number of players Any
Ideal for Getting people to know each other at the beginning of a party
What you will need Sticky notes (one for each player), about eight cocktail sticks or similar small items for each player

Odd or even

This game is a good one for those parties where perhaps some people are meeting others for the first time. It makes everybody circulate and meet each other, addressing each other by name so they soon get to know each other.

Preparation
Write the name of each party guest on a sticky note (or have a pencil and labels handy so guests can write their own names) and arrange your cocktail sticks into piles of eight. In the absence of cocktail sticks, beans or pebbles would suffice.

How to play
Hand each guest the label containing his or her name and a pile of eight cocktail sticks.

Players circulate and, using the label, address each other by their names. Suppose James approaches Sylvia. He takes some or all his sticks in his fist and says to her 'Sylvia, odd or even?' If Sylvia guesses correctly she takes one of James's cocktail sticks. If she is wrong, she hands James one of hers. Then, taking some of her sticks in her fist, she says 'James, odd or even?', and another stick changes hands according to the accuracy of James's guess.

After five minutes or so, when everybody has had time to meet everybody else, the host calls a halt and the player with the most sticks is the winner.

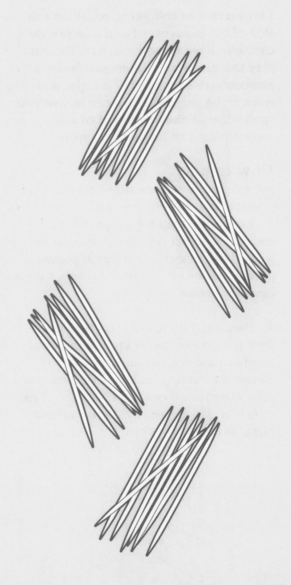

The horror game

Age range 12+
Number of players As many as can comfortably sit round a table
Good for A quiet period in a small party

The success of this game relies on the skill of the presenter (you!). So prepare carefully, have a good story ready and play the game only when you feel the atmosphere of the party is right; you want to be sure that you can weave your spell without the likelihood of silly interruptions to break the tension.

How to play
Seat the guests around the table. Place a baby wipe in front of each. You, with your box of props, should be at the head of the table with your props in a covered box at your feet. Nobody must see the props. The room should be as dark as possible, perhaps with the curtains drawn and lit by a single candle in a corner.

Tell the guests that you have recently discovered some gruesome remains of a body in the loft of your house and that they correspond with a rumour of a murder you heard about some time ago – which you will now relate. You then tell your story in as spine-chilling a manner as you can. A suggested framework follows.

Warning
* Do not invite young children to take part, and warn others that if they are of a particularly nervous disposition perhaps they should sit this one out.

'According to the rumour, a strange man who lived somewhere in this area claimed to have murdered a young tramp, and to escape detection had dismembered the body and hidden some parts of it in a cardboard box, which was never found. Well, I found what could be this box in the attic. According to the murderer, he first chopped off the victim's head and then cut out the eyes, and two things in the box look like decaying eyes. I'll pass them round under the table. [You pass round the two tomatoes]. Don't squeeze them too hard, because you don't want eyeball all over your fingers! What do you think? I have to pass them under the table because if you saw the eyes looking at you you'd faint.'

When the tomatoes are nearly back to you, resume the story.

What you will need Some of the following: a candle; a packet of baby wipes; two hard cherry tomatoes; a piece of rubber shaped like a tongue; two dried figs; a lock of hair; a damp sponge; two carrots; rubber gloves; a beetroot; a towel; a table with an overlapping plastic tablecloth

'He also removed the tongue, which I will pass round now. [Pass the piece of rubber round]. As you can feel, it has lost some of its flexibility over the years, and has hardened up a little, but you can still see traces of dried blood round the base. I'll let anyone who wants to examine it do so afterwards, but I warn you, it's not a pretty sight.'

Continue in this manner with the other objects.

The dried figs (or apricots) represent the ears. A lock of hair is, of course, a lock of hair. The squeamish will be especially horrified when you describe how the head was severed so that the killer could keep the brain. You must say, as you pass round the slightly damp sponge:

'Be careful with the brain. Although it has dried out somewhat, it's still a bit squashy and parts might come off and I wouldn't like any of you to find a bit of brain left stuck to your fingers afterwards.'

Tell your listeners that once the killer had dealt with the head, he turned his attention to smaller items of the torso. Pass round the carrots ('He took off the big toes') and the rubber gloves filled with soft earth and taped so that the earth cannot spill ('The hands are particularly

interesting, and show the victim was probably quite young').

This could be the end of the story, but there is an optional extra: the beetroot. The beetroot is the heart, but of course beetroots stain, and you will not want to stain the clothes of your listeners, or your tablecloth (which is why a plastic one is suggested). So if you use the beetroot, wrap it in a towel. Say:

'Lastly, the murderer removed the heart. Because some blood is not quite dried, I've wrapped it in a towel so that the blood will not stain your clothes. Be sure not to let the heart touch your clothes. When you've passed it on, wipe your hands on the baby wipe in front of you, as you wouldn't want to go home with blood on your hands.'

After the game
* To prevent the possibility of more sensitive guests having nightmares later, let them see the various body parts afterwards, when hopefully they will get the colour back into their cheeks and have a laugh about it all.

Murder in the dark

Age range 8+
Number of players Any number
Good for A party of mixed ages, best played in the evening when the lights can be switched off

This game is best played in a room large enough for people to move about in and it helps if the lights are out. The lights go on when the detective enters to solve the dastardly crime.

How to play

Once you know how many players are going to take part, you take that number of playing cards from the pack, ensuring that the cards you take include just one Ace and one Jack, the rest of the cards being ordinary cards from the two to the ten.

Shuffle the cards and ask each player to take one, not showing it to the others. Explain that the person who has the Jack is the murderer and the player who has the Ace is the detective.

Collect the cards and then ask the detective to reveal himself. Explain how the game works, which is as follows:

The detective goes out of the room and waits just outside the door. The lights in the room are switched off. The players are requested to move around the room (but if grandad and grandma are sitting in chairs they can stay there).

After a few seconds, the murderer (who is unknown to anybody but himself, remember) taps a victim on the shoulder and whispers 'I am the murderer and you are now dead'. The victim screams and lays down on the floor dead (or

The detective

* The success of this game is largely due to the detective, who shouldn't just ask a perfunctory question or two and then make a guess. He can ask questions like: 'Why are you looking shifty?', 'Did you dislike the victim?', 'Do you think a man or a woman did it?', 'What was your motive in killing him?', 'Have you moved since the murder?' or 'You look a suspicious character ... was it you?'.
* It is likely, of course, that many players will know who the murderer is (since the room might not be completely blacked out) so the detective is not allowed to ask questions like 'Where is the murderer standing now?'.

remains sitting comfortably in his armchair and feigns death).

When the scream is heard, all players must stand still where they are. Only the murderer is allowed to glide quickly away to another part of the room (if he wishes).

When the detective outside the door hears the scream, he counts to five (to allow the murderer to move) and enters the room, switching on the lights. He examines the corpse and begins to question anybody present in an effort to find the murderer.

During the questioning, only the murderer can tell a lie. All the others have to answer the detective truthfully.

Eventually the detective must decide who he thinks committed the murder and he must make an arrest by saying to the suspect 'I am arresting you for the dreadful murder of John Jones (naming the victim)'. If the detective is right, the killer confesses. If he is wrong, the right killer can now reveal himself, and if all agree, shuffle the cards and choose a new detective and murderer.

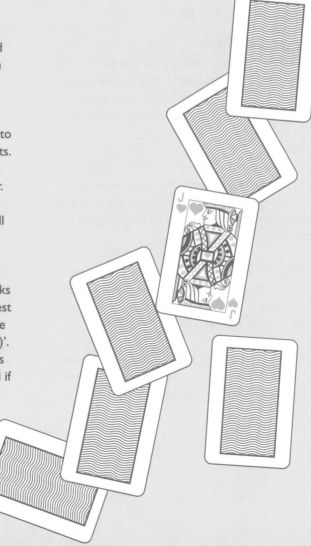

Squeak, piggy, squeak

Age range 6+
Number of players Any number
Good for Children's birthday parties, when all are of similar age and are reasonably well acquainted with each other
What you will need A chair for each player; a cushion; a blindfold

This game promotes physical contact between the participants and brings them all into the game.

How to play

One child is chosen and is given a cushion and then blindfolded. The blindfolded child is turned round three times in the centre of the room while the other children sit on chairs around the room.

He then feels his way around the room until he finds somebody sitting on a chair. Putting the cushion on her lap and sitting down on it, he says 'Squeak, piggy, squeak'. The child on the chair has to squeak like a pig, and can be asked to repeat the squeak.

He must then guess whose lap he is sitting on. If he is right, that player becomes the guesser for the next round; if not, the guesser must find another player to sit upon and guess again.

When a new guesser is blindfolded, the children quickly change seats. If a guesser is wrong three times, then another guesser is chosen.

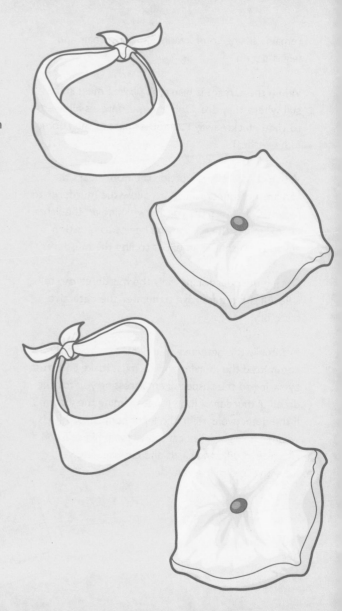

Age range 7+
Number of players 8+
Ideal for Livening up children's parties after a quiet game or two
What you will need Four sturdy chairs, a pack of cards

Royal court

This is a shouting and dashing game. The players need to be able to recognize the four suits in a pack of cards.

How to play

This game is best for 16 players. If you have this number, place the four chairs in the four corners of an imaginary square, facing inwards. The players stand facing inwards on the imaginary lines forming the square, with four players between each chair.

Remove from a pack of cards the Ace, King, Queen and Jack of each suit. Shuffle the 16 cards and spread them face down on the floor in the centre. On the command 'Go', each player grabs a card. A player who picks up an Ace runs to sit on a chair, calling out 'Ace of ...', adding whichever suit he has.

The other players whose cards are of the same suit go to his chair. The holder of the King sits on his knees with his feet on the floor, the holder of the Queen sits on that player's knees and the holder of the Jack on the third player's knees.

The first team to be seated correctly is the winner.

For other numbers

* If the number of players is divisible by three but not four (so 9, 15, 18), you could dispense with a suit and a chair. The number sequence of cards to be used is also variable to suit the number of players. Instead of Ace to Jack, you could use Ace to Queen, ten or nine.

Warning

* The host should let the players know that care is to be taken when playing this game as it could be painful for a 7-year-old if he gets the Ace and three heavy adults suddenly pile on top of him!

Put a cork in it

Age range 10+
Number of players Any number (in teams)
Good for A funny interlude in a party that does not involve moving about
What you will need A wine bottle cork (2.5 cm/1 in high); a supply of small pieces of tissue paper, a pencil and paper

This is a game in which anyone above about 10 years old can participate. It should present a few laughs.

Preparation

Write a number of questions on separate pieces of paper, about twice as many as there will be players. Cut out the same number of pieces of tissue paper, each about 5 cm (2 in) square.

How to play

Divide the players into two teams (not necessarily equal) and seat them in two groups. Hand the first player the cork and a piece of tissue paper, which she wraps round it. She then places the cork upright between her top and bottom teeth. Hand her one of the questions. She then has to read this out, with the cork in her mouth. She might have to repeat it, perhaps more than once.

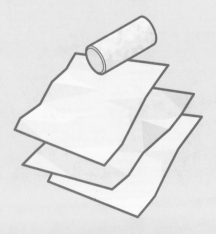

The first player from either team who correctly answers the question wins a point for the team.

When the question is answered, the cork and a fresh piece of tissue paper are handed to the first player from the second team, who reads out a second question. Continue until all members of both teams have read two questions. The team with the most points wins. An impartial referee (you) will need to decide who answers the question first.

Ten sample questions

* How old is dad?
* What was the artist Michelangelo's first name?
* Who is president of the United States?
* What is butter made from?
* Who invented the telescope?
* What have I got in my mouth?
* How much did my haircut cost?
* Who is married to Catherine Zeta-Jones?
* In which year did the First World War start?
* Who is sitting north-west of me?

Though some of these are not particularly hard questions, they might be difficult to ask with a cork in your mouth.

Age range 10+
Number of players 4–6
Ideal for A party with older people who want a quiet game
What you will need An empty wine bottle and a supply of matches or cocktail sticks (say 10 for each player)

Piling up matches

This game tests the steadiness of the hand and becomes more tense as more and more matches become balanced on the bottle.

How to play

Stand an empty wine bottle (the cork can be used in the previous game) in the centre of the table. The narrower the neck of the bottle the better. The players sit around the table, each holding ten matches.

The first player balances a match across the mouth of the wine bottle. This is not difficult. The second player does the same, then the third, and so on. Soon a number of matches are balanced more or less precariously on the bottle and it becomes more and more difficult to add another without disturbing those that are there. Sooner or later somebody will knock some matches off. A player who knocks matches from the bottle to the table must take the spilt matches into his hand, and the turn passes to the next player. The player who manages to get rid of all his matches first is the winner. Since there is an advantage in going first, on a second game the first player should be the player on the left of the player who started the previous game, thus giving each player a chance to go first.

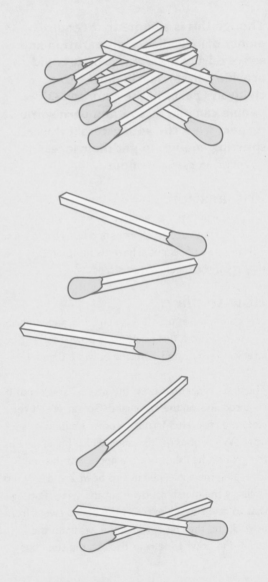

Dunking challenge

Age range 8+
Number of players Any number
Good for Children's parties, including playful not-so-young children

Though this is a game that requires plenty of ingredients, preparation and some tidying up afterwards, it could provide a hysterical highlight to a children's party in the summer. Older people can join in, too, and earn some respect from the youngsters if they're sporting enough to get their faces covered in syrup or flour.

Preparation

A timekeeper will be required, as well as two or more adults to act as referees and keep the 'course' tidy and free of potential hazards (it could become slippery if too much water is spilt).

How to play

The course is set up. Mark a start line, and at about 1.8 m (6 ft) from this point place bowl 1. At intervals of 90 cm (3 ft), place bowls 2, 3 and 4.

The first competitor dons the protective clothes if required and, on the command 'Go' (at which you start the stopwatch), runs to bowl 1 and kneels down. Without using his hands, which he keeps on the ground, he fishes out the apple with his teeth. Dropping the apple, he goes to bowl 2 and extracts similarly the marshmallow from the syrup. Putting that to one side, he extracts the boiled sweet from bowl 3, and then he extracts the egg from the custard in bowl 4. He runs back to the start line

Preparation steps

Step 1

plastic bowl + water + apple

Step 2

plastic bowl + syrup + marshmallow

Step 3

plastic bowl + flour + boiled sweets

Step 4

plastic bowl + custard + boiled eggs

What you will need Four large plastic bowls; three bags of flour; 3 litres (5 pints) of custard; two tins of syrup; clean water; an apple; a marshmallow; a boiled sweet and a peeled hard-boiled egg for each player; protective clothing (a suit of overalls or a plastic mac); a stopwatch; towels and a supply of water for cleaning-up purposes

where his time is taken and noted down by the timekeeper.

The competitor is allowed two minutes at each bowl. If he fails to extract an item from the bowl in two minutes, the timekeeper tells him to move on to the next bowl. Each 'missed' bowl incurs a two-minute time penalty.

After completing the course, the competitor is allowed to collect and keep his apple, his

marshmallow, his boiled sweet and his egg, although it is unlikely he will really want his custard-flavoured egg. Water and a towel should be at hand so that he can clean himself up.

A referee tidies the course, puts a new apple, marshmallow, boiled sweet and egg into the respective bowls, and the next competitor is ready to start.

Variation
* The game is perhaps better as a two-team game, but of course this requires another set of bowls and perhaps more syrup, flour and custard. When the first member of the team gets back to the start line, he touches the next member, who starts his run. As there is not therefore a gap between competitors, the referees must tidy and replenish the course as the race progresses. The timekeeper needs to set his watch when the first team completes the course and stop it when the second team completes. Provided the first finishers haven't cancelled out their winning margin by exceeding the second team's penalties, they are the winners.

Warning
* You should not press anybody to take part who is reluctant. Those with dentures shouldn't compete, nor those with smart clothes. Young girls might want to change out of their party dresses to compete. We suggest fresh apples and sweets for each competitor on hygiene grounds. Some people might still object to dunking their heads and mouths into bowls where others have gone before and their reservations should be respected.

Broken bottle

Age range 10+
Number of players Any number
Good for Outdoor parties where there is reasonable space to throw a ball
What you will need A tennis ball or a similar soft ball, plus a readiness to settle arguments as to whether a catch was a fair one or not

This is a catching game where every missed catch proves costly – a player who misses too many will find himself having to use one hand only, or making catches on his knees, until eventually he is out altogether.

How to play

Players form a circle, with one holding the ball, and proceed to throw the ball to each other. It is best if the ball is thrown across the circle rather than to someone close by. It is suggested that a rule be applied that a player must throw the ball to the player standing to the right of the one from whom he received it. In this way the ball should go round and round the circle. In every case the thrower should call out the name of the player he is throwing to, thus preventing two players trying to make the same catch.

To start, everybody catches the ball with both hands. However, as soon as a player misses a catch, he must put his left hand behind his back, and thereafter use his right hand only. If he misses a second catch, he must put his right hand behind his back and use his left hand only. On his third miss, a player must go down on one knee, but may use both hands again. If he misses again, he must go down on both knees.

If a player misses a fifth catch, he must stay down on both knees but put his left hand behind him and use his right only.

His sixth miss is the last that will be allowed him. He stays kneeling on both knees but must now catch with his left hand only, holding his right behind his back. Another miss and he is out.

Play continues as more and more drop out until only one player is left – the winner.

Occasionally, a throw will be so bad that it would be unreasonable to expect the catcher to catch it, especially if he is kneeling and cannot move towards the ball. In such cases those players still in the game may deem it an unfair throw, and the player who failed to catch the ball is not penalized, remaining in the game.

Age range 6–8
Number of players Six or more
Good for Outdoor birthday parties, particularly for young girls, since the theme is witches
What you will need A good-sized lawn; two or three black hats; pointed if possible; two or three brooms

Wicked witches

This is a game in which two or three children play witches. It entails a good deal of chasing and probably a certain amount of screaming.

Preparation

The wicked witches (two or three according to the number of players) will look and feel more wicked if they have black hats. If you are handy enough to make cones from cardboard and paint them black, that would be excellent. If not, any old black hats from an adult's wardrobe would do nicely.

How to play

If there are ten or fewer players, two witches would be sufficient – more than ten players perhaps require three witches.

The witches are chosen and they put on their hats and take their broomsticks and go and hide in a corner of the garden. If there is nowhere to hide

fully, it doesn't matter – they can stand in a corner huddled together and whispering to themselves.

The other children are asked to dance and skip about the lawn, knowing that sooner or later the witches will be coming to get them. So the daring children skip as close to the witches as they dare.

After a few seconds the witches decide to strike, and without warning they come shrieking and yelling from their corner trying to touch the other players. When a witch touches a player she calls 'Tag' and that player is turned to stone and must immediately stand still till the end of the game.

The witches can touch the players only by hand and must always take care not to touch them with the broomsticks, which doesn't count.

The game ends when all the players have been tagged and all is still. The last two or three tagged then become the witches for the next game and take over the hats and broomsticks and huddle away in the corner.

> **Warning**
> * Children running with broomsticks could cause accidents – tripping other children or inadvertently hitting them with the broomsticks. If you feel this is a danger play the game without the broomsticks.

Sinking ship

Age range 6+
Number of players Any number (in teams)
Good for An outdoor family party of all ages
What you will need A large bowl; a slightly smaller bowl; a small plastic cup

This is a game where all the family can join in, but its main attraction is to allow the young to play with water.

Preparation

Nearly fill the large bowl with water. Float the smaller bowl on the surface.

How to play

Form the players into two equal teams and line each team up on opposite sides of the bowl. One player from Team A is given the plastic cup and with this she takes as much water as she wants from the large bowl (but not less than half a cup full) and pours it into the smaller bowl; she then retires to the back of her team's line.

The first player from Team B then takes the plastic cup and does the same. In alternate turns each member of the two teams pours some water from the large bowl into the smaller one until the smaller bowl is on the point of sinking, and players have to be more and more careful pouring in the water.

Eventually a player pours into the smaller bowl enough water to make it sink. That player then leaves the game and the smaller bowl is emptied and set afloat again; players continue to fill it, one from each team alternately. One player is eliminated each time the bowl sinks.

Finally, all of one team is eliminated, and the other team wins.

Age range 6+
Number of players Four or more
Good for Large parties of children of the same age, such as birthday parties
What you will need The judgement of Solomon, as you will be asked to settle who won a close race

Tapping hands

This is a running game, which might lead to a scramble or two. Because of this, it is a good idea for an adult or two to act as referee.

How to play

All the players except one form a large circle. There could be, if space allows, about 1.8 m (6 ft) between them, so that anybody running round the edge of a circle of 12 children would have to run about 30 m (100 ft).

The children face inwards and clasp their hands behind their backs. The odd player (who can volunteer or be selected by the referee) is the first tapper. She runs round the circle until at any point she taps the hands of one of the players standing in the circle.

The tapper continues running, while the player tapped must run round the circle in the opposite direction. The two race to get back to the space created in the circle, the first there filling the space. If the tapper loses, she continues running and taps another player. If the tapper wins, the loser continues running and becomes the tapper.

To avoid a collision, it should be agreed that when the two runners pass, the tapper (who, after all gets a start) must run round the outside of the player tapped. To give everybody a chance to play, the tapper cannot tap a player she has already raced.

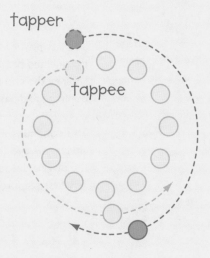

Balloon race

Age range 5+
Number of players Eight or more (in teams)
Good for Young children who like balloons
What you will need Two balloons (plus spares in case of accidents)

Most children's parties have balloons, and this is a way to use a couple of them in a game.

How to play

Two teams are formed and each team lines up in a row, with one player behind another.

The front players in each team are handed a balloon of a different colour (so that they can shout 'Come on red' and 'Come on blue').

On the command 'Go', the first player passes the balloon over her head to the player behind, and he passes it back similarly until it reaches the last player in the line.

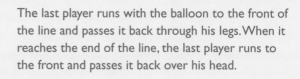

The last player runs with the balloon to the front of the line and passes it back through his legs. When it reaches the end of the line, the last player runs to the front and passes it back over his head.

This continues with the balloon being passed back alternately over the head and between the legs until the original leader of the line is back at the front. The first team to achieve this is the winner.

Age range 8+
Number of players Eight or more
(in teams)
Good for A bit of fun with balloons
What you will need Two balloons
(plus spares in case of accidents); a
blindfold for each player

Blind tunnel race

This is a game that is played between two teams and, to avoid possible embarrassment, it might be best to have a team of boys versus a team of girls. The fun in this game comes when a blindfolded team loses control of the balloon and its straight line begins to waver. Ensure that there is at least 90 cm (3 ft) between players so that they must reach for the balloon and hopefully get into a muddle.

How to play

Each team forms a line with one player behind another. Each player is blindfolded, and stands with legs apart. The first player in each team is given a balloon. If the teams are of mixed sex, they can be called Team A and Team B; if they are of the same sex, Girls and Boys. The object is to pass the balloon backwards through the legs from front to back. As soon as the last player of the team has the balloon safely in hand, she shouts 'About turn', announcing the name of the team – for example, 'About turn, Girls' – at which each member of the team must turn around 180 degrees, including the player who calls out.

The balloon is then passed back between the legs of each player as before, and when it reaches the end so that it is back with the player who started with it, she raises it high, shouting 'Girls win' or whatever the team name is.

Dressing-up relay

Age range 8–12
Number of players Eight or more (two teams)
Good for A silly relay item in a party where older children are in the majority
What you will need Two plastic bowls; two sets of old clothes; string for a start line

This is an exciting, if somewhat silly, game. Each set of clothes must have the same items, and there should be as many items as there are players on a team.

How to play

Pick two teams, equal in number, speed and strength. Lay a line of string at one end of the course as a start point, and place the two bowls with the clothing items about 20 m (66 ft) away. Remember there must be an item of clothing for each player.

At the word 'Go', the first player from each team runs to his bowl and puts on one item of clothing (say, the hat). He runs back to the start line, takes off the hat and hands it to the second runner, who puts it on and races back to the bowl. She adds a second item of clothing (say, the scarf). She runs back to the start line, takes them both off, hands them to the third runner, who puts them on, runs to the bowl and puts on a third item. He runs back to the fourth runner and so on.

The last runner should come running back to the start line wearing all the clothes. The bowl will be empty. It is best if the older runners go last, as they have more to do.

The first team to complete the course with a fully clothed player wins.

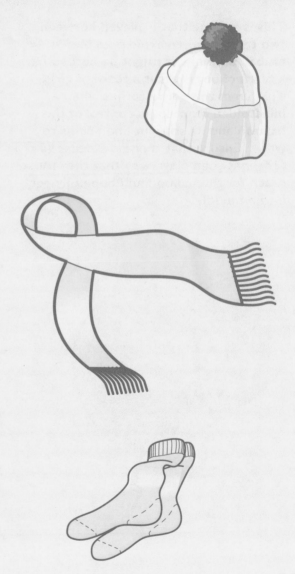

Age range 10+
Number of players Any even number
Good for An outdoor party of older children (who can catch)
What you will need Two balls or quoits; two canes; string

Spry

This is a catching game in which adults can play with older children. The ideal amount of players for this game is 12.

How to play

Select two teams. The two team leaders stand almost back to back with their teams facing them in a line about 3.7 m (12 ft) away. There should be 1.8 m (6 ft) between each team member. Canes could be laid on the ground to mark the leaders' position, and string for the teams' positions. The illustration shows the layout for six players per team.

The leader starts with the ball. He throws it to Player One, who returns it, then Players Two, Three,

Four, who return it. Player Five, however, instead of returning the ball, runs to the centre and becomes leader, throwing it to the other players in turn, all of whom return it except the original Player Four, who himself becomes leader. The other players then shift to the left again.

This is repeated until everyone on the team has reached their original starting positions. The first team to achieve this wins.

If a ball is dropped, the ball has to be returned to the player who threw it, and be re-thrown.

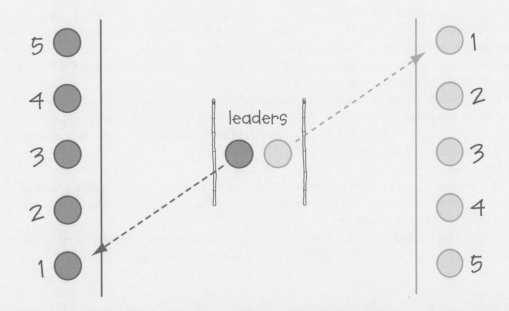

Sheepdog trials

Age range 6+
Number of players Any even number above six (in teams)
Good for Mixed parties of varying ages

This is a game that is played by teams of two, and has the attraction that a child can be paired with an adult.

How to play

First the 'course' has to be arranged. As big a room or clear space as possible should be used. Lay two chairs on their sides against one wall, so that the backs touch the wall and the legs provide an opening into which a person could crawl (see illustration opposite). The chairs make a sheep pen and the person is the sheepdog.

Around the floor, with a reasonable amount of space between them, should be placed a number of objects, perhaps about six. For example, a small cushion, an upturned wastepaper basket, a pile of three or four books, a cardboard box, a wine bottle and a biscuit tin – anything that can be bumped into without causing injury or damage. It is a nice touch, but not essential, if the objects can be labelled 1 to 6, with 6 being nearest the sheep pen and 1 closest to the opposite side of the room.

Teams of two are selected, and one person is the shepherd and the other the sheepdog. The sheepdog is blindfolded, and the object is for the shepherd to guide the sheepdog around the various obstacles in turn and into the sheep pen. The actual course is agreed beforehand (see illustration).

A timekeeper is appointed and he must keep the time. The sheepdog is positioned at the end of the room nearest obstacle 1, and is allowed to survey the course. He is then blindfolded, turned round three times and asked to kneel on the floor. When the timekeeper is ready (so when the second hand of his watch is at 12 o'clock), he calls out 'Go', and the sheepdog, guided by the shepherd, must find his way to the pen as quickly as possible.

The shepherd is limited in his instructions. He can say only: 'Forward', 'Back', 'Turn left', 'Turn right', 'Stop' and 'Go'. When the sheepdog turns left or right, he is allowed to add phrases like 'A bit more' or 'Not so much'.

If a sheepdog touches an obstacle, ten seconds is added to his total time, but he is only penalized once for each obstacle – if he knocks an obstacle over he is not penalized if he touches it again.

The sheepdog is not penalized for touching the pen on his way in, and he is deemed to have arrived in the pen when he touches the wall between the chair backs.

The time taken by each sheepdog should be written down. The fastest pair is the winner.

The sheepdogs and shepherds can then change places or the pairings can be changed.

What you will need A large space; two chairs; various articles to serve as obstacles (such as cushions, books, stools, cardboard boxes, wastepaper baskets, empty wine bottles, a cylindrical biscuit container); pieces of cardboard for labels; a stopwatch or a reliable watch with a second hand; a blindfold; a sheet of paper

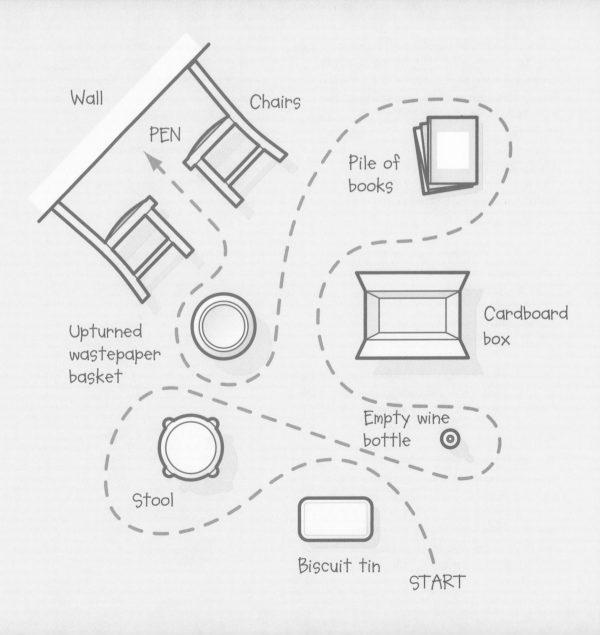

Wall

Chairs

PEN

Pile of books

Cardboard box

Upturned wastepaper basket

Empty wine bottle

Stool

Biscuit tin

START

In and out the egg cups

Age range 9+
Number of players 4–12 (in teams)
Good for Amusing a group of older children who like a test of skill
What you will need A table; up to eight egg cups; four table-tennis balls and 12 straws, according to the number of players (see below)

Blowing a table-tennis ball from one egg cup to another is a lot more difficult than it looks, and there will be much frustration as well as bouncing table-tennis balls in the air before this game is done.

Preparation

This is a team game, and the number of teams and the size of a team will depend upon the number of players. Suggested are:

* Four players – two teams of two
* Six players – two teams of three
* Eight players – two teams of four
* Nine players – three teams of three
* Ten players – two teams of five
* 12 players – four teams of three

You will need two egg cups per team (large enough to hold a table-tennis ball comfortably), one table-tennis ball per team and one straw per player.

How to play

The teams sit on opposite sides of a table, one player from each team sitting, and the others standing behind their team-mate. The sitting player places his table-tennis ball in an egg cup in front of him and positions the other egg cup a few centimetres beyond it (the player can choose the distance, and can alter it during the game if he wishes).

On the command 'Go', the first player attempts to blow the table-tennis ball from one egg cup into the other. If the table-tennis ball goes astray, his team-mates can retrieve it and place it back in the egg cup for a further attempt.

Once the table-tennis ball has been successfully blown from one egg cup to the other, then the seated player is replaced by another of his team, who has to perform the feat.

The winning team is the first one in which all its members have succeeded.

Age range 8+
Number of players Eight or more (in teams)
Good for Birthday parties with lots of children of the same age – as many as 16 players can easily be accommodated
What you will need A chair for each child; a small paper bag for each child

Bang bang relay

This game requires a lot of room and might equally well be played outdoors as well as indoors. Children love to make a noise and banging paper bags is always enjoyable.

How to play

The players are divided into two equal teams. Two rows of chairs are arranged facing each other with about 1.8–2.4 m (6–8 ft) between them. There also needs to be a bit of space at the back of the chairs. On each chair is a paper bag.

Each player sits on a chair (and on the bag). On the command 'Go', the player in chair 1 (see below) takes off in the direction shown, runs round the back of his own team's chairs and back to his place. He then picks up his paper bag, sits on his chair, blows up the bag and bangs it. The bang is the signal

Extra baggage

* It might be an idea to have at least double the number of bags as players. First, you might need to bang one to show youngsters how it's done, and second, the pleasure of banging paper bags is such that the children might want to repeat the game. Poppers or streamers could be used as an alternative to paper bags.

for the second player to take off, and he runs round the chairs in the same direction, sits, blows up his bag and bangs it, at which point the third player takes off and so on. The team whose last player bangs his bag first is the winner.

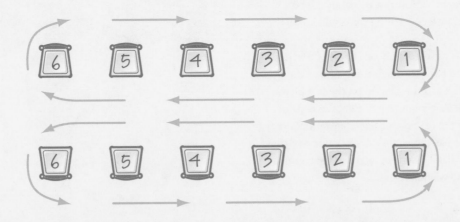

Pass the orange

Age range 5+
Number of players Eight or more (in teams)
Good for Parties of all ages
What you will need Two oranges

This is a well-known game that promotes a closeness between the players, but it can be annoying when the course is almost completed and the orange is dropped, so the whole team has to start again.

How to play

Two teams are chosen. Some say that taller players should form one team and shorter players the other, but it is not necessary – if tall players have to bend, that adds to the fun. The teams need not be equal, but if one team has an extra player it should be the 'stronger' team, as an extra player is a disadvantage.

The teams form up in two lines. The first player in each team is given an orange, which she places under her chin, holding it between chin and neck.

On the command 'Go', the first player transfers the orange from beneath her chin to beneath the chin of the next player. It must not be handled. The second then transfers it to the third, and so on.

If the orange is handled or drops to the floor, it must be passed back to the first player and the whole process started again. When the last player has the orange safely under her chin, she runs or walks back to the first player and transfers it. When the first player has the orange back under her chin, she raises her hand. The first team leader to raise her hand is the winner.

Variation

* This similar game can be played with 12, 16 or 20 players as a relay. Two teams are chosen and this time each team must be of an even number because the teams must be split into pairs. Each pair should be of more or less equal height. One pair from each team begins at one end of the room with an orange wedged between their foreheads. On the command 'Go', they must run (or walk or waddle) to the opposite wall, touch it and waddle back. If the orange is dropped, they must return to the start line and begin again. When one pair has successfully negotiated the course, the next pair places the orange between their foreheads (they can do this by hand) and does the same. The winning team is the first to have all its pairs complete the course.

Age range 5–8
Number of players Any
Ideal for A bit of fun at kids' parties
What you will need A sack (could be a duvet cover or sleeping bag) for each player (plastic bin liners, although more readily available, would be less satisfactory as they would probably tear); string for marking out the course

Sack race

This is a traditional race for outdoor children's parties. It usually provides a few tumbles and lots of laughs, but nobody should hurt themselves if the ground is grassy.

How to play

Mark out a course by stretching lengths of string for start and finish lines, about 15–20 m (49–66 ft) apart.

Each runner steps into her sack, gathers it round her waist and holds it up – she must not let it fall round her ankles during the race. Any fallers can get up and continue.

On the command 'Go', the runners jump or bounce to the finish line, the first to arrive being the winner.

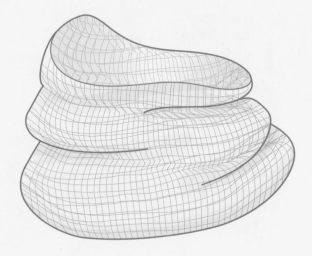

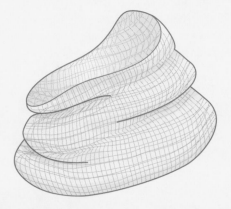

Sack shortage

* If you have, say, only four sacks and 16 children, organize heats. Four heats of four runners would suffice, with the first two in each heat going into two semi-finals, where the first two in each race meet in a final.

Quick on the draw

Age range 8+
Number of players Six or more (in teams)
Good for Family parties, since there is no upper age limit, and the only restriction on whether grandad plays is how fast he can run

This is a drawing and racing game that usually causes much amusement, due to the outlandish efforts of some players to draw fairly simple things.

Preparation

On about 20–30 slips of paper, write the names of a number of common objects – things that everybody will know, but that aren't necessarily easy to draw. The panel contains a suggested list. Fold the slips of paper and place them in a bowl on a table at one end of the room. Beside the bowl lay two piles of clean slips of paper and three pencils.

How to play

Choose two equal teams and sit them close to each other at the opposite end of the room to the table holding the bowl and the slips of paper.

Each team nominates a player to be the first to take part. When the referee says 'Go', the two players cross to the table (they need not race). When both are there, each takes a blank slip of paper from one of the piles and a pencil. Then one of them takes a slip from the bowl, unfolds it and lays it on the table, so that each player can see what is written on the slip simultaneously.

The player then has to draw as quickly (and as clearly) as possible the object written on the slip of paper. No words must be written on the drawing.

Each player rushes to be the first to hand the drawing to his team. He must then stand apart, and cannot give hints or encouragement to his team. The referee must keep an eye open for cheating.

Any member of the team can call out what he thinks the object in the drawing is. The first to correctly shout out the object scores a point for the team. Any writing accompanying the drawing automatically gives the point to the other team. The referee's decision is final on all matters.

Once the drawing has been identified, the next two players, one from each team, go to the table and another slip is taken from the bowl. Play can continue until all members of both teams have had, say, two turns.

What you will need Slips of paper
(about 10 cm/4 in would do); two pencils
(plus a spare); a bowl

Suggested subjects
* A cucumber
* The pearly gates
* A black hole
* A magazine
* A dolphin
* An aspirin tablet
* A squirrel
* A fried egg on toast
* A toffee
* A mobile phone
* A shooting star
* A frog
* A bar of soap
* A lipstick
* A CD
* A rose
* Charlie Chaplin
* A jumbo jet
* A hippopotamus
* A hedgehog
* A wedding ring
* A big toe-nail
* A crocodile
* Three pairs of socks
* A push-chair
* A fire

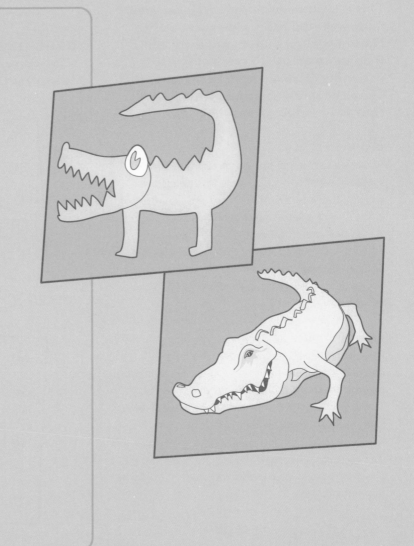

Acrostics

Age range 10+
Number of players Any number
Good for Family parties, as all ages can take part
What you will need A sheet of paper and a pencil for each player or team; a stopwatch or watch with a second hand

This is a game for anyone who can spell fairly well, and has a wide vocabulary. Naturally, older players will be better than those of, say, 10 years old, so in a gathering of mixed ages, perhaps teams of two or three could be formed, with the oldest helping the youngest.

How to play

A referee supplies all players, or teams, with small sheets of paper and a pencil. He then reads out a word of five letters or more. Each player writes the word down the left-hand side of the paper, and then writes the letters of the word in reverse order down the right-hand side of the paper. Each player or team then has three minutes to fill in the space between the pairs of letters with other letters to make new words.

When the referee calls time, everybody must put down their pencils, and all those who have completed proper words between each pair score a point for each word plus a bonus of ten points. Those who haven't completed all the words just score a point for each word.

The referee then reads out a second word and the players try again. After ten words, those players with most points win.

Examples

* The effort for the word TWENTY scores 16 points. The lower effort for NUMBER scores five points:

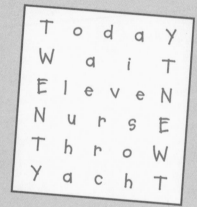

Age range 9+
Number of players Any even number over four
What you will need A sheet of paper and a pencil for each 'drawer' (see below); three additional sheets of paper; scissors; egg timer or stopwatch

Picture clues

With just one minute allowed, one team member has to draw as many words as possible for his team-mates to guess. This is a real test of working under pressure: not only do the children have to think of the simplest drawing possible in a very quick time, but they also have to be able to draw it well enough for their team-mates to guess.

Variation
* Team members can take it in turns to do the drawing with each correct guess.

Tip for beginners
* Stick to words that are easy to draw.

Preparation
Cut each of the three additional sheets of paper into four to produce 12 game cards and write a single word on each of them, using a range of objects, activities and emotions. For example, you could have six objects (table, dog, hat, bus, door, horse); three activities (running, smiling, clapping); and three emotions (happy, cross, angry). Then turn the cards face down on a table.

How to play
The players divide into two teams of at least two people each, and choose one player who will be the 'drawer'. This player selects a face-down card from the table and has to make a drawing of the word you have written. His team-mates have to guess what the word is from his drawing: he is not allowed to say anything or make any gestures. Play continues for one minute, with the drawer taking another face-down card from the table with every correct guess from his team-mates. At the end of the minute all the correct guesses are counted up and scored for the drawer's team. Play swaps over to the other team, and the winning team is the one with the most points.

(Car)

(Happy)

(Running)

(Hat)

(Door)

Word couplings

Age range 10+
Number of players Any number
Good for Parties where older children want to play word games with the adults
What you will need A sheet of paper and a pencil for each player; stopwatch

This is a word game with a difference – players must think of pairs of words. It is a good game, as perfect scores of 26 are rare, and it will usually produce an outright winner.

How to play

Give each player a pencil and piece of paper. Ask the players to write the letters A to Z down the left-hand side of the paper. Choose and announce a letter, say P. Each player has to go through the alphabet writing down a two-word phrase for each letter, the second word of the phrase beginning with the letter P.

Several two-word couplings suggest themselves; for A, P, for instance, Apple Pie, Active Player, Auto Pilot, Arnold Palmer (proper names are allowed). The only restrictions are that the two words must make a recognizable pair, and that no word can be used twice in the list.

After a time limit, say ten minutes, the player with the highest number of phrases wins.

You can play the game as often as you like, but avoid letters like J, X or Z for the second word. As well as P, good letters are B, H, R, S and T.

A perfect score of 26, with P as the key letter, could be obtained as follows:

P

A pple Pie
B iennial Plant
C hristmas Present
D ry Powder
E aster Parade
F ire Power
G oose Pimple
H arry Potter
I deal Pair
J unior Partner
K ings Pawn
L eading Part
Mobile Phone
N ew Potato
O pen Prison
P retty Picture
Q uiet Patch
R ose Pink
S and Pit
T hird Place
U gly Pig
V ictoria Plum
Window Pane
X mas Party
Y oung Person
Z oo Pass

Across and down

Age range 10+
Number of players Any number
Good for Parties where there are cerebral types wanting a testing game
What you will need A word grid; a pencil for each player; a dictionary

Those people who spend hours on newspaper crosswords may relish a game that gives the appearance of making up their own crosswords. But it can be very frustrating, especially when other players pick letters that are of no use to you at all.

How to play

Supply each player with a pencil and a sheet of paper. It is best if each piece of paper contains a grid like a crossword. For up to six players, a grid of six squares by six is a good size – for more than six players, perhaps seven by seven or eight by eight. Make a neat grid in advance and photocopy it for the players.

The first player calls out a letter of her choice, which each player must enter in a square on her grid. The letter may be entered in any blank square, but it must be done immediately and it cannot be moved later to another square.

When all players have entered the letter on their grids, the next player calls out a letter, and this is entered, and so on round the group.

The object is to enter the letters so that they make words, reading across or down. Words must consist of three letters or more. Proper nouns, foreign words and abbreviations do not count. The game ends when the grids are completed, and each player passes her grid to the left for checking. Each word scores the number of letters it contains. A letter can be used twice or more in different words; for instance, a line WANTON would score: WANTON (6), WANT (4), ANT (3) and TON (3). Not many lines like this will be achieved. The winner is the player with the highest total.

S	L	A	N	T	M
I	C	E	U	O	A
F	H	A	T	E	D
T	I	R	E	D	L
T	I	M	E	V	E
P	L	A	Y	X	Y

Across:
Line 1 slant (5), ant (3)
Line 2 ice (3)
Line 3 hated (5), ate (3), hat (3)
Line 4 tire (4), tired (5), red (3), ire (3)
Line 5 time (4), eve (3)
Line 6 play (4), lay (3)

Down:
Line 1 sift (4)
Line 2 no points
Line 3 ear (3), arm (3)
Line 4 nut (3), tee (3)
Line 5 toed (4)
Line 6 mad (3), ley (3)

TOTAL: 77

One at a time

Age range 10+
Number of players Any number
Good for Parties of all ages
What you will need A sheet of paper and a pencil for each player; stopwatch

Players cannot be at a loss for words when playing this game. A whole string of words can follow on from the starting word, and the player with the longest string wins.

How to play

A pencil and paper are given to every player.

Each player is then asked to write the same word (chosen by the host) at the top of his sheet. Begin with a word of four letters, for example 'Care'.

The object is for each player to write beneath the word another four-letter word that differs in one letter only from the original word. The player continues to make a string of words, each different from the word above it by one letter only. A word can only be used once.

At the end of a given time, activity stops and the player with the longest string of words wins.

Follow this by giving all players a five-letter word, and after this game a six-letter word. Usually, the longer the initial word, the harder the game gets. In fact, choose your words in advance, and make sure they are alterable by one letter. A simple word like 'Please', for example, can hardly be developed at all. Strings of four, five and six-letter words are shown.

CARE	RIVER	LETTER
CURE	RAVER	BETTER
CURT	RAVED	BUTTER
CART	RACED	BITTER
PART	PACED	LITTER
PERT	PARED	LATTER
PENT	CARED	LATHER
LENT	CARER	BATHER
LEND	CATER	RATHER
WEND	LATER	RASHER
WENT	MATER	DASHER
TENT	MATED	DASHED

Age range 10+
Number of players Any number
Good for Family gatherings that
include children aged 10 or more
What you will need A sheet of
paper and a pencil for each player; a
stopwatch or watch

Guggenheim

**This is a slightly more difficult version of
Categories (see page 140).**

Preparation

To make it easier for the players, draw the grids in
advance like the one in the diagram. The categories
can be chosen beforehand and written down the
left-hand column, or players can write them on the
day. There should be eight columns for the players
to write in their choice of word for each category.

How to play

Each player has a pencil and paper. You then choose
an eight-letter key word – open a book at any page
and pick the first eight-letter word to appear on the
left-hand side. You read this word to the players and
they write it across the top of the columns on their
sheets, one letter above each column.

Each player has ten minutes to write in each column
opposite each category a word that corresponds to

Scoring

* First of all, players score one point for each
  space filled in. Players then read out their
  words one at a time, column by column, and
  each player who has a word that nobody else
  has used scores an extra point for it.

the category, which must begin with the letter at the
top of the column. Because the letters are chosen at
random, the grid may be hard to complete. There
could be awkward letters, and some could be
duplicated, which means that players might need to
think of two instances of the category beginning
with the same letter. If the eight-letter word was
'Dividend', as below, three of the columns will need
filling with words beginning with D, and two with
words beginning with I. Words cannot be repeated.

	D	I	V	I	D	E	N	D
Flower								
Town								
Food								
Boy's name								
Colour								
Tree								

Dingo

Age range 10+
Number of players Any number
Good for Entertaining children while sharpening up their arithmetic

This game is played like Bingo. It is Bingo with dice, hence its name Dingo. It is suggested that players cross out the numbers on their cards as they achieve them, otherwise you would need to supply up to 15 counters or buttons for each player.

Preparation

You will need to make the cards, as illustrated. Six versions are suggested, the numbers being arranged on each to give them all similar chances of winning. Notice five numbers (17, 19, 27, 28, 29) are missing because in this game they are impossible to get. It doesn't matter, incidentally, if all players had the same cards because each player makes their own individual numbers with the dice. If you have a computer and printer, you could make and print a number of differing cards.

How to play

Each player is given a Dingo card, and each rolls the two dice to determine who goes first, the highest scorer having that honour.

The first player throws the two dice, and she can choose one of four different ways to use the two numbers thrown to cross off a number or numbers on her card. Suppose she throws a 2 and a 6, she can:

1 Use the two numbers separately, to cross off 2 and 6
2 Add them together, to cross off 8
3 Multiply them, to cross off 12
4 Join them as a two-digit number, to cross off 26

She can use her numbers in any of the four options, but one only. For instance, with 2 and 6 she cannot cross off both 8 and 26. She must choose. Usually it will pay to cross off the numbers over 12 first, if the opportunity occurs, as they are more difficult to achieve. The hardest numbers on the cards are 22 and 33, which can be obtained by only one throw (2, 2 and 3, 3).

Occasionally a player may find that she cannot use one or even both of her numbers, in which case she forfeits them. A player who throws a double can use the numbers as she wishes, and have another throw.

When a player has crossed off her number or numbers, she passes the dice and pencil to the player on her left, who has her turn, and so on. The first to cross off all her numbers wins.

What you will need Two dice;
a number of home-made Dingo cards; a
pencil

1	2				6
	8	9		11	
		15	16		
	20		22	23	
	26				30
		33		35	

	2	3		5	
7		9			12
	14	15	16		
		21	22	23	
	26				
				35	36

		3	4	5	
7			10	11	
	14	15	16		
			22		24
25					
31	32				36

1	2				6
	8	9			12
13	14				18
		21			24
	26				30
	32				36

1			4		6
	8		10		
		15	16		18
	20	21			24
25					
31			34	35	

	2	3	4		
		9	10	11	12
		15			18
		21			24
25					
		33	34	35	

Fifty

Age range 7–10
Number of players Any number
Good for A party where a group of young people want to do something on their own for a while
What you will need Two dice (plus pencil and paper to score if the players insist, but it is more fun without)

This is the simplest of all dice games, in that children can sit on the floor and play it with only two dice, keeping running totals of their scores in their heads.

How to play

The players sit, either on the carpet or round a table. To decide who goes first, they all roll the dice and the highest total goes first. If two or more tie for highest, they have a repeat throw among themselves to see who goes first.

When the first thrower has been decided, he throws the dice, and thereafter the turn to throw goes round to the left.

The only scoring comes from throwing doubles:

Before a player throws, he announces his score so far, and when he has made his throw, he announces his new score, passing the dice to the next player.

The winner is the first player to reach 50.

Each player's score rises gradually by steps of five, with the big moments coming with the throw of a double-six (25 points) or a double-three, when everybody laughs at the unfortunate player whose score reverts to nothing.

Double-six	scores 25 points
Double-five	
Double-four	All these score 5 points
Double-two	
Double-one	
Double-three	Loses all the score you have made so far

Age range 8+
Number of players Any number
Good for Those periods during a family party when a simple yet exciting game is required
What you will need One die; a pencil and a sheet of paper

Pig

In this game, players can decide for themselves when their turn ends. It is a question of being happy with what you've got or trying for a bit more at the risk of losing all.

How to play

All the players sit round a table and throw the single die in turn. The player throwing the lowest number goes first. If two or more tie, they throw again until the tie is broken.

The first player throws the die and announces the score. He can throw it again as often as he likes, keeping a running score by adding the result of each throw to his previous total. However, if he throws a

1, his turn ends, and he loses all his score for that turn.

Unless he throws a 1, therefore, a player must decide when he wants to stop. When he stops, his score is written down and the die passes to the player on his left.

The die is passed round with each player either recording a score or throwing a 1. The scores for each round are added up as play progresses and the first player to reach 101 wins.

On average, a 1 will be thrown every six throws, and a player whose score on one turn gets into the 20s might consider that a good score to stop at.

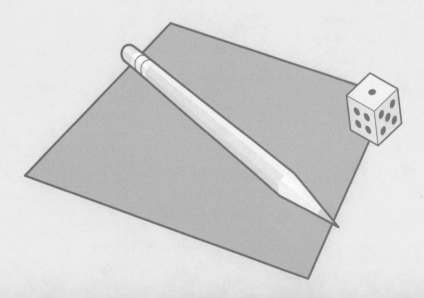

Beetle

Age range 8+
Number of players 2–8
Good for Parties with children who like drawing
What you will need A die; a sheet of paper and a pencil for each player

This is a race to draw a beetle (see illustration). Any more than eight players could make the game a bit tedious.

How to play

Each player throws the die to see who goes first, the highest scorer getting the privilege. The turn then passes from player to player to the left, and each player on her turn throws the die once.

As soon as a player scores a 1, she may begin to draw her beetle. A 1 stands for the body, and the body is always the first thing to be drawn. Once started, a player on each turn can add one item to the drawing provided she throws the right number. When the body is drawn, a 3 will add all three legs to one side of the body, a 6 will add the tail and a 2 the head. Once the head is attached to the body (but not before), each 4 thrown will add an eye, and each 5 thrown will add a feeler.

To draw the complete beetle, therefore, takes a 1, a 2, two 3s, two 4s, two 5s and a 6. But remember, the body has to come first, and the head has to be attached before the eyes and feelers can be added, so there will be wasted throws and it could easily take 20 or more throws to complete the drawing. The first to do so, of course, wins.

The beetle
It takes nine throws to complete, but some throws will get wasted.

1 = Body
2 = Head
3 = Legs (six)
4 = Eyes (two)
5 = Feelers (two)
6 = Tail

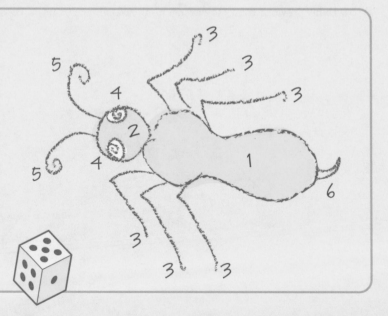

Age range 8–12
Number of players 2–8
Good for A children's party (it encourages a little simple arithmetic)
What you will need Two dice; a drawing of a clock face (see illustration); a pencil for each player

The clock face

In this game, the players throw the dice in turns and race to cross off all the numbers on a clock face. Each player's clock face must be kept in full view so that all players can see which number is being tried for with each throw.

Preparation

If you have a computer and a printer, you could make a clock face and print off a copy for each player to use.

How to play

Players throw the two dice to determine who goes first (highest score goes first). The turn thereafter passes to the left.

Players in turn throw the two dice and cross off the numbers 1 to 12 on the clock face as they score them, but they must be scored in the correct order from one o'clock to twelve o'clock.

For the numbers 1–6

A player can get the number with one die, or by adding the two together. So, if she is on four o'clock, she can get her four by throwing 4 with one of her dice, or by throwing 1, 3 or 2, 2. When on 1 to 6, she can also cross out two numbers at once if they are in sequence. For example, if she needs 2 for two o'clock, and she throws 2, 3, she can cross out both two o'clock and three o'clock.

For the numbers 7–12

A player can get these only by adding the numbers on her two dice. However, there are often two or three ways to get these numbers; for example, 7 can be obtained with a 6, 1 or 5, 2 or 4, 3.

Variation

* For a quicker game, you could allow players to cross off the numbers in any order. This means they can start crossing out from the first throw.

Drop dead

Age range 8+
Number of players 2–8
Good for A quiet period in a party when you can get the children seated round a table

This game provides the pleasure of throwing five dice, with each player's turn continuing for seven or eight throws while he racks up a good score.

How to play

Write the players' names on the score-sheet and record their scores for each round.

The first player throws the five dice (there's no advantage to throwing first or last). He scores the total of all the dots showing unless he throws a 2 or a 5 among the five dice. If any die shows 2 or 5, he scores nothing for that throw and furthermore he removes any die showing 2 or 5. He can continue his turn by throwing the remaining dice and scoring the total of the dots, again unless a 2 and/or a 5 are included in his throw.

A player's turn continues with him throwing the dice and adding his scores together as he goes, but every time he throws a 2 or 5, that die is removed. Eventually he runs out of dice altogether and his turn ends – he is said to have 'dropped dead'. His total is then entered on the score-sheet, and he hands the five dice to the player on his left.

Play ends when all the players have had five turns. Their scores are then totalled on the score-sheet, and the player with the highest total wins.

How a player's turn might develop is shown right.

Example

The player avoids a 2 or a 5 on his first throw, but loses dice on his second, fourth, fifth and eighth throws.

Throw 1
Score: 17 Running score: 17

Throw 2
Score: 0 Running score: 17

Throw 3
Score: 9 Running score: 26

Throw 4
Score: 0 Running score: 26

Throw 5
Score: 0 Running score: 26

Throw 6
Score: 6 Running score: 32

Throw 7
Score: 3 Running Score: 35

Throw 8
Score: 0 Running score 35

What you will need Five dice; pencil
and paper to score

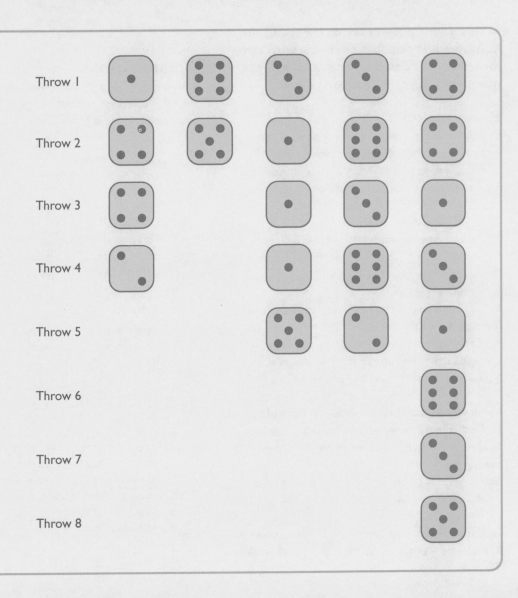

Throw 1

Throw 2

Throw 3

Throw 4

Throw 5

Throw 6

Throw 7

Throw 8

Chicago

Age range 8+
Number of players Any number
Good for Family parties where a game for all ages is required

In this game, players try to throw all the numbers it is possible to throw with two dice. They have two attempts to roll each number, using two dice each time.

Preparation

Draw up a score-sheet with all the players' names written across the top and the numbers 2 to 12 down the left-hand side. Add a line for totals at the bottom (see illustration, opposite).

How to play

There is no need to throw dice to see who goes first, as there is no advantage, and indeed on each throw a different player could start.

In the first round, all the players try to throw the lowest total possible with two dice, which is 2 (two 1s). Each player has two attempts, and a player who succeeds scores five points plus two points as a bonus (two being the number attempted).

In the second round, each player has two attempts at the number 3 (achieved by throwing a 2 and a 1). Success brings five points plus three. And so on to the last round, where success brings 17 points (five plus the bonus of 12). At the end, the scores are totalled, and the player with most points wins.

Opposite is a possible outcome of a game between four players – Lydia, Jonny, Isobel and Oliver – with the relevant scorecard shown.

Combinations

There are 36 ways in which two dice may fall, with 7 the likeliest number to result. The 36 ways result in these totals:

What you will need Two dice; a
pencil; a score-sheet

throw	Lydia	Jonny	Isobel	Oliver
2				
3				
4				
5				
6				
7				
8				
9				
10				
11				
12				
Total	43	49	33	25

Golf

Age range 10+
Number of players 2–6
Good for Parties that might include a golf fan or two who'd like a game that slightly simulates its scoring

This is a game where you play six 'holes' and try to play them in as few 'strokes' as possible. You end up with something that vaguely resembles a golf score.

Preparation
Draw up an overall score-sheet on which the players' names are listed down the left-hand side. The diagram shows a score-sheet for five players. The numbers relate to the numbers of the 'holes'.

How to play
It doesn't matter in which order you play, but you can each roll the dice, the highest scorer going first, the second highest going second and so on.

The first player rolls the dice and, according to how they fall, decides which hole he is going to play first. It will normally be the hole corresponding to any doubles or trebles he achieves in the throw. For example, if he throws 1, 2, 5, 5, 6, he will choose to play hole 5, since to complete hole 5 he has to have all five dice showing 5 uppermost.

If a player had the throw 1, 2, 5, 5, 6, he would set aside the two 5s and throw the other dice again. Any 5s he threw would be added to the first two, and he would then re-throw the dice. He would continue to throw all the dice not showing 5 until finally all showed 5. The number of throws he took would be the number to be recorded for that hole.

The dice are passed round and when all players have completed a hole, the first player tackles a second hole, and so on until all players have completed six holes. Each player's scores are then added together to give his score for the 'round'.

Of course, a player's option to choose the hole he wishes to play based on his first throw becomes less valuable as the game progresses. A player with only holes 2 and 4 to play, for example, might throw 1, 3, 3, 5, 6 with his first throw. He must still choose which of holes 2 and 4 to play and throw all the dice again having used one throw without achieving anything. Scores will thus tend to be bigger for the last hole played than for the first.

What you will need Five dice; pencil
and paper to score

	1	2	3	4	5	6	Total
Jack							
Sophie							
Ian							
Lucy							
Martin							

Yacht

Age range 10+
Number of players Two or more
(up to six is best)
Good for A small party looking for a
dice game that requires thought as well
as luck

This is one of the best dice games, and
can be enjoyed by players of all ages.
Throughout the game, players have to
make choices – do they risk all on going
for a high-scoring combination, or do
they settle for a safe but comparatively
small score?

Preparation

Prepare in advance a score-sheet as shown; if you
have a computer and printer, make half-a-dozen.

	Alan	Jane	Rose	Chas
Ones				
Twos				
Threes				
Fours				
Fives				
Sixes				
Little straight				
Big straight				
Full house				
Four of a kind				
Choice				
Yacht				
TOTAL				

How to play

Write each player's name at the top of one of the
columns on the score-sheet. Each player then
throws the five dice in turn to determine who goes
first – the player with the highest total throws first.
The turn to throw passes to the left.

The object is to throw as many as possible of the
patterns shown on the score-sheet. The panel, left,
describes the patterns and the scoring systems.

On her turn, a player throws the five dice and then
nominates one of the patterns to attempt. She must
announce it so that all can hear. She then has two
more throws in which she can re-throw as many of
the dice as she wishes.

For example, if a player throws 5, 5, 2, 2, 1, she might
nominate any of the following:
Fives She re-throws 2, 2, 1. She has a guaranteed
ten points.

Four of a kind She re-throws 2, 2, 1 and if in her
two re-throws she gets two more 5s, she scores
30 points – if she fails she scores nothing.

Full house She re-throws just the 1, hoping that in
her re-throws she might get a 5 (score 29) or a 2
(score 26).

Yacht She re-throws 2, 2, 1 hoping to get all 5s for
a score of 50.

What you will need Five dice; a
prepared score-sheet and pencil

Little straight She re-throws 5, 2, hoping to get 3,
4, giving her 30 points.

Choice She re-throws 2, 2, 1, hoping for a high
pip total.

A player can only score by getting the pattern she
nominated – if she gets another pattern she cannot

score (except if she goes for four of a kind and gets
yacht, where she scores for her four of a kind). A
player can nominate a pattern only once.

Her score is entered on the score-sheet after each
turn, even if it is 0, so that at the end of the game
each player will have had 12 throws. The player with
the highest total wins the game.

The Patterns
Ones Only the 1s score – one point each

Twos Only the 2s score – two points each

Threes Only the 3s score – three points each

Fours Only the 4s score – four points each

Fives Only the 5s score – five points each

Sixes Only the 6s score – six points each

Little straight 1, 2, 3, 4, 5 – scores 30 points

Big straight 2, 3, 4, 5, 6 – scores 30 points

Full house Three of one number and two of
another – for example 3, 3, 3, 5, 5 – scores total
pip value plus 10.

Four of a kind Four of any one number scores
total pip value of the four, plus 10.

Choice An attempt to score as many as possible,
irrespective of the pattern. The score is total pip
value, so 6, 6, 5, 5, 3 scores 25 points.

Yacht All five dice showing the same number
scores 50 points irrespective of the number.

A player who nominates little straight, big straight,
full house, four of a kind or yacht and fails to make
it scores no points for that throw.

Squares

Age range 9+
Number of players 2–8
Good for An undemanding dice game for a quieter period of a party

This is an attractive, simple game which can be amusing and frustrating at the same time.

Preparation

On a piece of cardboard of about 30 cm (12 in) square, draw up a grid of 36 squares, numbered as shown. Make a set of eight counters for each player by cutting squares or circles of card of a size that will fit into the squares on your grid. Each player's set of counters should be of the same colour, and different from everybody else's. If you use white card, you could leave one set of eight white and, with paints or coloured pencils, make sets of black, red, blue, green, yellow and so on.

How to play

The board is set in the centre of the table, with the players seated around. Each player throws the dice to determine who throws first (it is an advantage). The player with the highest score has the first turn and thereafter the turn passes to the left around the table.

The objective of each player is to get rid of his counters as quickly as possible by placing them on the board.

Each player on his turn throws the two dice and places a counter onto a blank square on the board according to the number thrown. The numbers on the two dice can be used in three ways: they can be added, subtracted or used as separate digits to make a two-digit number. Thus, a throw of 2, 5 could be used to cover the squares 3 (5–2), 7 (5+2) or 25. Both numbers thrown on the dice must be used in this way, and a number cannot be used singly. For instance, a player throwing 5, 2 could not use the numbers separately to cover both squares 2 and 5, nor could he use one number only and discard another (so that he could not cover the 2 and ignore the die showing 5).

There are special rules for a throw that produces a double. Any double except double-1 allows a player to put a counter on any number on the board he wishes. This is useful, since eight numbers (17, 18, 19, 20, 27, 28, 29, 30) can be covered only by throwing a double. A double-1, however, incurs a penalty. The player to the right of the thrower is allowed to remove one of the thrower's counters from the board and return it to the thrower's pile.

Each player is allowed one throw of the dice on each turn. If the throw cannot be used – for example, if it is 4, 5 and both squares 1 and 9 are occupied – then the turn passes without the thrower being able to place a counter on the board.

The winner is the first player to place all his counters on the board. If there are six or more players, it is possible for the board to be full before any player has got rid of all his counters, in which case the player with fewest counters left wins.

What you will need Two dice; a
home-made board; a set of eight counters
for each player (see page 366)

1	2	3	4	5	6
7	8	9	10	11	12
13	14	15	16	17	18
19	20	21	22	23	24
25	26	27	28	29	30
31	32	33	34	35	36

Block game

Age range 8+
Number of players 2–6
Good for A small party where perhaps a few people would like a quiet game

The Block Game is the basic game of dominoes, and there are several ways of playing it, some being more popular in particular countries than others. A simple game for four players is described first, with variations given later.

How to play

The full set of 28 dominoes is spread face down on the table and shuffled around. Players take seven dominoes each and look at them. The usual way to see your dominoes during the game is to stand them on one of their long edges with the spots facing you, in such a manner that you can see your hand but the others players cannot. The object is to get rid of all your dominoes.

The player holding the double-6 goes first by laying it in the centre of the table. The turn now moves to the left, with the next player being required to lay a domino of which one side is a 6 against the starter domino. If the domino played is the 6–4, then the next player must lay a domino that matches either

the 6 or 4. This is laid against the 6 or 4 already on the table. Thus a chain is formed, and each player on his turn can play a domino to either end of it. If he hasn't a domino that will go, he passes.

It is customary when playing a double to the table to place it at right angles to the chain, as the illustration opposite shows. Corners can be turned when necessary in a similar way.

The first player to get rid of all his dominoes wins that round and the other players are debited with the total number of spots on the unplayed dominoes in their hands. The scores are recorded and it is customary to play five games, after which each player's scores are added up and the player with the lowest total is the winner.

For two or three players

If there are two or three players, it is customary to leave the undealt dominoes face down in a 'bone yard' (so-called because originally dominoes were made of bone). A player who cannot go must take a domino from the bone yard. He can play this to the centre if it goes. If not, he adds it to his hand and passes. The last two bones in the bone yard must not be taken. When the bone yard is exhausted (so there are only two bones left), the player merely passes. If no player holds the double-6, the highest double held goes first.

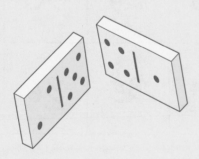

What you will need A standard set of
dominoes; pencil and paper to score

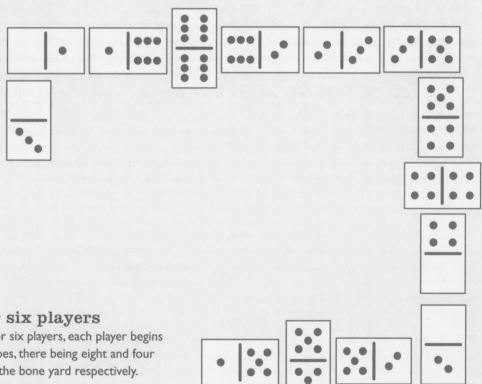

For five or six players
If there are five or six players, each player begins
with four dominoes, there being eight and four
dominoes left in the bone yard respectively.

Sebastopol
* In this variation, when a double is played
  it is laid across the chain, and each end is
  available to be played on – a new chain is
  begun at right angles to the previous one.

Blind Hughie

Age range 8+
Number of players 2–5
Good for Introducing young children to dominoes
What you will need A standard set of dominoes

This is a domino game that requires no skill and can be played by young children (perhaps with adult supervision).

How to play

To choose a dealer, the dominoes are shuffled face down and each player turns one over. The player with the highest double is the dealer; if no doubles are turned, the highest total spots deals.

The dominoes are turned over again and reshuffled. The dealer gives dominoes face down to all players including herself: if two or three players, seven dominoes each; if four or five players, five dominoes each. The dominoes not dealt are put aside and not used in the game.

The players do not look at the faces of their dominoes, but lay them in a neat row face down in front of them.

The player on the dealer's left turns over her left-hand domino and places it in the centre of the table. The next player on her left then turns over her left-hand domino. If one end matches one of the ends of the domino on the table, then she places the matching ends together to begin a chain. If her domino will not go, she turns it over again and places it face down at the right-hand of her row.

The next player then turns over her left-hand domino and plays it to the table or not in the same manner, and so on round the table.

The first player to get rid of all her dominoes wins. If the game gets blocked and nobody can go, there is a re-deal.

Age range 8+
Number of players Four
Good for When specifically four people would like a domino game
What you will need A standard set of dominoes

Ends

This is a game where a little skill can be exercised. It is different to most domino games in that dominoes are passed from one player to another.

How to play

The dominoes are placed face down on the table and shuffled. Each player takes seven.

Players arrange their dominoes so that they can see them and the player with the double-6 plays it to the table.

Players in turn to the left then play a domino to the table so that one end matches one of the ends of the chain, as in the Block Game (see page 368).

If a player cannot go, she asks the player on her left for a domino that will go. If she gets one, she plays it to the table and the player on her left then has her turn. This is where the player asked for a domino can show some skill. If she has two that will go, she hands over one that will enable herself to go on her next turn.

If the player asked for a domino does not have one that will go, she must ask the player on her left, and so on. When a suitable domino is passed over, it is passed back round the table to the original player who asked for it, and she plays it. Play then proceeds as usual.

If the question goes all round the table with nobody being able to supply a suitable domino, the original asker can play whichever domino she likes, and play again proceeds.

The winner of the game is the first player to get rid of all her dominoes.

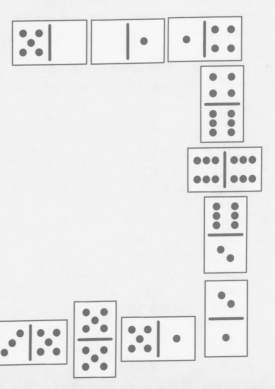

Fives and threes

Age range 8+
Number of players 2–5
Good for Up to five players who want a more advanced domino game

This is a dominoes game where the best players are good at arithmetic, since the object is to make the totals at each end of the domino chain add up to a number that divides by five or three. Children quick at sums should shine.

How to play

The first player is chosen by spreading the dominoes face down on the table and each player picking one. Highest double goes first – if nobody has a double, all pick a second domino and so on. The dominoes are then returned face down and the whole lot shuffled.

If two or three are playing, each player takes seven dominoes; if four play, each takes six; and if five play, each takes five. Remaining dominoes are placed to one side and take no part in the game.

The first player lays any domino to the table; the next player on the left can then lay a domino against it providing one end matches one end of the domino on the table, as in the Block Game (see page 368). A player must go if he can.

The object of the game is to score points by laying a domino such that the total of spots at each end of the chain is a multiple of either five or three.

If the total is nine, it scores three points (three 3s), if it is ten, it scores two points (two 5s) and so on. Doubles are laid across the chain and both ends count, enabling higher scores. For example, double-6, double-3 makes 18 (for six points), while double-6, double-4 makes 20 (for four points). The panel shows the scoring multiples.

Play continues in rotation for as long as a player can lay a legitimate domino. It does not end if one player gets rid of all his dominoes, but only when no player can go. A player who does get rid of all his dominoes, however, scores an extra point for going out of the round.

After each round, the first player is the one to the left of the previous first player. A running score is kept of all the players' points, and the first to 41 is declared the winner.

Scoring multiples

3	scores 1	(for one 3)
5	scores 1	(for one 5)
6	scores 2	(for two 3s)
9	scores 3	(for three 3s)
10	scores 2	(for two 5s)
12	scores 4	(for four 3s)
15	scores 8	(for five 3s and three 5s)
18	scores 6	(for six 3s)
20	scores 4	(for four 5s)

What you will need A standard set of dominoes; pencil and paper to score

Example game

The illustration shows three hands, A, B, C, and how the game might develop. A goes first and lays 4, 5 for three points (the ends total 9). B lays 4, 1 for two points (the ends total 6). C lays 5, 2 for one point. A lays 2, 4 for one point. B lays the double-4 for three points. C lays the double-1 for two points. A lays the 4, 3 for one point. B lays the 1, 2 for one point. C lays 2, 3 for two points. A, on his turn now cannot go. B lays his double-3 for three points. C lays 3, 1, which doesn't score. This is the position in the game as laid out, with B on nine points, A and C on five. A can go now, and can score three points with 1, 6. And so on.

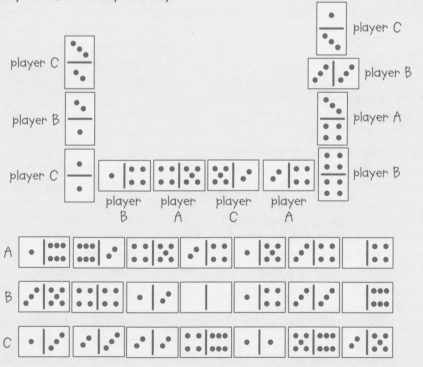

Bergen

Age range 8+
Number of players 2–4
Good for A group of dominoes enthusiasts looking for an interesting game

This is a fascinating game where points are scored in a way that doesn't apply to any other domino game – the object is simply to make both ends of the chain the same. But it is not always as simple as it looks.

How to play

From the shuffled face-down set, players take six dominoes each (if two or three players) or five each (if four players). The remaining dominoes form the bone yard.

The first player to play is the one holding the lowest double, the double-blank. If nobody has this, ask for double-1 and so on. If there are no doubles out, the lowest domino is played.

The game follows the Block Game (see page 368) and others previously described in that successive players must play to the chain in the centre a domino that matches one end of the chain. If a player cannot go, she must draw a domino from the bone yard. If this matches, she can play it, but if not she misses her turn, which passes to the player on the left. The last two dominoes in the bone yard are not drawn. A player who cannot go when there are only two dominos remaining in the bone yard misses her turn.

The object of the game is to score points by making both ends of the chain the same. If this is achieved

with an ordinary domino (that is, not a double), you score two points for a 'double-header'. If it is achieved with a double, you score three points for a 'triple-header'.

The illustration of a game in progress explains this part of the scoring. Player A lays 1, 1 (the lowest double in play) and scores two points. B plays 1, 4 (no points), C plays 1, 6 (no points). D plays 6, 2 (no points). A plays 2, 4 (two points). B plays double-4 (three points). C plays 4, 5 (no points). D plays 5, 0 (no points). A plays 4, 3 (no points). B has to draw from the bone yard, gets 3, 6 and plays it (no points). C plays 0, 6 (two points). D plays double-6 (three points) and so on.

Play continues until one player gets rid of all her dominoes and scores two points for doing so.

If play is blocked and nobody can go, the player with the lowest hand scores one point. The lowest hand is that which doesn't contain a double. If two or more hands are without a double, then that with the lowest total of spots wins – if tied, each get a point. If all hands contain a double, the point goes to the player with the least doubles – if tied, the player with the lowest double gets the point.

A running score is kept during successive games of the points scored by all players. With two players, the first to 15 points is the winner, with three or four players, the winner is the first to ten points.

What you will need A standard set of dominoes; pencil and paper to score

Example game

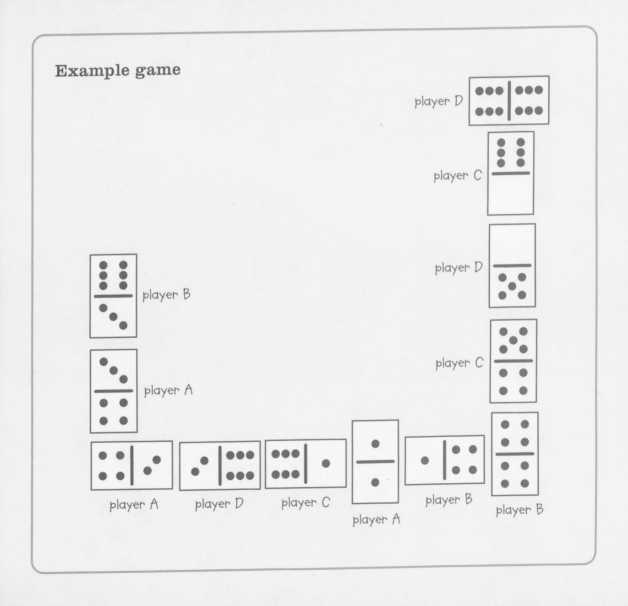

Index & solutions

Index by age

Index

A

Aces up 13
Across and down 349
Acrostics 346
Activity codes 128
Add a letter 175
adventure walks:
  Insect hunt 285
  It's categorical 282
  Secret trails 284
  What am I like? 283
Aim game 234
All in together 213
alphabet and letter games:
  Add a letter 175
  Alphabet sentences 168
  Beat the boat 174
  Dot-to-dot letters 171
  Food store 268
  Grid challenge 176
  I love my love 270
  Letter ladders 177
  Lose your letters 134
  Next letter 265
  Postman's dog 266
  Spelling bee 173
  Take away one 170
  Unscramble the letters 172
  see also word games
Alphabet sentences 168
Animal Olympics 196–7
Animal, Vegetable or Mineral
  310
Authors 68–9

B

Back to the beginning 151
Ball against the wall 245
ball games:
  Aim game 234

Ball against the wall 245
Bat that! 237
Box drop 235
Broken bottle 330
Dodge that ball 220
First to 100! 247
Hit the hole 280
Hot potato 218
In and out the egg cups 340
Pass it round 232
Pat ball 255
Piggy in the middle 236
Queen-i-o 240–1
Roll around 233
Rounders 248–9
Simon says 238–9
Sixty-six 26
Spot 243
Spry 337
Upsy-downsy 242
Web ball 244
Balloon race 334
Banana relay 297
Bang bang relay 341
Bat that 237
Battleships 164–5
beach games:
  Big fish, little fish 281
  Boat races 278
  Castle destroyer 276
  Castle magic 274–5
  Hit the hole 280
  In the swim 279
  Tot it up 277
  Up, up and away 273
  Where's the treasure? 272
Beanbag bowls 203
Beat the boat 174
Beetle 356
Beggar my neighbour 27

Bergen 374–5
Big fish, little fish 281
Bingo , bango 44
Bisley 20–1
Black Jack 82–3
Blind hookey 80–1
Blind Hughie 370
Blind tunnel race 335
Block game 368–9
Bloodhounds 301
Boat races 278
Boodle 72–3
Bowled over 195
Box drop 235
Boxes 120
Brag 92–3
  Three-stake brag 94–5
brain teasers:
  Back to the beginning 151
  Colour coded 150
Broken bottle 330
Bubble car 211
Build it up 106
Busy hexagon 133

C

Canfield 10–11, 24–5
Card for card 304
Cardgo 44
Castle destroyer 276
Castle magic 274
Catch the thief 127
Categories 140
Chain drawings 98–9
Chase-the-ace 66
chasing and catching games:
  Big fish, little fish 281
  Colourful croc 222
  Fire and ice 253
  Get back 250–1

Red letter day 263
Snake chase 226
Tail end 252
What's the time, Mr Wolf?
  254
Cheat! 46–7
Chicago 360–1
Cinderella 217
circle games:
  Farmer's in his den 185
  Hunt the shoe 303
  I sent a letter to my love
    183
  In and out the dusty
    bluebells 184
  Ring-a-ring o' roses 182
  Skip to my Lou 180–1
  The Clock 14–15
Clock face 357
Clock patience 14–15
codes:
  Activity codes 128
  Dice code 124–5
  Spy letters 132
Colonel 38–9
Colour coded 150
Colour collecting 271
Colourful croc 222
Coming round the
  mountain 188
Concentration 52–3
Consequences 137
copying games: Follow my
  leader 224
Count me in 193
counting games:
  Ball against the wall 245
  Count me in 193
  First to 100! 247
  Slithering snakes 118

Solutions

Page 133
Busy hexagon
There are an amazing 114 triangles.

Page 143
House builder

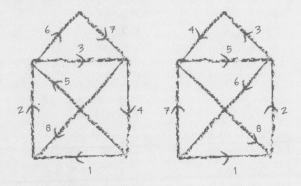

Page 167
Magic square

2	9	4
7	5	3
6	1	8

Acknowledgements
Executive Editor Jane McIntosh
Editor Amy Corbett
Design Manager Tokiko Morishima
Page Make-up Dorchester Typesetting
      Group Ltd
Senior Production Controller Amanda Mackie
Illustrator Sudden Impact Media